THINKING FRAGMENTS

THINKING FRAGMENTS

Psychoanalysis, Feminism, and Postmodernism in the Contemporary West

JANE FLAX

■

UNIVERSITY OF CALIFORNIA PRESS
BERKELEY   LOS ANGELES   OXFORD

University of California Press
Berkeley and Los Angeles, California

University of California Press, Ltd.
Oxford, England

©1990 by
The Regents of the University of California

Library of Congress Cataloging-in-Publication Data

Flax, Jane.
    Thinking fragments : psychoanalysis, feminism, and postmodernism
in the contemporary West / Jane Flax.
        p.   cm.
    Bibliography: p.
    Includes index.
    ISBN 0-520-06586-7 (alk. paper)
    1. Psychoanalysis and philosophy. 2. Feminism—Philosophy.
3. Postmodernism. 4. Philosophy, Modern—20th century. I. Title.
BF175.4.P45F58 1990
150'.88042—dc19   89-4797
                                                                         CIP

Printed in the United States of America
1 2 3 4 5 6 7 8 9

The paper used in this publication meets the minimum requirements of American Na-
tional Standard for Information Sciences—Permanence of Paper for Printed Library
Materials, ANSI Z39.48-1984.   ∞

To the memory of my father,
Seth Flax,
and to Kirsten, Phyllis, and Fred
—companions in and out of the night

Contents

The wounded surgeon plies the steel
That questions the distempered part;
Beneath the bleeding hand we feel
The sharp compassions of the healer's art
Resolving the enigma of the fever chart.

Our only health is the disease
If we obey the dying nurse
Whose constant care is not to please
But to remind of our, and Adam's curse,
And that, to be restored, our sickness must
grow worse.

The whole earth is our hospital
Endowed by the ruined millionaire,
Wherein, if we do well, we shall
Die of the absolute paternal care
That will not leave us, but prevents us
everywhere.

T. S. Eliot, "East Coker"

Acknowledgments

I suppose many authors experience the process of writing as rather traumatic. This is certainly so in my case, although not so much the actual writing as the events surrounding it. I began final preparatory work for writing this book in the summer of 1985. In January 1986, Eugene Frankel, my husband of fifteen years, was finally diagnosed as having pancreatic cancer. On May 6, 1986, he died.

The basic draft of this book was completed in the spring of 1987. I would never have been able to finish it and go on with my life without the steadfast care of friends. Above all I am indebted to Phyllis Palmer, who went through every step of the process for over a year, and to Kirsten Dahl, whose calls from New Haven kept me going through many a dark night. Mervat Hatem, Yvonne Hoffman, Shelley Rockwell, and Jean Kondo Weigl provided reliable, empathic support and continuity. Elizabeth Abel, Janet Adelman, Ted Brown, Nancy Chodorow, Peter Lyman, Harvey Mendelsohn, Judy Stacey, and Barrie Thorne were there at surprising and crucial moments.

Interwoven with the process of death, the writing continued. In addition to these friends, my work is heavily indebted to ongoing, long-term conversations with Sandra Harding and Nancy Hartsock. Naomi Schneider, my editor, was unusually supportive. Her faith in the worth of this project and my ability to finish it was essential to its completion.

One of the most surprising discoveries for me was how separate yet intermingled loss and love remain. The courage and resilience of my son, Gabriel Flax Frankel, encouraged me in many ways, but I owe special thanks to Fred Risser for both going on and beginning again.

Part One

The Conversation

One

Something Is Happening

On Writing in a Transitional State

*Whatever happens, every individual is a child of his time;
so philosophy too is its own time apprehended in thoughts.
It is just as absurd to fancy that a philosophy can transcend
its contemporary world as it is to fancy that an individual
can overleap his own age, jump over Rhodes. . . .*

*One more word about giving instruction as to what the
world ought to be. Philosophy in any case always comes on
the scene too late to give it. As the thought of the world, it
appears only when actuality is already there cut and dried
after its process of formation has been completed. . . .
When philosophy paints its grey in grey, then has a shape
of life grown old. By philosophy's grey in grey it cannot be
rejuvenated but only understood. The owl of Minerva
spreads its wings only with the falling of dust.*

G. W. F. Hegel,

Philosophy of Right

In this book I represent, interrogate, juxtapose, and construct conversations between three important modes of contemporary Western thought: psychoanalysis, feminist theories, and postmodern philosophies. I am not a neutral participant in or a disinterested facilitator of these dialogues. At least three purposes motivate their evocation: a desire to grasp certain aspects of the texture of social life in the contemporary West; a fascination with questions of knowledge, gender, subjectivity, and power and their interrelations; and a wish to explore how theories might be written in postmodern voices—nonauthoritarian, open-ended, and process-oriented.

In part these purposes arise out of my work as I juggle at least four identities and practices: therapist, philosopher, feminist, and political theorist. I chose to construct conversations within and among these three modes of thinking because each appears to be the best available

informant/speaker in relation to at least one of my purposes or practices. As a therapist I cannot escape questions of subjectivity and of
its formation and deformations. Psychoanalytic theories most powerfully address these concerns. As a philosopher trained in the post-
Kantian epistemological era I find questions of knowledge and its
limits unavoidable. Postmodernism offers the most radical and unsettling disruptions of and in this epistemological terrain. As a feminist
and a woman I confront the omnipresence and centrality of gender
and the lived experience of its structures of dominance and subordination. Feminist theories have presented gender as a central object of
inquiry. As a political theorist I cannot ignore questions of power and
justice. Each theory makes important contributions to rethinking
these traditional concerns.

The conversational form of the book represents my attempt to find
a postmodern voice, to answer for myself the challenge of finding
one way (among many possible ways) to continue theoretical writing
while abandoning the "truth" enunciating or adjudicating modes
feminists and postmodernists so powerfully and appropriately call
into question. Although I have many disagreements with particular
aspects of postmodern thinking, its self-analytic spirit (which is not
always exemplified by the primary exponents of postmodernism and
even less by their disciples) is one of its most important contributions.
An integral and especially important aspect of postmodernist approaches is a refusal to avoid conflict and irresolvable differences or to
synthesize these differences into a unitary, univocal whole. In this
spirit I will not attempt to resolve conflicts within or between the
theories discussed here, nor will the conversations among them result in any new, grand synthesis. Instead of a conclusion I will raise
further questions about this conversational mode of writing and the
adequacy of all its voices, including my own.

The longer I work and write, the more intertwined the issues of
knowledge, self, gender, and voice become. Any theory that is blind
to or erases one or more of these issues is less and less satisfactory.
Unfortunately, I have also become increasingly convinced that psychoanalysis, feminist theories, and postmodernism are each partially
constituted by and through precisely such blindnesses and erasures.
This is one reason I decided to put them into conversation with one
another. Like other postmodernists I do not believe that there can

ever be a perfectly adequate, unified theory of the "whole." My treatment of these theories is not based on such a premise. But I do think that theorists can provide more or less space for a variety of voices and that they can be criticized for ignoring or repressing certain questions that are germane to their own projects.

My attempts to understand these issues are also increasingly complicated by two additional problems: the paradoxical, simultaneously fragmenting, and pervasively bureaucratized qualities of social life and the radical critiques of claims to truth and the self-understanding of intellectuals posed by psychoanalysts, feminists, and postmodernists. These problems necessarily form part of the context of this book. Among other consequences, questions of voice and meaning become more salient but less amenable to resolution. How is it possible to write? What meanings can writing have when every proposition and theory seems questionable, one's own identity is uncertain, and the status of the intellectual is conceived alternately as hopelessly enmeshed in oppressive knowledge/power relations or utterly irrelevant to the workings of the technical-rational bureaucratic state?

I believe many persons within contemporary Western culture share such feelings of unease, of being without a secure ground or point of reference, although they are not always acknowledged and discussed or articulated and experienced in the same ways.[1] Something has happened, is happening, to Western societies. The beginning of this transition can be dated somewhat arbitrarily from after the First World War in Europe and after the Second World War in the United States. Western culture is in the middle of a fundamental transformation; a "shape of life" is growing old. The demise of the old is being hastened by the end of colonialism, the uprising of women, the revolt of other cultures against white Western hegemony, shifts in the balance of economic and political power within the world economy, and a growing awareness of the costs as well as the benefits of scientific and technological "progress."*

---

*It will soon become evident to the reader that my use of such words as *transitional* or *transformative* is not meant to imply that changes in Western culture are moving us in any particular preset (much less "progressive") direction. I do not believe that there is an inexorable, inner logic to history that events and analysis will necessarily reveal more clearly and completely. Furthermore it is evident to me that the use of such words as *us* or *our* in

Western intellectuals cannot be immune from the profound shifts now taking place in contemporary social life. These transformations have deeply disrupted many philosophers' self-understanding and sense of certainty. One of the paradoxical consequences of this breakdown is that the more the fault lines in previously unproblematic ground become apparent, the more frightening it appears to be without ground, the more we want to have some ways of understanding what is happening, and the less satisfactory the existing ways of thinking about experience become. All this results in a most uncomfortable form of intellectual vertigo to which appropriate responses are not clear.[2] It is increasingly difficult even to begin to know how to comprehend what we are thinking and experiencing. Each mode of thinking I discuss both contributes to and offers at least one way of accounting for this confusion. Each of these accounts focuses primarily on one fragment of a fragmenting culture. Feminists stress the disruptive effects of challenges to and transformations in previously ex-

---

relation to Western culture is extremely problematic. One's sense of and location within Western culture are shaped and differentiated by race, class, age, ethnicity, gender, and sexual preference (see, for example, the essays in Henry Louis Gates, ed., *'Race,' Writing and Difference* [Chicago: University of Chicago Press, 1986]; Cornel West, "The Politics of American Neo-Pragmatism," in *Post-Analytic Philosophy*, ed. John Rajchman and Cornel West [New York: Columbia University Press, 1985]; and Cherrie Moraga and Gloria Anzaldua, eds., *This Bridge Called My Back: Writings by Radical Women of Color* [Watertown, Mass.: Persephone Press, 1981]). How to identify and do justice to both possible commonalities and differences within people's experiences in the contemporary West will be a persistent tension in and goal of this book.

The "West" itself, of course, does not exist in a vacuum. It is part of a world system. The West's place within the world system is itself in transition, as is the system as a whole. (The concept of a "world system" is complex, controversial, and variously defined but nonetheless useful. Important variants are represented in Barbara Hockey Kaplan, ed., *Social Change in the Capitalist World Economy* [Beverly Hills, Calif.: Sage, 1978]; Samir Amin, Giovanni Arrighi, Andre Gunder Frank, and Immanual Wallerstein, *Dynamics of Global Crisis* [New York: Monthly Review Press, 1982]; Theda Skocpol, *States and Social Revolutions* [New York: Cambridge University Press, 1979]; and Janet Henshall Momsen and Janet Townsend, eds., *Geography of Gender in the Third World* [Albany: University of New York Press, 1987].) The West is not internally homogeneous either; there are many important differences within Europe and between European cultures and American ones. Nonetheless the existence of numerous particularities does not negate the possibility or meaningfulness of shared experiences.

isting gender systems. Psychoanalysts echo and extend Freud's claim that psychoanalysis undermines our belief and pride in a particular and definitive human excellence—reason. Postmodernists also question the nature and powers of reason, but they locate the decline and changes in our beliefs about it within a story about the death of a "metanarrative"—the Enlightenment.[3]

Initial encounters with postmodernism were most disruptive of my previous intellectual frameworks—feminism, psychoanalysis, and critical theory. Paradoxically, I found myself trying to make sense of this experience by locating it within the metanarrative postmodernists themselves construct. Even though I ultimately found this approach limited and unsatisfactory, I will try to evoke and define some of the problems that concern me by introducing their story first.

The Dream Is Over: On Theorizing in a Postmodern State

Postmodernist stories about contemporary social transformations have at least one common organizing theme: There has been a breakdown in the metanarrative of Enlightenment. Social transformations are understood as symptoms of or episodes in this breakdown. The breakdown of this metanarrative forces philosophers to confront questions of voice, terrain, purposes, and meaning that are suspended during and by periods of consensus. To many contemporary philosophers it appears that the Enlightenment has failed. The grand ideas that structured, legitimated, and lent coherence to so much of Western science, philosophy, economics, and politics since the eighteenth century no longer appear compelling or even plausible. The Enlightenment now seems more like an inherited set of beliefs, rent by all too self-evident internal contradictions. The political and philosophical aspirations and claims typical of Enlightenment thinking appear to have been falsified by that which it was supposed to predict yet cannot account for: the subsequent course of Western history.

Enlightenment ideas that now seem problematic include such interdependent concepts as the dignity and worth of the "monadic" (socially isolated and self-sufficient) individual and the interconnections between reason, knowledge, progress, freedom, and ethical action.[4]

Essential to all Enlightenment beliefs is the existence of something called a "self," a stable, reliable, integrative entity that has access to our inner states and outer reality, at least to a limited (but knowable) degree. Enlightenment metanarrative also provides a privileged place for science and philosophy (especially epistemology) as forms of knowledge. If philosophy loses its privilege in relation to knowledge and truth, then the legitimacy of the philosopher's rule over this terrain is also necessarily called into question.[5]

Certainly it is true that almost as soon as these ideas were posited by philosophers such as Diderot or Kant, they were attacked, at least in part, by others (e.g., Rousseau). Nonetheless, the critics of the Enlightenment remained outside the mainstream—on the "margins" of philosophy, as Derrida would say.[6] "History" seemed to prove that such critics were cranks or "romantics." They stubbornly refused to acknowledge the unprecedented progress being made in Western politics, economics, and science throughout the eighteenth and nineteenth centuries.

More recent events in Western history have posed fundamental challenges to the self-certainty of reason and its "science." The anti-Enlightenment cranks now seem more like prophets. It is no longer self-evident that there is any necessary connection between reason, knowledge, science, freedom, and human happiness. Indeed, the relation between these now appears to be at least partially and irresolvably antagonistic. The escape from tutelage through reason and knowledge that Kant believed was also the path to freedom may, it seems now, lead instead into an ever more terrifying enslavement to the products of that knowledge.

The inherent connections Enlightenment thinkers posited between science, progress, and happiness appear disturbingly ironic when we contemplate Hiroshima, Auschwitz, or the possibility of a "nuclear winter." It appears at least plausible that we are now inescapably enmeshed in a "dialectics of enlightenment" in which, as Horkheimer and Adorno assert, enlightenment reverts to myth.[7] These myths include ones that justify political uses of terror waged on a mass scale made possible only by the existence of "advanced" science and technology. For example, the governments of the United States and the USSR both claim to be the ultimate bastion and guarantor of freedom, progress, and human emancipation. Each sees itself as the "shining city on a hill" where those eighteenth-century ideals can become fully real at last. Yet the United States and the USSR are engaged in a system of mutually assured destruction, aptly called MAD, in which the entire planet is held hostage. Putting the planet at perpetual risk of annihilation is justified in the name of freedom and human emancipation.

It now also appears possible that economic development may not or may not only provide freedom from want, as political economists from Smith through Marx to contemporary Keynesians and neoclassical theorists believe. Rather, as Weber asserted, the price of such progress in the West may be an ever-encroaching bureaucratic "iron cage."[8] The economic comfort of some persons in the West may also depend on or result in the underdevelopment of the Third World and the emergence of permanent underclasses and regions within the First World. Indeed, when contemplating their place in the world system, well-off Westerners would do well to recall Adorno's response to the Holocaust:

The guilt of a life which purely as a fact will strangle other life according to statistics that eke out an overwhelming number of killed with a minimal number of rescued, as if this were provided in the theory of probabilities—this guilt is irreconcilable with living. And the guilt does not cease to reproduce itself, because not for an instant can it be made fully, presently conscious. This, nothing else, is what compels us to philosophize.[9]

Necessary Ambivalence

Yet philosophers' (including postmodernists') relations to the Enlightenment are necessarily ambivalent. It is a legacy that many of us can neither fully accept nor reject, neither destroy nor preserve. Appealing alternatives to its characteristic set of beliefs are lacking. The socially prevalent ones seem to be fanatical theocracies, unrelenting dogmatism, absolutist states, chaos, or a moral relativism so paralyzing it elides into nihilism.

If we are not to be paralyzed by adopting the "angel of history's" view of the past—"one single catastrophe which keeps piling wreckage upon wreckage and hurls it in front of his feet"—we need some ways to make (or create) sense out of all the social and philosophical debris.[10] We also need some ways to (re)locate the practices of philosophizing within contemporary social contexts because part of the family myth we inherit as children of the Enlightenment is that we ought to be able to *think* our way out of these confusions. Yet the utility, meaning, and legitimacy of thinking itself are called into question once its problematic and conventional foundations and foundational illusions are exposed.

The feeling that new ways of thinking are a necessary part of the solution to contemporary dilemmas is not altogether an illusion. Because we continue to contemplate the inadequacies of our thinking, it cannot be completely misguided or irrelevant to look for "revolutionary" modes of philosophy that "glimpse the possibility of a form of intellectual life in which the vocabulary of philosophical reflection inherited from the seventeenth century would seem as pointless as the thirteenth century philosophical vocabulary had seemed to the Enlightenment."[11]

The extent and depth of our social and intellectual confusion indicate a need for "new maps of the terrain (viz. of the whole panorama of human activities) which simply do not include those features which previously seemed to dominate."[12] However it is necessary to understand both the limitations of any "revolutionary" philosophy and the power of thought itself isolated from other human capacities or forms of action. Thinking, as both feminists and psychoanalysts insist, is not the only or an innocent source of knowledge. Even revolutionary philosophies bear the marks of the tradition out of which they arose and against which they rebel. The rebellion of a revolutionary philosopher is characterized as much by a mostly unconscious ambivalence toward the past as by an absolute break with it. Precisely this ambivalence is what is most interesting because analysis of it can elucidate the power of the past and of persisting conflicting wishes. Yet the stronger the ambivalence, the more difficult it may be for those caught up in it to engage in such analysis or even to recognize its existence. These wishes may become a source of social and intellectual paralysis or destructive behavior and ideas as readily as constructive change.

Furthermore, as I know from my own work, there seems to be a temptation inherent in more abstract forms of thinking: to confuse the word and the deed. Those of us who love philosophy are not immune from the fantasies of "infantile omnipotence" that are so powerful in unconscious processes. These fantasies include the belief that if one wishes or thinks something, it will inevitably occur—that the wish or thought is the necessary and sufficient cause of a desired or feared result. In intellectual life these fantasies sometimes result in an overestimation of the power of thinking and its centrality to human life. Naturally, such fantasies, a particularly attractive form of "solace" against deeply felt helplessness or despair, recur most powerfully in times of stress or confusion.[13] So philosophers need to find ways to improve consciousness of and develop critical perspectives on our own more grandiose and self-deluding ideas. However, postmodernism alone is not a sufficient antidote to philosophic delusions. Feminists and psychoanalysts offer alternative models of learning and ways of making sense of experience. They speak of and to worlds outside texts, literature, and language. Feminists and psychoanalysts also show us that thinking is not the only or even necessarily the best source of knowledge. Creating conversations between feminists, psychoanalysts, and postmodernists will reveal how narrow the limits and constricting the boundaries of postmodern narratives are as alternatives to traditional philosophic practices.

Philosophy as Analyst and Patient

Psychoanalytic theory and practice have much to offer philosophers, including postmodernists, and feminists. According to analytic theory, ambivalence is an appropriate response to an inherently conflictual situation. The problem lies not in the ambivalence, but in premature attempts to resolve or deny conflicts. The lack of coherence or closure in a situation and the existence of contradictory wishes or ideas too often generate anxiety so intense that aspects of the ambivalence and its sources are repressed. It is often better in such a situation to analyze the sources of the ambivalence and one's inability to tolerate it. It is equally important to examine why, when lacking absolute certainty, the will becomes paralyzed.

This perspective forces me to question the temptation to construct a "successor project" to fill the void left by the failures of the Enlightenment.[14] It also reminds me of the dangers of a defense against the anxiety induced by disorder and irresolvable conflict especially typical of intellectuals. One strives to achieve a grand synthesis in which apparently contradictory ideas are shown to be merely parts of some coherent whole. For example, postmodernists construct their own metanarratives of the "death" of the Enlightenment or the "metaphysics of presence," thus violating their own principles of "deferral" and indeterminacy. Reason (this time disguised as "language") reappears, persistently pursuing its cunning plan, despite the apparent dominance of entropic forces in the world.

Contemporary conditions call for ways of philosophizing more akin to an analytic search for understanding. In this search the process of discovery and the dialogue within and by which discovery is facilitated are intrinsic aspects of any claim to truth. The goal of analysis is not to achieve closure or a final truth that renders further investigation unnecessary. Rather, the analyst hopes that in and through the process of analysis a patient will overcome some of the internal barriers to the desire for self-understanding. Although the analysis will be "terminated," the analytic process will continue with the former patient now able to be her own analyst. For the termination process and hence the analysis to be successful, both analyst and patient must accept that all closure is to some extent arbitrary, temporary, and conventional.

Concepts of understanding and meaning are not unproblematic. There are also many unresolved questions about the kinds of knowledge that can be generated within, or based on, psychoanalytic processes. I will return to some of these questions later. Nonetheless, I would still argue that the model of the simultaneously receptive and self-consciously "construction-building" analyst is particularly appropriate to our historical moment.[15] To view oneself as a heroic lawgiver, "foundation builder," neutral judge, or deconstructor who has the right to evaluate the truth claims and adequacy of all forms of knowledge places the philosopher outside of a time in which such un-self-reflective certainty seems more like a will to power than a claim to truth. I think what we can best offer at such times is to facilitate conversations between different ways of thinking, being especially careful to search for and include those voices that sound foreign to or critical of our "native" ones.

Unlike the postmodernist concepts of conversation, however, my analytic and feminist experiences compel me to stress the subjective and intersubjective aspects of "conversation" or its absence. Postmodernists too often ignore or obscure the nonlinguistic aspects of humans—hence the many important ways that gender and other social relations and internal psychic life structure speakers and narrative-linguistic forms are rendered invisible by and within postmodernist stories. As the following chapters show, paying attention to these aspects may profoundly change both the subjects and the structures of conversation.

Two

Transitional Thinking
Psychoanalytic, Feminist, and Postmodernist Theories

Profound yet little comprehended change, uncertainty, and ambivalence seem pervasive in the contemporary West. This transitional state makes certain forms of thought possible and necessary and excludes others. It generates problems that some philosophies seem to acknowledge and confront better than others. In our time these problems include issues of self, gender, knowledge, and power. Certain philosophies best present and represent "our own time apprehended in thought." Like dreams, they allow us insight into the primary process of our age. Throughout this book I will argue that psychoanalysis, feminist theories, and postmodern philosophies are such modes of thought and can be best understood in this way. These modes of thought are transitional ways of thinking. Each has some insight into central social issues, the ambivalences of the present, and of its own status within it. In important ways each mode of thinking also has anticipatory moments that offer glimpses of a future that will not be a mere repetition of the past. These transitional modes of thinking are both symptoms of the state of our culture and partial, necessarily imperfect, tools for understanding it. They illuminate the problems most characteristic and deeply felt within our society and some of the roots of our helplessness to resolve that which makes us miserable.

Each way of thinking takes as its object of investigation at least one facet of what has become most problematic for myself and many others in our transitional states: how to understand and constitute self, gender, knowledge, social relations, and cultural change without resorting to linear, teleological, hierarchical, holistic, or binary ways of thinking and being. Each mode of thinking also provides a partial critique and corrective to the weakness of the others. Hence by creating conversations in which each theory in turn is the dominant but not exclusionary voice, I can assess both the insights and the limitations of each mode of thinking separately and together in relation to these problems.

In this book each voice will have a chapter in which it will predominate. The voices will be heard in this order: psychoanalysis, feminist theories, and postmodern philosophies. However, because in each chapter the other two voices will interrogate and critique the predominant one, the reader needs some sense of the character of each before any is discussed in detail. In the remainder of this chapter I will provide an overview of each mode of thinking especially in relation to questions of self, knowledge, gender, and power and of some of the tensions and complementarities between them.

Transitional Thinking 1: Psychoanalysis

The psychoanalytic assumption of unconscious mental activity appears to us, on the one hand, a further development of that primitive animism which caused our own consciousness to be reflected in all around us, and, on the other hand, it seems to be an extension of the corrections begun by Kant in regard to our views on external perception. Just as Kant warned us not to overlook the fact that our perception is subjectively conditioned and must not be regarded as identical with the phenomena perceived but never really discerned, so psycho-analysis bids us not to set conscious perception in the place of the unconscious mental process which is its object. The mental, like the physical, is not necessarily in reality just what it appears to us to be. It is, however, satisfactory to find that the correction of inner perception does not present difficulties so great as that of outer perception—that the inner object is less hard to discern truly than is the outside world.

Sigmund Freud,
"The Unconscious"

> *The lament of the paranoiac shows also that at bottom the self-criticism of conscience is identical with, and based upon, self-observation. That activity of the mind which took over the function of conscience has also enlisted itself in the service of introspection, which furnishes philosophy with the material for its intellectual operations. This must have something to do with the characteristic tendency of paranoiacs to form speculative systems.*
>
> Sigmund Freud, "On Narcissism"

For all its shortcomings psychoanalysis presents the best and most promising theories of how a self that is simultaneously embodied, social, "fictional," and real comes to be, changes, and persists over time. Psychoanalysis has much to teach us about the nature, constitution, and limits of knowledge. Furthermore, often unintentionally, it reveals much about what Freud calls the "riddle of sex" and the centrality of this riddle to the formation of a self, knowledge, and culture as a whole. Psychoanalytic theories also help us understand power in its noninstitutional forms—how relations of domination become woven into the fabric of the self and how desire and domination become intertwined.

No account of psychoanalysis can be complete without an attempt to grapple with its founding father, Sigmund Freud. Yet despite the many commentaries on his work, grappling with Freud is still not easy. Difficulties arise from at least two sources: the mythological and foundational functions the "idea" of Freud performs within the psychoanalytic community and the complexity of Freud's own work. Ambivalence, ambiguity, antimonies, and paradoxes pervade Freud's theories. The mythological and foundational functions of the idea of Freud have begun to be confronted both within and outside of the psychoanalytic community. However, commentators on Freud's work still tend arbitrarily to reconcile the antimonies in his theories or merely to cancel out one pole in favor of the other.[1] Furthermore most commentators on both Freudian and post-Freudian psychoanalysis tend to ignore or discount the pervasive yet obscuring and distorting effects of the riddle of sex on all aspects of psychoanalytic theories and practice.[2]

A more fruitful approach is to accept the existence of these antimonies and to investigate why Freud could neither recognize nor reconcile them. In Chapter 3 I will discuss Freud's writings as a series of puzzles in which central problems within Western philosophy and social life are addressed, revealed, and concealed. Freud's work is paradoxical because it culminates and defends major tendencies within Enlightenment thinking, especially its individualism, empiricism, and rationalism. Yet at the same time his theories undermine the very epistemological and psychological aspects of Enlightenment thought he attempts to rescue.

Freud's work also reveals some of the external and internal sources of relations of domination, especially those rooted in the "family romance"—sexuality, gender, and the tensions between men and women, desire, cultural conventions, and the demands of the social order. At the same time such revelation functions in part to conceal some sources of domination more deeply, especially those rooted in and supporting asymmetric gender relations. Without full acknowledgment and investigation of Freud's own antimonies and ambivalence, we risk entering into and replicating the series of displacements, contradictions, and repressions that characterize his work as much as a radical break with the past.

Indeed this is what has happened in the subsequent development of psychoanalytic theory. Post-Freudian theorists are often more "prisoners of sex" than Freud. Although Freud's theories are riddled with ambivalence and antimonies, he also provides some of the tools to recover the missing or repressed terrain within them. Freud at his best tried to provide an account of psychological development as simultaneously a bodily, intrapsychic, interpersonal, and social-historical process. This is precisely what I find most appealing in and powerful about his work. However, subsequent psychoanalytic writers tend to split mind and body, nature and culture, self and other, reason and unreason, and male and female into irreconcilable, naturalistic, or essentialist dualisms. Freud was not always at his best, however. There are many important dualisms with his own theories: culture versus nature, self versus other, oedipal versus preoedipal, drive theory (economics of the libido) versus object relations theory, mind versus body, and analyst versus patient.

Much of the character or even existence of these splits is rooted in gender relations and Freud's anxieties about them. Gender relations continue to have a primarily unconscious influence on the structure and content of post-Freudian psychoanalytic theory. This influence permeates Lacanian and object relations psychoanalysis, two especially important contemporary forms of psychoanalytic theory. Much of the repressed material in psychoanalysis concerns the mother's power in the infant's real and fantasy life (and the infant's in the adult's) and the fear of female sexuality and the (potential) autonomy of women. Part of what is missing in psychoanalysis is a feminist consciousness of the power of gender in our social and intrapsychic lives and in our theories about them.

Freud deals with this material primarily by displacement and denial. He displaces and lessens preoedipal fears of annihilation of the self by transforming them into oedipal ones (castration). He evades the centrality of the preoedipal mother-child relationship by insisting that the oedipal struggle is the crucial event in the life history of an individual and culture as a whole. He discounts the possibility of any real relationship between self and m/other by positing primary narcissism as the original human state and the infant as a drive-governed organism rather than an object-seeking one.

Contemporary psychoanalysis posits diametrically opposed views of the relationship between self and other. However opposed the views of Lacan and object relations theorists appear to be, they share a common difficulty.[3] These sons of Freud inherit his anxieties about the power of mothers, women, and female sexuality. Lacan and many others deny that any genuine relatedness between two selves is possible. Lacan's work is important to psychoanalysts and feminists because, unlike the ego psychologists once dominant in the United States, he stresses the inherently strange and nonsocial qualities of desire. However, he is so unnerved by his discovery of the desire of the m/other that his discovery results in the (theoretical) annihilation of the self. For Lacan the self cannot "really" exist precisely because it comes into being in and through the desire of the m/other. The desire of the other for Lacan entails a loss and permanent alienation of the self. Thus Lacan merely inverts Freud's theory of primary narcissism. In Lacan's theory there are only others, never a self; even the self is an other to itself. Analysis can go no further than confronting the patient with this ontological estrangement.

In contrast, object relations theorists believe it is possible to be a "true" self, but only in and through a relationship with a "good enough" mother who exists for the child and in the theory as an object. Object relations theory is also important to the development of psychoanalysis, feminism, and philosophy, especially in its emphasis on preoedipal (mother-child) relations in the formation of a self and on play as a source of knowledge. Ultimately, this form of psychoanalytic theory is much more compatible with feminist and postmodernist projects than is Lacan's work. However, despite the centrality of the concept of reciprocity in object relations theory, the mother never appears as a complex person in her own right, with her own processes that are not simply isomorphic to those of the child. Furthermore, not so coincident with the emergence of the child as object seeking is the disappearance in this theory of many forms of desire, sexuality, and embodiment in both mother and child.

In his clinical work Freud confronts the need for concepts of subjectivity that can do justice to a self that is simultaneously embodied, social, desiring, autonomous, and interrelated with others. However, neither he nor subsequent psychoanalytic theorists have been able to develop such concepts. Contemporary psychoanalysis presents us with objects without desire or desire without related objects. These continuing failures within psychoanalytic theory are partly rooted in its gender biases and blindness. Equally important, barriers to adequate theories of subjectivity arise out of the persistent confusions in psychoanalysis about criteria for and the status of the knowledge or truth claims produced in and through the analytic situation. The continuing influence of Enlightenment philosophies of knowledge such as empiricism have made it difficult for psychoanalysts to generate epistemologies that are more appropriate to their own practices. The obscuring effects of both empiricism and gender have made it difficult for psychoanalysts fully to understand or use the richness of clinical material and the complexities of the relationship between patient and analyst. The insights of postmodern and feminist theories can contribute to better analysis of these difficulties within psychoanalysis.

Transitional Thinking 2: Feminist Theory

Have you any notion how many books are written about women in the course of one year? Have you any notion how many are written by men? Are you aware that you are, perhaps, the most discussed animal in the universe? . . . How shall I ever find the grains of truth embedded in all this mass of paper? I asked myself, and in despair began running my eye up and down the long list of titles. . . . It was a most strange phenomenon; and apparently—here I consulted the letter M—one confined to the male sex. Women do not write books about men—a fact that I could not help welcoming with relief, for if I had first to read all that men have written about women, then all that women have written about men, the aloe that flowers once in a hundred years would flower twice before I could set pen to paper.

Virginia Woolf,
A Room of One's Own

Feminist theory is developing rapidly. In fact feminist theory is not even a discipline, if this is defined as a delimited area of intellectual discourse in which a general consensus exists among its practitioners as to subject matter, appropriate methodology, and desirable outcomes. There is lively controversy among persons who identify themselves as feminist theorists on each of these components.[4]

Nonetheless it is possible to identify underlying goals, purposes, and constituting objects in feminist theorizing. A fundamental goal of feminist theorists is to analyze gender: how gender is constituted and experienced and how we think—or—equally important—do not think about it. The study of gender includes but is not limited to what are often considered the distinctively feminist issues: the situation of women and the analysis of male domination (or patriarchy). Feminist sensitivity to the effects of gender has begun to radically transform approaches to questions of self, knowledge, and power. Because within contemporary Western societies gender relations have been ones of domination, feminist theories have compensatory as well as critical aspects. Feminist theorists recover and explore the aspects of societies that have been suppressed, unarticulated, or denied within male-dominant viewpoints. The histories of women and our activities have to be written into the accounts and self-understandings of entire cultures.

In this process, however, our self-understandings change. Feminist theories call for a transvaluation of values—a rethinking of our ideas about what is just, humanly excellent, worthy of praise, moral, and so forth. Because we live in societies in which men have more power than women, it makes sense to assume that what is considered most worthy of praise may be those qualities associated with men and that "praise" of the stereotypically female may actually be used as a means of keeping women in their separate and not equal places. Thus feminist theorists offer normative as well as critical theories that honor the philosopher's ancient responsibility to articulate visions of justice and the good. Such visions, perhaps paradoxically to a modern way of thinking, are meant to be practical; they must answer a question central to human life—how *shall* we live?

Although feminist theorists may share a common object of investigation (gender), there is by no means consensus on the answers to questions that arise once gender is rendered problematic and in need of explanation(s). These questions include the following: What is gender? How is it related to anatomical sexual differences? How is gender constituted and sustained in one person's lifetime and more generally as a social experience across time? How does gender relate to other sorts of social relations such as class or race? Does gender have one history or many? What causes gender to change over time? What are the relations between gender, sexuality, and a sense of individual identity? What are the relations between heterosexuality, homosexuality, and gender? Are there only two genders? What are the relations between forms of male dominance and gender? Could or would gender "wither away" in egalitarian societies? Is there anything distinctively "male" or "female" in modes of thought and social relations? If there is, are these distinctions innate and/or socially constituted? Are gender distinctions socially useful and/or necessary? If so, what are the consequences for the feminist goal of attaining "gender justice"? What are the important determinants of differences *among* men and *among* women as well as between men and women? To what extent are our current concepts of "objectivity," science, and knowledge gender-bound or biased? Are there now and/or could there ever be gender-neutral methods of research or social theories? What would they be?

Confronted with such a bewildering set of questions, one can easily overlook the fundamental transformation in social theory that has occurred, at least among people who are aware of feminist theories. The single most important advance in and result of feminist theories and practices is that the existence of gender has been problematized. As in the development of any new kind of knowledge, one of the greatest difficulties is to make the familiar seem strange and in need of explanation. Gender now appears to be a powerful and virtually all-pervasive force in the organization of many societies, in ways of thinking, and in the constitution of each person, male and female. Feminist theorists introduced the concept of "gender system" to focus researchers' attention on aspects of gender including these two: Gender is socially constructed, and it becomes an independent and determining factor in the organization of society.

Gender's apparent naturalness derives from at least three sources: the existence of social conditions that no longer exist or are in rapid transition, the existence of male dominance, and the previously unexamined identity between gender and anatomical sexual differences. I will discuss each of these sources in greater detail in Chapter 5.

Social Conditions

The emergence of feminist theories was made possible at least in part by the reemergence of feminist movements in the late 1960s. The existence of contemporary feminist movements is rooted in and has contributed to the emergence of transitional cultures in the United States and elsewhere. In these cultures there have been radical transformations in social experience such that once widely shared categories of social meaning and explanation have broken down. From a North American feminist perspective important transformations include changes in the structure of the economy, the family, the place of the United States in the world system, the intensification of the "legitimation crisis" (the declining authority of previously powerful social institutions), and the emergence of political groups with increasingly divergent ideas and demands concerning justice, equality, social legislation, and the proper roles of the state. In such a "decentered" and unstable universe, questioning even the most apparently natural facets of human existence, such as gender, seems plausible. Such questioning itself produces further conflict because cultural instability also makes old modes of social relations more attractive. The new right and conservative politicians like Ronald Reagan both call on and reflect a desire to go back to a time when people of color, women, and countries were in their "proper" places. Gender relations can become an arena in which people attempt to defend against the anxieties of living in transitional cultures.

Male Dominance

The existence of male dominance itself has obscured the problematic nature of gender relations. Men as a relatively, although differentially, privileged group have less to gain from exposing the arbitrary and unjust aspects of gender relations. They benefit from these inequities in many ways. In Western culture as in most others, gender is a differentiated and asymmetric division and attribution of human traits and capacities. Through gender relations two types of persons are created: males and females, each posited as an exclusionary category. One can be only one gender, rarely the other or both. The actual content of being a male or female and the rigidity of the categories themselves are highly variable across cultures and time. There are also many important differences in any one society between women (and between men). Nevertheless gender relations so far as we have been able to understand them have been (more or less) relationships of domination. That is, the organization of gender systems has been (more) defined and (imperfectly) controlled by one of its interrelated parts—the male. Thus feminists insist that the concept of power must be extended to include and account for asymmetric gender relations.

Male dominance exists in any system in which men as a group oppress women as a group, even though there may be hierarchies among men (and women). Typically in male-dominant societies, men have more access to and control over the most highly valued and esteemed resources and social activities (e.g., in a religious society men will be priests, and women will be excluded from the most important religious functions or considered polluting to them). Male dominance has material bases in men's violence against women (e.g., rape) and in their control of women's labor power, sexuality, and reproductive capacity. It also has a psychodynamic base as a defense against the infantile mother and men's fear of women. Male dominance has assumed many different forms throughout history; it has been (and still is) exercised against different women in varying ways, but it still remains a dynamic force today. No account of a society can be adequate if it lacks a subtle and particularized analysis of gender relations.

This relation of domination and the existence of gender as a socially constructed system have been concealed in many ways, including defining women as a "question" or the "sex" or the "other" and men as the universal or at least ungendered "species being." In a wide variety of cultures and discourses, men tend to be seen as free from or not determined by gender. In contemporary academia, for example, male researchers do not worry about how being a man or studying men may entail gender bias, but feminist theories by their very association with women are assumed to be political (not scholarly) or trivial (not something you have to work at to understand because people just "are" their gender). Rarely have male scholars self-consciously studied the "psychology of men" or "men's" history or considered the possibility that how men feel about women and their own gender identities may affect every aspect of their thinking about and acting in the world. This denial of men's own location in and determination by gender systems has practical consequences as well. Male scholars tend not to read feminist theories or to think about possible implications for their own work. Women are left with the responsibility for thinking about gender, but because we do it, such work is devalued or segregated from the "mainstream" of intellectual life. Such devaluation and segregation are present in both psychoanalytic and postmodernist discourses.

Category Confusions

Another barrier to our comprehension of gender relations has been the equating of gender with "sex." In this context sex means the anatomical differences between male and female. These anatomical differences appear to belong to the class of "natural facts" or "biology." In turn biology is equated with the pre- or nonsocial or natural. Gender then appears to be constituted by two opposite terms or distinct types of being—male and female. Because male and female seem to be opposite or fundamentally distinct types of being, we tend not to think of gender as a social relation. We attribute "difference" to individuals' possession of distinct qualities. Gender is viewed as a "natural" attribute of "the self." We do not see it as a consequence and symptom of particular, historical, and socially constructed cultures. Furthermore, we draw moral and political conclusions from this distribution of natural properties. If gender is as natural and intrinsically a part of us as the genitals we are born with, it would be foolish or even dangerous to attempt either to change gender arrangements or not to take them into account as a pregiven limit on human activities.

Or would it be so foolish? What, after all, is natural in the context of the human world? We might see many aspects of our embodiedness or biology as pregiven limits to human action, but Western medicine and science do not hesitate to challenge them. For example, few Westerners would refuse to be vaccinated against diseases to which our bodies are naturally susceptible, although in some cultures such actions would be seen as violating the natural order.

As Weber and others have pointed out, Western science tends to "disenchant" the natural world.[5] Increasingly, the natural ceases to exist as the opposite of the "cultural" or social. Nature becomes the object and product of human action; it loses its independent existence for us. Ironically, the more such disenchantment proceeds, the more humans seem to need something that remains outside their powers of transformation. Until recent developments in medicine like "sex change" operations, one such area seemed to be anatomical differences between men and women. Thus in order to "save" nature from ourselves, we equate sex, biology, nature, and gender and oppose these to the cultural, social, and human.

Concepts of gender then become a complex metaphor for ambivalence about human action in, on, and as part of the natural world. But in turn the use of gender as a metaphor for such ambivalence blocks further investigation of them, for the social articulation of these equations is not really in the form I stated previously but rather—sex, biology, nature, and women: cultural, social, and male. Women in the contemporary West are sometimes seen as the last refuge not only from the "heartless" world, but from an increasingly mechanized and fabricated one as well. Even postmodernist discourses are marked by contradictory and ambivalent metaphors of gender and nature. What has remained masked in many modes of thought is the possibility that our concepts of biology and nature are rooted in social relations; they do not merely reflect a pregiven structure of reality (or language). To understand gender as a social relation, feminist theorists have begun to deconstruct the meanings we attach to biology, sex, gender, and nature.[6] These efforts at deconstruction and their so far ambiguous and contradictory results will be discussed in more detail in Chapter 5.

Gender Rethought

Having begun at least to identify these barriers to our thinking about gender, we can now see that it has at minimum three dimensions. First, it is a social relationship that is both independent and autonomous from and at the same time shaped by other social relations such as race and economic status. It is a form of power and affects our theories and practices of justice. Second, it is a category of thought, that is, thinking is both subtly and overtly gender-bound and biased. Thus traditional concepts of epistemology must be transformed to include analysis of the effects of gender on and about thinking. Unless we actively seek out the effects of gender on both society and our thinking about it, our knowledge (about knowledge and societies) will be inadequate. Every culture constructs ideas about gender, and in turn these ideas help structure and organize all other forms of thinking and practice as well—often in surprising and unexpected ways. For example, gender helps structure our ideas about nature and science, the public and the private, and the rational and the irrational. Third, gender is a central constituting element in each person's sense of self and in a culture's idea of what it means to be a person. Thus adequate accounts of subjectivity would have to include investigation of the effects of gender on its constitution and expression and on our concepts of "selfhood." Each culture identifies and sorts out somewhat differently a possible range of human attributes and activities and assigns some to one group and some to another. This sorting out is justified among other ways by a concept of gender. Individuals are in turn defined in part by and through their membership in one of these gendered groups. Gender also partially structures how each person experiences and expresses his or her self. For example, the expression of aggression may vary by gender. There may also be gender-based differences in how one forms, experiences, and maintains intimate relations with others or in how one resolves conflicts between the competing demands of work and family life. These differences not only reflect the influence of externally defined "sex roles" but evoke and depend upon feelings that are part of the very fiber of the self. Hence such feelings are not readily accessible to our rational consciousness, even though they may exert a powerful influence over what we do.

Feminist Theories and the Obscuring "Riddle of Sex"

Feminist theorists have made tremendous progress in the past fifteen years. However feminist theories themselves are not exempt from the obscuring effects of gender on our thinking about the self, knowledge, social relations, and gender systems. To understand the promise and limitations of feminist theories as well as their particular object—gender—we must locate feminist theories within the wider experiential and philosophical contexts of which they are both a part and a critique. To progress further, feminist theorists need to enter into dialogues with the "other(s)" to increase our own self-consciousness, facilitate the recovery of repressed material within feminist theory, and improve our theoretical and methodological sophistication. Precisely because men have different sorts of gender-bound experiences, "male discourses" read with feminist sensitivities may offer important insights into aspects of gender that our female experiences impede us from seeing.

Both psychoanalysis and postmodernism have much to contribute to feminist discourses. Psychoanalytic theories of the constitution of femininity can increase our awareness of gender-based distortions and repressions within feminist theories. Postmodernist philosophies can make us more critical of our epistemological presuppositions. Feminist theories cannot be exempt from the implicit or explicit critiques of universalizing claims to knowledge made by psychoanalytic and postmodernist theorists. There cannot be, nor should we expect there to be, a feminist equivalent to a falsely universalizing Marxist or empiricist "science." Any feminist standpoint will necessarily be partial and will to some extent merely reflect our embeddedness in preexisting gender relations. According to postmodernism, there is no force "outside" our social relations and activity (e.g., history, reason, progress, science, some transcendental essence) that will rescue us from such partiality and embeddedness. Each person who tries to think from the standpoint of women may illuminate some aspects of society that have been suppressed within the dominant view. But none of us can speak for "woman" because no such person exists except within a specific set of already gendered relations—to "man" and to many concrete and different women.

Furthermore, among the important lessons feminist theorists can learn from postmodern philosophies is to pay attention to the interconnections between knowledge claims, especially to absolute or "neutral" knowledge, and power. Our search for an "Archimedes point" may conceal and obscure our entanglement in a "discursive formation" or episteme in which truth claims may take some forms and not others.[7] Such entanglement entails political as well as epistemological consequences. Any episteme requires the suppression of discourses that differ with or threaten to undermine the authority of the dominant one. Hence within feminist theories a search for a "defining theme of the whole" or "a feminist viewpoint" may require suppressing the important and discomforting voices of persons with experiences unlike our own. This may be a necessary condition for the apparent authority, coherence, and universality of our own beliefs or experiences.

The very search for a cause or "root" of gender relations or, more narrowly, male domination may partially reflect a mode of thinking that is itself grounded in particular forms of gender or other relations in which domination is present. Perhaps "reality" can have "a" structure only from the falsely universalizing perspective of the dominant group. Perhaps only to the extent that one person or group can dominate the whole can "reality" appear to be governed by one set of rules, be constituted by one privileged set of social relations, or be told by one "story." Criteria of theory construction such as parsimony or simplicity may be met by the suppression or denial of the experiences of the "other(s)." The preference for such criteria may also reflect a desire to keep the others out.

Transitional Thinking 3: Postmodern Philosophies

The postmodern would be that which, in the modern, puts forward the unpresentable in presentation itself; that which denies itself the solace of good forms, the consensus of a taste which would make it possible to share collectively the nostalgia for the unattainable, that which searches for new presentations, not in order to enjoy them but in order to impart a stronger sense of the unpresentable. A postmodern artist or writer is in the position of a philosopher: the text he writes, the work he produces are not in principle governed by preestablished rules, and they cannot be judged according to a determining judgment, by applying familiar categories to the text or to the work. The artist and the writer, then, are working without rules in order to formulate the rules of what will have been done. *Hence the fact that work and text have the characters of an event. . . .*

Finally, it must be clear that it is our business not to supply reality but to invent allusions to the conceivable which cannot be presented. And it is not to be expected that this task will effect the last reconciliation between language

*games (which, under the name of faculties, Kant knew to
be separated by a chasm), and that only the transcendental
illusion (that of Hegel) can hope to totalize them into a real
unity. But Kant also knew the price to pay for such an illusion is terror. The nineteenth and twentieth centuries
have given us as much terror as we can take. We have paid
a high enough price for the nostalgia of the whole and the
one, for the reconciliation of the concept and the sensible, of
the transparent and the communicable experience. Under
the general demand for slackening and for appeasement, we
can hear the mutterings of the desire for a return of terror,
for the realization of the fantasy to seize reality. The answer
is: Let us wage a war on totality; let us be witnesses to the
unpresentable; let us activate the differences and save the
honor of the name.*

Jean-François Lyotard,
The Postmodern Condition

Postmodern philosophies of knowledge can contribute to a more accurate and self-critical understanding of our theorizing and the intentions that underlie it. Postmodern philosophers, especially Foucault,
also offer a radical rethinking of the meanings and operation of power
that is particularly appropriate to transitional states. However, postmodernist discourses are deficient in their treatment of issues of gender and self, and there are also important absences in their discussions of power and knowledge. Like feminist theory, postmodern
philosophy is not a unified and homogeneous field. The persons and
discourses associated with postmodernism include Nietzsche, Foucault, Derrida, Deleuze and Guattari, Lyotard, Rorty, Cavell, Barthes,
semiotics, deconstruction, psychoanalysis, archaeology, genealogy,
and nihilism.[8] Postmodernists share at least one common object of
attack—the Enlightenment—but they approach this object from
many different points of view and attack it with various methods and
for diverse purposes.

Despite their many differences, these discourses are all "deconstructive"; they seek to distance us from and make us skeptical about
the ideas concerning truth, knowledge, power, history, self, and language that are often taken for granted within and serve as legitima-
tions for contemporary Western culture. According to postmodernists, many of these still predominant ideas are derived from the
distinctive set of philosophical and political assumptions characteristic of Western thinking at least since the Enlightenment. Hence they

seek to displace the metanarrative of Enlightenment through a variety
of rhetorical strategies. Because they believe philosophy occupies a
constituting and legitimating position within this metanarrative, it
follows that its deconstruction is the responsibility of the postmodernist and (at least *qua* philosophers) their most salient contribution
to contemporary Western culture. To carry out this deconstruction,
postmodernists construct stories about the Enlightenment in which
the disparate views of a variety of thinkers, including Descartes,
Kant, and Hegel, are integrated into (and reduced to) one "master
narrative." This master narrative then serves as an adversary against
which postmodernist rhetoric can be deployed.

According to postmodernists, "the Enlightenment" story has these
major themes and characters:[9]

1. A coherent, stable self (the author). The most distinctive and
valued property of this Enlightenment self is a form of reason capable
of privileged insight into its own processes and into the "laws of nature." If, as in Kant's philosophy, reason necessarily has limits on
what it can know, these limits in turn can be known by reason.

2. A distinctive and privileged mode of story telling—philosophy
(the critic and judge). The philosopher stipulates the criteria for adequate story telling, and, it turns out, only philosophy can fully satisfy
these criteria. Only philosophy can provide an objective, reliable, and
universalizable "foundation" for knowledge and for judging all truth
claims.

3. A particular notion of "truth" (the hero). True knowledge represents something "real" and unchanging (universal) about our
minds or the structure of the natural world. The "real" is that which
has an existence independent of the knower; it is not merely created
or transformed by the mind in the process of knowing.

4. A distinctive political philosophy (the moral) that posits complex and necessary interconnections between reason, autonomy, and
freedom. Especially important and problematic to postmodernists is
the Enlightenment belief that conflicts between truth, knowledge,
and power can be overcome by grounding claims to authority in reason. The Enlightenment hope is that utilizing knowledge in the service of legitimate power will assure both freedom and progress.
Knowledge can then be both "neutral" (e.g., grounded in universal
reason, not in particular "interests") and socially beneficial.

5. A transparent medium of expression (language). Enlightenment philosophers posit or presume a realist or correspondence theory of language in which objects are not linguistically or socially constructed; they are merely made present to consciousness by naming or by the right use of language.

6. A rationalist and teleological philosophy of history (the plot). Events in the plot do not occur randomly; they are connected by and through an underlying, meaningful, and rational structure comprehensible by reason. The pregiven purpose of history is the progressive perfection of humans and the ever more complete realization of their capabilities and projects.

7. An optimistic and rationalist philosophy of human nature (character development). Humans are said to be intrinsically good, able to reason and to be rationally governed. Goodness will naturally unfold and be expressed as people's external circumstances become more favorable (e.g., as authority becomes enlightened, and the natural world is better controlled and utilized through science).

8. A philosophy of knowledge (an ideal form). Science serves as the exemplar of the right use of reason and the paradigm of all true knowledge. Science "progresses" (e.g., acquires ever more accurate knowledge of the "real" world) by applying and improving its own unique "logic of discovery." The objects of scientific investigation exist "out there," independent of the scientist or subject.

Postmodern philosophers try to reveal the internally contradictory nature of each of these claims. They also posit a set of ideas at least partially outside Enlightenment beliefs. Postmodern philosophers also claim their deconstructions can open up spaces in or from which different and more varied ideas and practices may begin to emerge. The partial and problematic qualities of their achievements and claims can best be seen when postmodernists enter into conversations with psychoanalysts and feminists.

"Masters of Suspicion": Postmodern Positionings

For someone accustomed to more conventional philosophies, reading the postmodernists can be a frustrating endeavor. These authors do not offer a set of logical and sustained arguments or a synthetic or even coherent viewpoint. Instead they present a series of "positions" and a heterogeneous polyphony of voices.[10] This style or styles is congruent with postmodernism itself. Among the characteristic traits and purposes of postmodernist thought is the displacement of epistemology and metaphysics by rhetoric. Postmodernists intend to replace the search for and enunciation of truth, which they believe has dominated Western philosophy since Plato, with the art of conversation or persuasive speech. In conversation the philosopher's voice would be no more authoritative than any other. A problem is that this voice still tends to override or direct too many others. It also retains the privilege of defining what "game" is to be played and its rules.

Certain themes, devices, and moves recur in postmodernist rhetoric. Radical and dramatic claims are frequently put forth and tend to cluster around certain highly charged themes. One of the most important claims is that Western culture is about to experience or has already experienced, but has been denying, an interrelated series of deaths. These include the deaths of Man, History, and Metaphysics. Postmodernists' "death" announcements are dramatic proclamations and partially metaphorical ways of stating a complex set of interdependent ideas. At this point I will only indicate some of the information each is meant to convey.

1. *The Death of Man.* Postmodernists wish to destroy all essentialist concepts of human being or nature. They consider all concepts of Man to be fictive devices that acquire a naturalistic guise both in their construction and in repeated use within a language game or set of social practices. In order to become authoritative in a culture dominated by the "will to truth," the conventional origins of all concepts of Man must be disguised. In fact Man is a social, historical, or linguistic artifact, not a noumenal or transcendental Being.

In their view Man is actually "decentered." His attempts to impose a fictive or narrative order or structure on experience or events are constantly preconstituted and undermined by desire, language, the unconscious, and the unintended effects of the violence required to impose such an order. Man is forever caught in the web of fictive meaning, in chains of signification, in which the subject is merely another position in language.

As a purely fictive character, Man has nothing that could serve as the basis for his stepping outside this web or for breaking free from it. There is no "Archimedes point," no moment of autonomy, no pure reason or constituting consciousness with independent, nonlinguistic, or nonhistorical access to the Real or Being of the World.

2. *The Death of History.* The idea that History has any intrinsic order or logic is another fiction of Man. Man constructs stories he calls History in order to find or justify a place for himself within time. Man wishes for time to exist for him; he wants to be at home in time—for time to be his home. He creates "master narratives" in which History is his, the subject's, coming to Be in and through time.[11] At the end of this story/time, Man's reason or labor will be made fully Real, and thus nothing will be alien to or estranged from him. He will be the Sovereign Subject forever.

The idea that History exists for or is his Being is more than just another precondition and justification for the fiction of Man. This idea also supports and underlies the concept of Progress, which is itself such an important part of Man's story. The notion of Progress depends on the idea that there is some pregiven goal toward which Man is steadily moving. This goal or purpose is meant for Man; it expresses or realizes him at his best. The closer he comes to it, the closer he comes to himself, to his essence.

Such an idea of Man and History privileges and presupposes the value of unity, homogeneity, totality, closure, and identity. This story requires positing one innate quality of Man that is best—reason, the capacity to labor, or the political life. All other qualities of Man should be subordinated to or serve the One. In juxtaposition to this story and to displace it, the postmodernists tell another, different one. The real is flux. History is a series of random events with no intrinsic order and no necessary laws that produce causality or even continuity. There is thus no empirical or logical reason to privilege unity, homogeneity, closure, or identity over difference, heterogeneity, alterity, and openness.

Furthermore there may be ethical or political reasons for reversing the value placed on unity over difference or homogeneity over heterogeneity. In order to make the whole appear Rational, the contradictory stories of others must be erased, devalued, suppressed. Any appearance of unity presupposes and requires a prior act of violence. Only by forcibly suppressing elements of the flux can History acquire a structured and unitary appearance.

It follows from this view of the Real and History that conflict and violence are endemic to the story of Man in time. There is no end to History, no closed totality in which the "stages" are pregiven, cumulative, irreversible, or progressive. There can be no guarantee that after a finite amount of struggle our work will succeed and be finished forever. The always temporary victor of a particular conflict may succeed in imposing his story as the whole truth, but all such victories and stories are in principle unstable and reversible. Furthermore no combatant can justly claim, though many do, to be merely the vehicle or instrument for an extrahistorical or social Good. There is no transcendental or disinterested position from which such a Good could be identified or from which it could be said that the Truth or the Good did in fact triumph in a particular instance.

3. *The Death of Metaphysics.* Western philosophy has been under the spell of the "metaphysics of presence" at least since Plato.[12] Most Western philosophers took as their task the construction of a philosophic system in which something Real would and could be represented in thought. This Real is understood to be an external or universal subject or substance, existing "out there" independent of the knower. The philosopher's desire is to "mirror," register, mimic, or make present the Real. Truth is understood as correspondence to it.

For postmodernists this quest for the Real conceals most Western philosophers' desire, which is to master the world once and for all by enclosing it within an illusory but absolute system they believe represents or corresponds to a unitary Being beyond history, particularity, and change. In order to mask his idealizing desire, the philosopher must claim that this Being is not the product, artifact, or effect of a particular set of historical or linguistic practices. It can only be the thought of the Real itself.

The philosopher also obscures another aspect of his desire: to claim a special relation and access to the True or Real. He claims that, in a sense, the presence of the Real for us depends on him—the clarity of his consciousness, the purity of his intention. Only the philosopher has the capacity for Reason, the love of wisdom (philo-sophia), the grasp of method, or the capacity to construct a logic adequate to the Real. Just as the Real is the ground of Truth, so too philosophy as the privileged representative of the Real and interrogator of truth claims must play a "foundational" role in all "positive knowledge."

Hence, too, the importance of epistemology within modern philosophy. Epistemology serves as the means to purge, clarify, or delineate the philosopher's consciousness, for himself and for the benefit of other philosophers.

Postmodernists attack the "metaphysics of presence" and the Western philosopher's self-understanding in a number of ways. They question the philosophies of mind, truth, language, and the Real that underlie and ground any such transcendental or foundational claims. However from feminist and psychoanalytic perspectives it sometimes appears that the underlying purposes of this attack are unclear and ambiguous. At times it seems to me that postmodernists are engaged in the same strategic operations in relation to modern philosophies that Kant applied to older concepts of reason: to subject them to critique in order to resituate them on firmer ground over which the philosopher can then reassert the continuing legitimacy of his exclusive command. Nonetheless postmodernist critiques of the "metaphysics of presence" in many ways complement, correct, and strengthen psychoanalytic and feminist deconstructions of mind, truth, language, reality, and philosophy. Feminist theories are much more sensitive to the "play" of gender (including its obscured presence in postmodernisms), and both feminists and psychoanalysts have clearer understandings of the complexities of subjectivity and selfhood.

Postmodernists' positions on "metaphysics" include:

1. *"Metaphysical Minds."* There is and can be no transcendental mind; on the contrary postmodernists claim that what we call the mind or reason is only an effect of discourse. There are no immediate or indubitable features of mental life. Sense data, ideas, intentions, or perceptions are already preconstituted. Such experiences only occur in and reflect a variety of linguistically and socially predetermined practices. The problem of the relation between the "mind" and "things in themselves" becomes infinitely more complex. One cannot even assume that the mind has some universal, transcendental, a priori categories or concepts that always preshape experience in the same, even if unknowable, ways. Instead the categories or concepts by and through which we structure experience are themselves historically and culturally variable. "Mind" is no more homogeneous, lawful, and internally consistent in or over time than is History.

2. *"Metaphysical" Truth.* Truth for postmodernists is also an effect

of discourse. Each discourse has its own distinctive set of rules or procedures that govern the production of what is to count as a meaningful or truthful statement. Each discourse or "discursive formation" is simultaneously enabling and limiting. The rules of a discourse enable us to make certain sorts of statements, but the same rules force us to stay within the system and to make only those statements that conform to these rules. A discourse as a whole cannot be true or false because truth is always contextual and rule dependent. Instead discourses are local, heterogeneous, and incommensurable. No non-discourse-dependent or transcendental rules exist that could govern all discourses or a choice between them. Truth claims are in principle "undecidable."

3. *"Metaphysical Language."* Postmodernists claim that notions of language as a transparent or neutral medium are wrong. Each of us is born into an ongoing set of language games that we must learn in order to be understood by and to understand others. The meaning of our experience and our understanding of it cannot be independent of the fact that such experience and all thought about it are grasped and expressed in and through language. To the degree that thought depends on language, thought and "the mind" itself will be socially and historically constituted. Recent theories of language seem to render impossible or meaningless any claim that there can be a historical or transcendental standpoint from and by which the Real can be apprehended and reported in or by thought.

4. *The "Metaphysics" of Reality.* The Real is unstable and perpetually in flux. Western metaphysics creates a false appearance of unity by reducing the flux and heterogeneity of experience into binary and supposedly natural or essentialist oppositions that include identity/difference, nature/culture, truth/rhetoric, speech/writing, and male/female. The construction of these qualities through and as opposites reveals the philosopher's desire for control and combination. The members of these binary pairs are not equal. Instead the first member of each is meant to dominate the second, which becomes defined as the "other" of the first. Its identity is determined only by its being as the negative of the first. The other has no independent or autonomous character of its own; for example, "woman" is defined as a deficient man in discourses from Aristotle through Freud. Once these oppositions are seen as fictive, asymmetric, and conditions of possi-

bility for the philosopher's story, then a premise that underlies all variants of the metaphysics of Presence can be revealed: To be other, to be different than the defining One is bad. It is better to be defined and determined as the lesser other of the One than to be outside Being altogether.

5. *The "Metaphysics" of Philosophy.* Philosophy is necessarily a fictive, nonrepresentational activity. As a product of the human mind, philosophy has no special relation to Truth or the Real. The philosopher merely creates stories about these concepts and about his own activities. His stories are no more true than any other. There is no way to test whether one story is closer to the truth than another because there is no transcendental standpoint or mind unenmeshed in its own story. Philosophers should seek instead an infinite "dissemination" of meanings. They should abjure any attempt to construct a closed system in which the other, "deferred," or "excess" are "pushed to the margins" and made to disappear in the interest of coherence and unity.

Postmodernist Moves: Deconstruction, Interpretation, and Dissemination

Deconstructive readers are disrespectful of authority, attentive to suppressed tensions or conflicts within the text, and suspicious of all "natural" categories, essentialist oppositions, and representational claims. They are willing to play with the text, to disrupt its apparent unity, to rescue its heterogeneous and disorderly aspects and its plurality of meanings and voices. They are not to think of themselves as author(ities) or as un- or dis-coverers of Truth, but rather as potentially interesting members of an ongoing conversation. Their responsibility is to offer listeners a variety of moves from and against which further movement becomes possible.

In a deconstructive reading one looks for what has been suppressed within a text or story. This strategy can work as well for a feminist interested in the effects of gender or an analyst tracking the unconscious as for a literary critic. Given the premise that the Real is always heterogeneous and differentiated, it follows that whenever a story appears unified or whole, something must have been suppressed in order to sustain the appearance of unity. Like repressed material in the unconscious, the suppressed within the story does not lose its power; it affects the character of the whole. Recovering the suppressed allows the strains and self-divisions that are an at least equally important part of the story to reappear. This rereading transforms the story's meaning for us and lessens its hold on or power over us. The deconstructionist is particularly interested in the strategies a work uses to claim its representational authority and to hide the necessary failure of any and all representational projects. Such failures provide further evidence for the untruth and impossibility of any theory or claim to representational knowledge.

In some ways deconstruction is a radical form of hermeneutics.[13] Like the hermeneutic reader the deconstructionist is interested in the meaning of the text. The deconstructionist wishes to push the text to the limits of its own explanatory force. Also like the hermeneutic reader the deconstructionist believes there is no meaning outside the text. Both assume the text's meaning is internally generated and gains its force from its own strategies, not from its capacity accurately to "represent" something about an "external reality."

In both hermeneutics and deconstruction claims to representational knowledge are to be replaced by concepts of understanding and methods of interpretation. Both the hermeneutic and the deconstructive reader believe knowledge is a subset of and is made possible by larger contexts of meaning or understanding. The legitimacy or authority of a knowledge claim arises out of and depends upon a set of linguistic practices and communicative interactions. Truth claims or knowledge are inseparable from *pragmatics*—from practice of and skill in contextual "know-how." Such know-how includes knowing how to speak and how to hear within and by the rules of the appropriate language game. Philosophy may be able to describe how understanding is possible in particular contexts; it cannot create a universalizing theory of knowledge (an epistemology) that can ground and account for all knowledge or test all truth claims because these are necessarily context dependent. Pragmatics, knowing how we understand one another and the different ways we do so, should replace epistemology. All understanding is interpretative and depends upon and must be expressed in and through preexisting contexts or language games. Therefore there is no uniquely privileged standpoint outside the text from which a speaker could claim to understand the whole "objectively."

No speaker can claim special or unique authority. Each reader or speaker can offer an interpretation of a text or the rules of a game. These interpretative moves can have an effect only if other players within the game then take them up. The other players will respond to and evaluate them by such criteria as the intrinsic interest of an interpretation, whether it is intelligible, and whether it generates new moves or adds to the richness, depth, or pleasure of our understanding within the game.

Postmodernist writers diverge from traditional hermeneutic thinking when they attack the idea that there is a cohesive "depth" meaning to a text that can be recovered by an adequate interpretation and serve as a standard against which interpretations can be evaluated. Derrida, for example, argues that no text has *a* meaning or authority to which the interpreter must defer.[14] Any text contains many unresolvable antimonies so that no one correct reading exists, and many contradictory ones are possible. Rather than recover or construct a "deep" meaning for the text, Derrida prefers "dissemination"—a constant and open-ended disruption and displacement of a text's authority through interventions that create an infinite stream of interpretations of and meanings for it.

Playing in the Graveyard?
The Politics of Postmodernism

This engagement in and preference for play, fragmentation, and differentiation has a serious purpose, at least in the work of writers like Foucault, Lyotard, and Deleuze and Guattari. Their skeptical and disrespectful polemics are partially strategic devices meant to disrupt and erode the power of the grand "normalizing" discourses that put into action and legitimate patterns of domination characteristic of the post-Enlightenment Western states.[15] The power of these discourses was not delegated to them by the state. In fact the modern state and the "human sciences" exist together in a complex, mutually interdependent network in which knowledge and power are inseparably intertwined. However, although the relations between knowledge and power are a central element within postmodernist discourses, the character of these relations and their implications that follow for philosophy (including postmodernism) are far from clear. At times the postmodernists seem to be saying that all knowledge is basically the same, so that philosophy can be as useful (or as useless) within knowledge/power networks as any other mode of thinking. Hence it can be as disruptive of the modern state to deconstruct the "metaphysics of presence" as to disrupt one of its central bureaucracies.

However, postmodernists sometimes argue that "knowledge" is not a homogeneous entity. There are many incommensurate and local language games. From this perspective the game of philosophy is of interest only to those who play it. Those engaged in other games (e.g., state/power/law/economy) may tolerate postmodernist or other philosophic practices precisely because of their irrelevance to and in the others. Hence postmodernists may be playing with texts while a fundamentally oppressive and destructive social system continues unfazed and unaltered. "Local" knowledges may be somewhat unmarked by the dominant network; yet for precisely that reason they may lack leverage against it. But to the extent that a knowledge is complicit in the network, how can it serve as a focus of resistance?

These ambiguities remain unresolved and often even unremarked within postmodernist discourses. Nonetheless postmodernists, especially Foucault, do identify many interesting connections between knowledge, self, and power. Like feminists and psychoanalysts they emphasize the workings of power that are often obscured within other discourses about it, such as Enlightenment liberal ones.

For example, Foucault argues the modern state must appeal to principles of reason and norms of "human nature" in order to have its laws considered legitimate and just. However, if human nature and reason are not inherently orderly and regular, the grounding of such laws would itself be unstable and constantly open to challenge by other interpretations and interpreters. The modern state thus depends on the creation and widespread acceptance of a fictive but persuasive account of "human nature" and on the emergence of a group of "experts" whose story about such questions will be considered authoritative and final.

The human sciences create such a fictive subject—Man, a Being with a fixed and lawful essence that is knowable by and through the methods and investigations of the human sciences. According to their own story, these sciences merely "discover," they do not create, such laws. The laws are said to be descriptive. In fact they are prescriptive as well because by and through them moral as well as statistical "norms" of human behavior are specified. Those who do not act in accordance with such laws are said to "deviate" from them. Deviations from norms that are by definition rational and natural are dangerous to a political order founded on the regularities of "human nature." Hence such deviant behavior must be studied, regulated, and punished. The entire population must be put under surveillance and (ideally) trained to govern itself by self-consciously or unconsciously accepting these "laws of human nature" as regulatory principles for its own behavior.

The Enlightenment demand for the foundation of all legitimate authority in Reason and Truth ironically results in a system of ever more pervasive and decentralized exercises of power by subjects over themselves under the anonymous and often unacknowledged "tutelage" of the "experts" and their "expertise." Man becomes more and more a "subject"—"subject" to laws that, it is claimed, constitute and reflect his inner Being. Subjection to such laws is said to constitute freedom and autonomy and to assure the accumulation of happiness, rationality, and progress for the population and species as a whole. We can be both determined and "free."

These many, often invisible, exercises of power are consolidated and coordinated by patterns of institutionalized practices and knowledge claims within a "discursive formation." Power ceases to be graspable in representational concepts. It is not the effect of a central, easily identifiable Will or Institution. Rather, power operates as innumerable instances of constraints; its effects can be seen whenever a population appears to be homogeneous, unconflicted, orderly, and unified. Such order always depends upon the subjection of localized, fragmented knowledges, which is a necessary condition for appearance of the "totalizing" discourses of authority.

By interrogating and disrupting these totalizing logics, postmodernists hope to open up spaces in which suppressed heterogeneity, discontinuity, and differences will reappear. The inherent instability of power relations can once again be set in motion if the artificial unity imposed by the fictive narrative of the human sciences is dissolved. To escape the homogeneity of the dominant discourse, we must juxtapose to it alternative modes that repudiate the truth claims and pretense of omniscience of the discourses that now watch over us. These alternative deconstructive discourses must necessarily pay attention to varieties of experience and value whatever they can find of the local and particular. They cannot offer *a* viewpoint, *a* universal subject, *a* way to liberation, development, or happiness, or *a* truth that will set us free—not even deconstruction or postmodernism itself.

No Conclusions

Conversations between psychoanalytic, feminist, and postmodernist theories will continue. In the chapters that follow I will discuss each mode of thinking in more detail. My analysis of each mode will identify the purposes of the theory as defined by the writers themselves; examine the theory through the lens of the other two and in this process identify important absences, "lacks," and repressions within that theory; utilize an understanding of what each theory lacks to account for why the theory fails to achieve the ends it poses for itself; and evaluate each theory's actual and potential contribution to a deeper understanding of knowledge, gender, self, power, and transitional Western culture.

No neat integration, new synthesis, or *Aufhebung* of psychoanalysis, feminist theories, and postmodern philosophies will emerge from this sympathetic quarrel among and with some of the most important modes of contemporary Western theorizing. Nor will I "solve" the problems or provide new theories of self, gender, knowledge, or power. I do not think any such outcome is either possible or desirable. Integration or synthesis would necessarily negate or deny irreducible differences between and among these discourses. To search for synthesis would presume that a theoretical jump over "the Rhodes" of our transitional and fragmented culture is possible through the exercise of a "pure" ahistoric reason.

Instead I will offer a possible approach to the practice of postmodern philosophy, one that is self-reflective about its methods and the limitations of knowing and of reason as the basis for knowledge and about knowledge as a source of power. Like many contemporary writers I have numerous questions concerning our and my expectations about adequate theorizing and desirable modes of social life. Although none of these questions is resolvable, giving reasons for why and in what sense one theory or concept of knowledge, self, gender, or power is better than another is still possible and necessary. Such arguments are not offered to "privilege" one theory or concept over another in any absolute or final sense, but rather to make my thinking clear enough that readers can enter into the argument and continue it in their own ways.

I have also tried to confront a philosophical tradition and temptation—to speak as a disembodied, impersonal truth teller or critic. Adopting such a voice entails denying the limitations in vision necessarily imposed by any person's social location, including my own, which happens to be white, female, materially comfortable, someone who benefits in many ways from being a citizen of a rich and powerful First World country. I also feel pulled between the practices and knowledges arising out of the various kinds of work I do, as psychoanalytic therapist, teacher of political theory in a predominantly black university, writer, and mother.

There may be no ways out of these dilemmas. Yet there may be at least better or worse ways of living with them. The better ways would seem to include a continuous struggle to be conscious of how philosophies and persons respond to differences and ambiguities: our fear of erasing them, our desire to do so.

Freud claims the inability to tolerate ambiguity is one of the most pronounced characteristics of the neurotic. Further questions emerge and are partially confronted in the last chapter: Do any of these three modes of thought point us toward cures for our inability to tolerate differences and unease? Or are Western culture and its most promising philosophies suffering a "sickness unto death"?

Part Two

The Selves' Conceptions

Three

Freud

Initiation and Omission in Psychoanalysis

But in thus emphasizing the unconscious in mental life we have conjured up the most evil spirits of criticism against psychoanalysis. Do not be surprised at this, and do not suppose that the resistance to us rests only on the understandable difficulty of the unconscious or the relative inaccessibility of the experiences which provide evidence of it. Its source, I think lies deeper. In the course of centuries the naive self-love of men had had to submit to two major blows at the hands of science. The first was when they learnt that our earth was not the center of the universe but only a tiny fragment of a cosmic system of scarcely imaginable vastness. This is associated in our minds with the name of Copernicus, though something similar had already been asserted by Alexandrian science. The second blow fell when biological research destroyed man's supposedly privileged place in creation and proved his descent from the animal kingdom and his ineradicable animal nature. This revaluation has been accomplished in our own days by Darwin. . . . But human megalomania will have suffered its third and most wounding blow from the psychological research of the present time which seeks to prove to the ego that it is not even master in its own house, but must content itself with scanty information of what is going on unconsciously in its mind. We psycho-analysts were not the first and not the only ones to utter this call to introspection; but it seems to be our fate to give it its most forcible expression and to support it with empirical material which affects every individual. Hence arises the general revolt against our science, the disregard of all considerations of academic civility and the releasing of the opposition from every restraint of impartial logic.

Sigmund Freud,
"Fixation to Traumas—
The Unconscious"

In a scientific program, the founding act is on an equal footing with its future transformations; it is merely one among the many modifications that it makes possible. . . . On the other hand, the initiation of a discursive practice is heterogeneous to its ulterior transformations. . . . The initiation of a discursive practice, unlike the founding of a science, overshadows and is necessarily detached from its later developments and transformations. As a consequence, we define the theoretical validity of a statement with respect to the work of the initiator. . . . In keeping with this distinction, we can understand why it is inevitable that practitioners of such discourses must "return to the origin." . . . If we return, it is because of a basic and constructive omission, an omission that is not the result of accident or incomprehension . . . this nonaccidental omission must be regulated by precise operations that can be situated, analyzed, and reduced in a return to a text in itself, to a primary and unadorned text with particular attention to those things registered in the interstices of the text, its gaps and absences. We return to those empty spaces that have been masked by omission or concealed in a false and misleading plentitude . . . this return, which is a part of the discursive mechanism, constantly introduces modifications . . . the return to a text is not a historical supplement that would come to fix itself upon the primary discursivity and redouble it in the form of an ornament which, after all, is not essential. Rather, it is an effective and necessary means of transforming discursive practice. A study of Galileo's works could alter our knowledge of the history, but not the science, of mechanics; whereas, a reexamination of the books of Freud or Marx can transform our understanding of psychoanalysis or Marxism.

Michel Foucault,
"What Is an Author?"

My return to the texts of the initiator and founder of the discursive practice of psychoanalysis has two purposes. One is to identify and evaluate what these texts can contribute to an understanding of a transitional culture, thinking, self, gender, and justice. The second is to examine to what extent postmodernist and feminist theories can elucidate or transform the "precise operations" regulating the constructive omissions that initiate and structure these texts. Despite the many problems with and controversies about his ideas, Freud has never been displaced or replaced as initiator and governing patriarch within psychoanalysis, although almost from the beginning there have been rebellious children who have wished or claimed to have done so. Even the most defiant among the progeny, for example, Karen Horney or Heinz Kohut, have found it necessary to claim the father's blessing or consent by positioning themselves within or as an extension or completion of some facet of his work.[1] The question or challenge—Is it psychoanalysis?—is adjudicated if not resolved by returning to *the* text, Freud's writings, for legitimation.

The return to Freud has motivations beyond the rules governing discursive practices or the politics and psychodynamics of the practitioners of psychoanalysis. No contemporary writer offers a theory of the human self matching the scope or complexity of Freud's. Although he fails to carry out his project, Freud specifies compelling criteria for an adequate concept of a human being. Any such concept would have to include and account for a being that is simultaneously embodied, desiring, rational, speaking, historical, social, gendered, subject to laws both "immutable" and unconscious and temporal, and capable of autonomy from social and biological determinants. Psychoanalysis as a discursive practice incorporates and transcends the boundaries between biology, politics, history, anthropology, philosophy, and linguistics. It includes a theory of mind, psychosexual development, gender, knowledge, and politics as well as a therapeutic practice and method of training. The scope and depth of Freud's work are part of its continuing appeal to myself and others.

Beyond the sheer scope and scale of his ideas, there are other reasons why periodic returns to Freud have occurred within twentieth-century Western intellectual history.[2] Like other great initiators Freud was exquisitely sensitive to and sometimes unconsciously reflective of the most important tensions and conflicts within his culture. Because in many important ways Freud's culture is still our own, we can read his work for "clue(s) to the less fully articulate experiences and reactions of ordinary men."[3] His discourses resonate with contemporary social and individual wishes and offer some hope of solutions to deeply felt problems. In these discourses, however, as in psychotherapy, what is not said, or what is avoided, is often as significant as the manifest content of thought. What is most interesting to me in Freud's work are the gaps, the acts of repression and displacement within his texts. I am interested in making sense of these gaps, but not by relating them to or speculating about the history and psychodynamics of

Freud as a unique and specific individual. Rather, his work provides instances of and clues to the mechanics of and motivations for more widely shared acts of repression. Much of his (and our) repressed material has to do with gender and the implications of the concept of the unconscious for Enlightenment notions of self and knowledge. Both feminists and postmodernists have begun to reveal these contents, often utilizing Freud's own concepts in deconstructions of his texts. However much more work remains to be done.

Two of the most useful tools for such work have been Freud's concepts of ambivalence and repression. *Ambivalence* refers to affective states in which intrinsically contradictory or mutually exclusive desires or ideas are each invested with intense emotional energy. Although one cannot have both simultaneously, one cannot abandon either of them. Freud's writings about self, knowledge, gender, and justice are pervaded by ambivalence. Such ambivalence is not necessarily a symptom of weakness or confusion in Freud's thinking. It is often a strength to resist collapsing complex and contradictory material into an orderly whole. Indeed Freud more often makes errors precisely when he attempts to *repress* his ambivalences. Freud, as we will see, is deeply conflicted about epistemological issues such as how knowledge (including psychoanalysis) is constituted and how it can be evaluated and about his role as discursive "founder." Sometimes he attempts to satisfy his positivistic superego by imposing a reductive and inappropriate order on his material. Other errors in his thinking arise when he attempts to deny or repress aspects of his own ambivalence in order to make "authoritative" pronouncements on issues that had become particularly controversial within the psychoanalytic community (e.g., clinical technique). Freud's (beloved but restrictive) position as founder induced pressures for codification that necessarily conflicted with his own desire to "play"—to be directed by his impelling curiosity and by his continual pleasure in creating and remaking ideas. Postmodernists and feminists are both intrigued by Freud's ambivalences and sometimes unable to sustain or do justice to them. Postmodernists appropriate Freud's concept of the "decentered" self but radically reduce its complexity and consequences. Some feminists simply reject all of psychoanalytic theory because of the truly ignorant and offensive ways Freud sometimes analyzes women.

Postmodernist writers correctly attribute *some* of Freud's ambivalence and repressive operations to his complex commitment to Enlightenment ideas. In the first part of this chapter, I discuss Freud's ideas of the self, sexuality, the unconscious, and knowledge and show how they both incorporate and undermine central Enlightenment precepts. But postmodernists can account for only some of the absences and constructions in Freud's texts. Feminist theorists correctly claim that Freud's acts of omission and repression are at least also equally rooted in his anxieties about gender. In the second part of this chapter, I argue that the "great riddle of sex" does pervade and structure many aspects of Freud's theories, including such supposedly gender-neutral subjects as psychoanalytic technique.[4] Freud's inability fully to "penetrate" this riddle blocks his capacity to grasp certain essential features of inner and outer reality. This inability in turn prepares the ground for Freud's and subsequent psychoanalysts' complicity in, rather than critical exposure of, a fundamental form of domination in our culture: one based in gender relations. Freud's tendency to conceptualize gender as a "biological" and hence unchangeable aspect of human life also leads him to an overly pessimistic account of the "inevitability" of repressive social relations.

Although feminist and postmodernist deconstructions of Freud's work offer many valuable insights into the operations of and nonaccidental omissions in his texts, they are inadequate for many reasons. One of the most important is that neither feminists nor postmodernists engage in a sustained consideration of what can be learned about self or knowledge from analysis of the psychoanalytic situation itself. In this regard they replicate rather than deconstruct one of Freud's most striking and puzzling omissions. I will return to this "empty space" often as the chapter unfolds. New theories developed within psychoanalysis since Freud have often incorporated rather than undone or analyzed many of Freud's constructive omissions as well. Therefore it is important to continue to identify and analyze these omissions because they have become part of the "discursive mechanisms" of contemporary psychoanalysis, as we will see in Chapter 4.

Some Fundamental Concepts in
Freud's Psychoanalysis:
Self, Sexuality, and the Unconscious

Freud's theories are not monolithic or uniform. They underwent several major revisions, and concepts from earlier formulations often coexist uneasily with later ones. Freud's ideas in 1893 differ in many important respects from those of 1914 or of 1937, as he himself admits.[5] His theories increase steadily in complexity, especially as clinical experience forces him to confront the bewildering multiplicity of determinations for even the (apparently) simplest type of psychic event. The arrogant Freud of 1893 who believes he can construct a determinist theory of the mind on the model of Helmholz's physics bears only a small resemblance to the more mature Freud. As his work proceeds, Freud increasingly resembles an explorer whose discoveries and experiences more and more exceed his own expectations and his ability to make sense out of them or to fit them into his theoretical frameworks. One sometimes has the sense he wishes he had never opened "Pandora's box" at all. In 1931, for example, Freud publicly acknowledges his difficulties in grasping the nature of preoedipal experience, which, he discovers to his surprise, plays such a central role in women's psychological development.[6] Freud's initial excitement about the power of analytic treatment gradually gives way to increasing modesty about its efficacy. Eventually he begins to despair at its limitations in confronting the unrelenting power of unconscious forces.

The growing complexity of and many ambiguities in Freud's work, however, should not obscure the persistence with which he pursues and develops certain ideas. These ideas and the gaps and omissions in his investigations are contributions to and symptoms of transitional thinking and culture. At stake within Freud's writings are questions that recur throughout contemporary thought and social life, including: What is the nature of the human being? What are the sources, limits, and powers of our knowledge about our selves and (and in) the physical world? What is the nature of human sexuality? Are there any "natural" rules governing or limits to its expression? What is gender? How and why do gender relations have their current forms? Can these forms be changed, and what would be the risks and benefits of doing so? How are relations of domination established, maintained, and replicated? To what extent are such relations a necessary and unalterable aspect of human life? How are we to understand mental illness and its relation to mental health? What do we mean by therapeutic "cures"—are they possible and, if so, why? Freud was troubled, at times almost tormented, by uncertainty about the answers to all these questions. Yet his attempts to respond to them and his frequent refusals to settle for premature closure or avoidance of their difficulties have much to offer those who live in and think about our own era of uncertainty and transition. As we pursue his writings on self, knowledge, gender, justice, and therapy, some of these constructive commissions and omissions will become more evident.

The Constitution, Limits, and Powers of the Individual Self

As postmodernists claim, Freud's writings on the constitution, limits, and powers of the self both challenge and reinforce Enlightenment views of humans as essentially rational beings. Freud's writings reflect and are structured by a distinctive ontology that conflicts with and contradicts other important theorists' ideas. In his view humans are originally and primarily desiring creatures. Our being is not defined by the capacity to reason, as Plato and Kant believe; by the ability to speak, reason, and engage in political deliberation, as Aristotle argues; or by the power to produce objects of value and need, as Marx claims. "The core of our being," according to Freud, consists of "unconscious wishful impulses" that cannot be destroyed. At best our more rational "secondary processes" will be able to direct "along the most expedient paths the wishful impulses that arise from the unconscious." Unconscious wishful impulses, most of which are forever inaccessible to our preconscious or conscious, will nonetheless remain the dominating force in our mental life.[7]

Freud's view of humans is thus profoundly materialistic. The basic purpose of human life, insofar as there is one at all, is to satisfy innate human needs. However the nature of our needs and our desire is far from clear in Freud's writings. As is well known, he conceptualizes these needs in two different, somewhat contradictory ways: instinct theory and object relations theory. According to instinct theory the origin of all instincts is somatic; stimuli arise from the body and are felt by us as a need or drive. The nervous system and the entire "psychical apparatus" are governed by the "constancy (or Nirvana) principle"—any stimulus is experienced as causing an increase in tension and hence is potentially unpleasurable.[8] The purpose of the mental apparatus is to reduce this tension by somehow altering the inner source of stimulation. The aim of an instinct "is in every instance satisfaction, which can only be obtained by abolishing the condition of stimulation in the source of the instinct." The "purpose" or ideal of the apparatus is to remain in a constant, unchanging state, which is infeasible, for it would require that the organism "maintain itself in an altogether unstimulated condition."[9] Because human organisms cannot ward off all stimuli, we instead try to find ways to discharge the tensions they produce. We experience as satisfaction and pleasurable whatever does away with a need. Hence organisms are governed by the "pleasure principle"—a need to reduce tension (unpleasure) through instinctual satisfaction. Freud claims, "what we call happiness . . . comes from the (preferably sudden) satisfaction of needs which have been dammed up to a high degree."[10]

Humans are a closed system with a finite amount of libidinal and aggressive energy. Connections with others are made only when one individual chooses to invest some of this energy in another. The purpose of such a connection is always narcissistic. Others exist for us as means to satisfy our needs, to relieve frustration, or to restore equilibrium. Freud distinguishes between "narcissistic" and "anaclitic" attachments to "objects" (other persons), but closer examination reveals that the purpose of both kinds of attachment is self-satisfaction, not concern for the other as an independently existing being. In narcissistic object-choice one may love "what he is himself (actually himself) . . . what he once was . . . what he would like to be . . . (or) someone who was once part of himself." In anaclitic object choice one may love "the woman who tends" or "the man who protects."[11]

If we could maintain psychic equilibrium solely by our own efforts, we would have no innate need to relate to other persons. Thus in this view humans are not inherently social; they have no desire or capacity to seek out or experience another person as an independently existing self. True reciprocity is not possible, although we may cover up or rationalize our selfishness with delusional ideologies such as romantic love. Object attachments can even be dangerous to the self. Because there is a limited supply of energy, the amount we invest in others will become a net loss if our need is no longer satisfied. It is possible that the more the self invests energy in others, the more depleted it will become. With each object attachment the self risks "melancholia," a loss of energy and self-respect.

Ambivalence is always present in love relationships. Love can easily turn to hate or sadism, and these in turn can be exercised on the self or on its (former) object. In later formulations of instinct theory, the death drive and the nirvana (constancy) principle precede Eros and the pleasure principle; "the relation of hate to objects is older than that of love." [12] Love violates the constancy principle; the always imperfect responses of objects raise tension levels and can create unpleasure. Hate is an "expression of the pain-reaction induced by objects" and "remains in constant intimate relation with the instincts of self preservation." [13]

This view of humans and human relationships is somewhat contradicted by aspects of Freud's post-1914 work, especially his introduction of concepts such as the superego, positive transference, and object love. In Freud's later theories the self is partially determined by the quality of its relations with others and how these relations are taken in and processed. Freud now claims the ego develops by introjecting objects, especially "sexual" ones, which the child has to give up. By introjecting the object the child takes it "inside." By identifying with the object, the child retains "inside" what he or she has to give up in the "outside" world. [14]

In Freud's development of the notion of the superego, he also seems to erase the radical disjunctions posited earlier between self, other, and culture. The superego is the "residue" and dissolution of the oedipus complex. Superego development entails and requires the internalization not only of individual parents but also of the past and contemporary injunctions of the culture as a whole. In turn parents, especially the father, derive part of their authority from their role as representative of the laws of culture. Through the development of the superego, aspects of the "external world" become part of the self and powerfully affect the character of our "internal" experience. Even the id is partially structured by the effects of object relations and their internalization.

In order for the internalization of a relationship with another person to be possible, there cannot be such a radical disjunction between the self and other as Freud's theory of narcissism seems to imply. The existence of internalized personal relations, continually affecting the thinking and feeling of the self, negate the idea of the mind as a purely private, drive-governed, or self-enclosed space. In Freud's later accounts of the formation of both the ego and the superego, human relationships arise from motives other than the simple need to reduce frustration or restore an imbalance in the libidinal economy.

Despite the many contradictions between the economic drive

model of mind and motivation and the object relations model, Freud (unlike subsequent analysts, such as Lacan and Winnicott) never abandons either theory. Nor does he seem happy with the tensions between the two. Despite the claims of later object relations theorists, Freud seems driven to incorporate object relations material *within* an economic model.[15] The economic drive model and the theory of narcissism remain the primary explanations for psychical phenomena, even object-related ones. For example, Freud explains the dissolution of the oedipus complex, at least in boys, mainly in economic terms. The boy has an intense libidinal and narcissistic investment in his penis. This investment comes into conflict with the potential consequence of his object love for the mother—castration. "Normally, in this conflict the first of these forces triumphs; the child's ego turns away from the Oedipus-complex." Thus "the Oedipus-complex succumbs to the threat of castration."[16]

Freud also sensitively explores some of the vicissitudes of object love. He acknowledges the incredible power of the attachment to objects, even dead ones, over the self. "Melancholia," for example, is both an object-related and a "constitutional" illness. In melancholia "loss of the object became transformed into a loss in the ego," and "the shadow of the object fell upon the ego."[17]

However Freud explains the power of objects for the self in economic terms, not as later object relations theorists would, by an innate need for attachment or object love. Attachments are formed by investing the *idea* of a person or relationship with libidinal energy. When a person no longer satisfies us, we must retrieve the invested energy, or the world or the self will feel empty. The normal processes of mourning or the pathological processes of melancholia are both means of detaching the energy from the object and recapturing it for the ego. The Nirvana principle continues to govern, even in the sphere of Eros or object attachments. Freud's continuous attraction to reorganizing his material in this way partially reflects and conceals his anxieties about gender and "science," as we will see later in this chapter.

Sexuality and the Unconscious

Freud's concept of humans as desiring creatures is, of course, intertwined with and grounded in theories of sexuality and the unconscious. The "principal constituents of the theoretical structure of psychoanalysis" include the theories of the unconscious, "the etiological significance of sexual life and of the importance of infantile experiences," as well as the theories of resistance and repression.[18] However, although these theories are among the most powerful and unsettling aspects of his work, they are somewhat contradictory and ambiguous. Freud's ideas support both radical and "normalizing" or regulatory concepts of sexuality. On the one hand he conceptualizes sexuality as the unfolding of innate, pregiven, psychosexual stages (oral, anal, phallic, and genital). "Not only the deviations from normal sexual life but its normal form as well are determined by the infantile manifestations of sexuality."[19] Libidinal satisfaction is a basic human need. Different "zones" of the body become the primary focus of such satisfaction at preset points in psychic development. In "what is known as the normal sexual life of the adult . . . the pursuit of pleasure comes under the sway of the reproductive function." The varied impulses of childhood are combined "into a unity, an impulsion with a single aim"—genitally oriented, heterosexual intercourse.[20]

Freud is somewhat ambiguous about whether "normality" is meant in a descriptive or prescriptive way. He describes "lingering over" earlier (nongenital) zones or stages as "immature" "fixations" and asserts that "every pathological disorder of sexual life is rightly to be regarded as an inhibition in development." Throughout his life he insists that neurosis is *caused* by "sexual instinctual forces."[21] Any deviation from mature genital heterosexuality would thus seem to be *prima facie* evidence of mental illness or "abnormality."

Yet at the same time Freud says that even in cases of the most perverse sexual behavior, such as intercourse with dead bodies, "we should not be too ready to assume" that such people are gravely ill. People can be "sick" in the "single sphere of sexual life" and "normal" in other respects. Deviations from heterosexuality also are not necessarily *prima facie* evidence of illness. Homosexuals should not be separated from "the rest of mankind as a group of a special character." All persons "are capable of making a homosexual object-choice and have in fact made one in their unconscious." There is only one form of sexuality. The "natural" state of a child is "polymorphous perversity," not heterosexuality or genitality. Thus "the exclusive sexual interest felt by men for women is also a problem that needs elucidating and is not a self-evident fact."[22]

Freud is also ambiguous about how opposed or disjunctive "natural" and "civilized" sexuality are. On the one hand he claims psychosexuality is not historically variable. How sexuality is expressed may be and always is modified by culture, but culture does not create the drives themselves. There will always be antagonism between libido or desire and culture, between "natural" beings and "cultural" persons. Nonetheless the opposition between nature and culture is not so absolute as it may first seem. Demand or desire is not a purely bodily sensation. A *trieb* (drive) is always a mental representation of a need or want. "The concept is thus one of those lying on the frontier between the mental and the physical."[23] A somatic demand must be translated into a psychic one before the organism can recognize and act on it. This process of transformation renders the drives vulnerable to cultural influences. The purity of the "natural" is further diminished with the increasing complexity of Freud's conception of the unconscious. Freud's initial conception of the unconscious is relatively straightforward. It expresses itself through and is the locus of "primary process." The characteristics associated with the "system Ucs." include *"exemption from mutual contradiction, primary process* (motility of cathexis), *timelessness,* and *substitution* of psychic for external reality."[24] Although primary process is simultaneously psychic and somatic, reason is conceptualized as a "secondary" process located within the ego or conscious mind. However, as Freud turns his attention from the unconscious to the ego, he discovers that the ego has its own processes of denial and defense. According to the later structural theories, aspects of the ego or superego, as well as demands of the id, may be repressed. "Conscious mind" and ego no longer coincide.

Freud now introduces the concept of the "dynamical unconscious," which includes repressed libidinal wishes, other kinds of knowledge about the self, and its relations to ego or superego objects and activities. Parts of the unconscious may even not be repressed— "all that is repressed is Ucs., but not all that is Ucs. is repressed."[25] The boundaries between ego, superego, and id and the distinctions between the psychic, somatic, and cultural are no longer clear, fixed, or impermeable. Because the ego originally develops out of the id, it is foremost a "body-ego" and is not isolated from the superego. The superego itself is simultaneously biological and cultural; it is the "outcome" of both historical and biological factors, including the oedipus complex and "the lengthy duration in man of his childhood helplessness and dependence."[26]

As postmodernists argue, the self in Freud's theories becomes increasingly fragmented, decentered, and heterogeneous in its qualities and dynamics. Forces are always affecting our "rational" thought and behavior, but these forces can be (at best) only imperfectly known or comprehended. The agency of our knowing is "contaminated" by the influence of these unconscious forces, including desire and authority. The ego is the only agency of the mind capable of thinking. It alone can submit mental processes or perceptions to "reality testing" or order events in time. However the ego is not always a reliable witness or source of information because in its relations with the id, the ego "too often yields to the temptation to become sycophantic, opportunist and lying, like a politician who sees the truth but wants to keep his place in popular favor."[27]

The ambiguities in the theories of the libido and the unconscious are also their strength and utility. Precisely because the concept of instinct (or drive) is simultaneously psychic and somatic, it offers the possibility of overcoming the mind-body dualism, which reappears in later psychoanalytic theories. Many aspects of embodiment and non-narcissistic object relations disappear in Lacanian theory. In some versions of object relations theory, instinct is purposively abandoned. Bodily experience and the non-object-related aspects of desire tend to disappear as well. "The body" or "biology" is assigned to the concerns of medicine or psychiatry, and psychoanalysis is reformulated as a science of "persons." This considerably weakens and restricts psychoanalysis and knowledge more generally because one never encounters a "person" without a body. Contemporary medicine and science in turn are often all too willing to conceptualize bodies as if they exist independent of persons, desire, and agency.

By conceptualizing sexuality as the driving force of human development and illness, Freud had no choice but to include bodies, fantasy, and object-related dimensions of experience within his theory. However often he may have been tempted to reduce desire to "biology" or chemistry, its object-related aspects pushed him back toward interpersonal relations. But his attention to the obdurate and conflictual nature of desire kept him from "normalizing" sexuality and reducing it to whatever dictates a culture imposes concerning its "natural" and appropriate expression. His insistence on the polymorphic and frustrating aspects of desire, on the frequent failures of objects to conform to one's wishes, provides a powerful challenge to our cultural ideology with its emphasis on heterosexuality, romanticism, and denial of the complexity of desire and its frequent noncoincidence with "love."

No subsequent psychoanalytic theory has been able to abandon libido theory and still account for embodiment or to transcend mind-body dualisms. No purely biological theory has been able to account for the interpersonal, cultural, and fantasy elements of human experience or mental illness. Although the many inadequacies of instinct theory and Freud's concept of sexuality may tempt us to abandon them, these ideas are still important. They operate as a demand and warning not to succumb to either a dualistic or a simplistically unitary view of mind-body relation. Freud's ideas about sexuality and embodiment can thus be appropriated by feminist and postmodernist discourse, but they require further analysis by them.

The Structure(s) of Mind
and Problems of Knowledge
The Fragmenting Mind

As postmodernists argue, Freud's increasingly complex structural theories undermine the concepts of mind upon which Enlightenment concepts of knowledge depend. Freud constructs powerful and complex theories of the mind that contradict and challenge many contemporary epistemologies. Unlike many philosophers Freud conceptualizes the mind as fully embodied, inherently conflictual, dynamic, nonunitary, and constituted in and through processes that are intrinsically different and cannot be synthesized or organized into a permanent, hierarchical organization of functions or control. Both the rationalist's faith in the powers of reason and the empiricist's belief in the reliability of sense perception and observation are grounded in and depend on the mind's capacity to be at least partially undetermined by the effects of the body, passions, and social authority or convention. However, Freud's theories of mind render such beliefs highly problematic. His later theories incorporate the qualities postmodernists prefer—heterogeneity, flux, and alterity. The distinction between inner and outer determinants of experience breaks down.

The mind's structure and processes become increasingly fragmented, fluid, and subject to complex and often unconscious alterations. The equation of mind and conscious thought or reason or the psychical and conscious becomes untenable.

Each aspect of the mind—ego, id, and superego—is now described as constituted in and through inner *and* outer experiences. Each is simultaneously psychic, somatic, object related, and cultural-historical. The id is the "reservoir" of libido and hence is simultaneously psychic and somatic. It also contains "object cathexes" and is in some way interpersonal as well. The id is historical and social because it contains important "phylogenetic acquisitions"—each individual inherits the entire cultural development of the species and its systems of rules, especially the incest taboo. The "ego-structures of previous generations" leave behind their "precipitates in the id of their progeny."[28]

The ego is a "surface-differentiation" of the id; it is "that part of the id which has been modified by direct influence of the external world." However "the ego is not sharply separated from the id; its lower portion merges into it." The ego is "ultimately derived from bodily sensations [and] may thus be regarded as a mental projection of the surface of the body." It is also interpersonal because it is "formed to a great extent out of identifications which take the place of abandoned cathexes by the id." The ego is social and historical as well. Because it is closely connected to the superego, it carries out "repressions in the service of and at its behest."[29] The entire ego structure may be radically modified, even driven into death, by the superego's powerful destructive energies.

The superego has "intimate relations" with the id and direct access to its cathectic (charged) energies, especially aggression, which it can utilize for its own purposes, independent of or against the ego. The superego is interpersonal because it is a derivation and result of the oedipus complex. This derivation brings it "into relations with the phylogenetic acquisitions of the id." As "heir to the Oedipus complex," it is derived from the id's (repressed) object attachments (the child's desire for the parents, fear of castration, etc.). Hence "the super-ego is always close to the id and can act as its representative *vis-a-vis* the ego."[30] But it also acts as the representative of morality because the entire social history of the species is internalized along with the authority of the father. A paradoxical consequence of this double derivation is that the locus of our conscience, of morality, is also inter-connected with and overdetermined by our instincts, especially aggression. The "highest" and "lowest" aspects of humanity are closely, sometimes inextricably, connected.

It is increasingly difficult to locate any aspect of the mind capable of engaging in or sustaining autonomous, "pure" thought (i.e., thought not affected by bodily experience, libidinal wishes, authority relations, or cultural conventions). Because even parts of the ego may be dynamically repressed, privileged, much less relatively complete, insight into the mind's operation is unattainable. Bias cannot be "con-trolled for" if its source is the dynamically unconscious repressed ma-terial that is in principle inaccessible to the conscious mind.

Freud's claim that the ego may be modified by its own defensive processes as well as by its ongoing struggle with the superego and the id thus undermines the Enlightenment belief in the intrinsic and nec-essary relationships between reason, self-determination, and free-dom or emancipation. The ego may devise elaborate rationalizations for the construction and maintenance of reason's own prison. It may seek accommodation with or even glorify tutelage as readily as ex-press the will to freedom. Neither the ego's "empirical observations" nor its "transcendental meditations" can be fully trusted or their reli-ability assumed. Under the unconscious influence of unresolved wishes, the ego may become rigid, trapped by and within a compul-sion to repeat. In this syndrome present events are unconsciously ex-perienced and reconstructed in the shape of the past. Old battles are continually fought on now familiar terrain. The capacity to observe and interpret present events is damaged, for they are unconsciously viewed through the prism of the past; the new is transformed into a mere replication of the old.

"Being able to give reasons" for one's choice of action or definition of self-interest cannot be taken as unproblematic evidence of ration-ality or freedom from the unconscious either. A "rational reconstruc-tion" of the reasons for a choice or belief may on analysis turn out to be an elaborate rationalization of or reparation for an irrational wish or fear. Reason can become the ally or servant of unreason in other ways. In alliance with the superego, on behalf of present forms of authority, it can suppress wishes for truth as well as pleasure. Out of fear of a punitive superego, the ego may learn to comply with the authorities (familial, intellectual, or political). It may even convince itself that in so doing it is pursuing truth or is expressing its own will. The self can be so dependent on and attached to its capacity for self-deception that its very sense of "reality" is threatened if its rationalizations begin to become undone.

Dreaming of Science

Freud's work thus does anticipate and support the critiques of traditional theories of mind currently articulated by postmodern philosophers. The mind loses its privileged status as a private internal space. It can be neither a Lockean blank slate, as required by neo-Baconian empiricism, nor any variety of monad, as envisioned, for example, by Descartes or Sartre. Radical individualism also becomes untenable, as do epistemologies that rely on the possibility of accurate self-observation and direct, reliable access to and control over the mind and its activities.[31]

Although his concepts of the mind and the unconscious undermine the splits between mind and body and reason and unreason upon which both rationalist and empiricist theories of knowledge depend, Freud never abandons a positivistic notion of science and the desire for psychoanalysis to be conceptualized and accepted as such a science. He "always felt it as a gross injustice that people always refused to treat psychoanalysis like any other science."[32] The subsequent course of psychoanalysis, especially in the United States, has been profoundly influenced by the positivistic aspects of Freud's thinking. For this reason, as well as to comprehend Freud's texts more adequately, we must explore what he understood "science" to be. His dreams of science, like many dreams, conceal unconscious wishes and defensive operations, which I analyze later in the chapter.

Although concerned about the adequacy of existing scientific theories, training, and practices (especially medicine) as models for psychoanalysis, Freud was deeply influenced by the scientism of his day. Psychoanalysis is not to be one more "poetic narrative," "modernist fiction," or philosophic account of the human life story. Philosophy and psychoanalysis represent irreconcilable and antagonistic claims to the representation of truth. Science *alone* can provide knowledge that "corresponds" to reality. Hence only through scientific means can truthful information be obtained about "what concerns human beings most of all—their own nature." Psychoanalysis deserves our interest not only as a method of treatment, but above all "on account of the truths it contains" about such essential matters.[33]

Freud felt obligated to "keep down" his own inclination "to speculation" and instead pursued the study of medicine. His "original purpose" was not to be a physician but to satisfy "an overpowering need to understand something of the riddles of the world in which we live and perhaps even contribute something to their solution."[34] Only by founding a new science could he make such a contribution. "Strictly speaking there are only two sciences: psychology, pure and applied, and natural science": Psychoanalysis is "a specialist science, a branch of psychology."[35]

Freud's concept of the scientific method contains a curious mixture of rationalist, especially neo-Kantian, and empiricist tenets. There is only one scientific method, and "the intellect and the mind are objects for scientific research in exactly the same way as any non-human things."[36] All science is "based on observations and experiences arrived at through the medium of our physical apparatus." However primary sense perception cannot yield direct information about reality itself. Although "reality will always remain 'unknowable,'" the scientist can obtain "insights" into "connections and dependent relations which are [really] present in the external world." "Somehow" these really independently existing relations can be "reliably reproduced or reflected in the internal world of our thought."[37]

The psychoanalyst, like the physicist, discovers "technical methods of filling up gaps in the phenomena of our consciousness."[38] The analyst infers or interpolates processes that are unknowable in themselves but are assumed really to exist to account for the phenomena directly observed. For example, if a patient makes a slip of the tongue (substitutes an inappropriate word for the correct one), the analyst infers that an unconscious process is occurring that can account for both the making of the slip and its particular content. The patient's agreement with the analyst's interpretation and her or his ability to use it by producing further associations are taken as evidence for the correctness of the analyst's understanding of both the patient and the unconscious processes themselves. The analyst uses the analytic situation and the technical methods of analysis (e.g., free association) "just as a physicist makes use of experiment."[39]

However, while analysts, like any scientist, strive to understand something "real" in and about the "external world," they must recognize that the truth value of the inferred processes is always provisional and open to question. Such inferences, as in any science, are merely hypotheses or approximations. Freud treats such hypotheses as "conjectures" that must be open to refutation. However he does not believe that observation is always "theory laden" or dependent. Theoretical inferences or constructs are merely "intellectual scaffolding," and Freud "look[s] forward to their being modified, corrected, and more precisely determined as further experience is accumulated and sifted." [40]

The hypothesis or inference of the existence of unconscious psychical processes "enabled psychology to take its place as a natural science like any other." [41] Like other sciences, psychoanalysis insists that "there are no sources of knowledge of the universe other than the intellectual working over of carefully scrutinized observations." [42] Previous psychologies failed because they could not account for the observed and observable phenomena that psychoanalysis studies. These "psychology[ies] of consciousness never went beyond the broken sequences which were obviously dependent on something else." [43]

Psychoanalysis is distinguished by the search for this "something else" and the rejection of any knowledge "derived from revelation, intuition or divination." [44] The analyst attempts to grasp the real that underlies surface appearances and can account for the empirically observable gaps in or deviations from "normal" consciousness (e.g., dreams, slips of the tongue). This search for and belief in a strictly empirical and deterministic reality distinguishes psychoanalysis from philosophy or religion. Psychoanalysis does and must share the *Weltanschauung* of the other natural sciences. Freud insists, wrongly in my view, that it has no distinctive *Weltanschauung* of its own.

Freud's account of the scientific *Weltanschauung* is shaped at least as much by the influence of Enlightenment philosophy as by scientific practice per se. Like other Enlightenment thinkers Freud makes his case for the superiority of science partially by contrasting (idealized) methods, purposes, and results of science to those of religion or philosophy. Science remains indispensable and irreplaceable because the scientist *alone* is committed to obtaining true knowledge. Truth is knowledge of "what exists outside of us and independently of us and, as experience has taught us, is decisive for the fulfillment or disappointment of our wishes." [45]

Unlike the philosopher, the scientist does not indulge in "the over-valuation of the magic of words and the belief that the real events in the world take the course which our thinking seeks to impose on them." Unlike religion, science does not seek to give us the "illusion" that the real world will "fit in with our instinctual wishful impulses." Science alone attempts realistically to "take account of our dependence on the real external world." Science is the only basis for "improvements" in the quality of human life. Despite the "dependent relations" and the fragility of the ego and reason, "our best hope for the future is that intellect—the scientific spirit, reason—may in process of time establish a dictatorship in the mental life of man."[46]

The Analytic Situation:
Knowledge from Practice

Much as Freud desired it otherwise, psychoanalysis simply does not and cannot fit within empiricist or rationalist models of science or knowledge. Psychoanalysis does offer a radically new *Weltanschauung*, although many of its epistemological, ontological, and ethical implications have not been adequately explored or developed. It is impossible to comprehend the nature of this *Weltanschauung* apart from or outside of a sustained consideration of the psychoanalytic situation itself, although philosophers (including postmodernists) and feminists often treat psychoanalytic theory as if it exists in isolation from and has no interrelations with analytic practices.

The primary "research tool" of psychoanalysis is the analytic situation. The analytic process and the knowledge it generates cannot be understood by or located within traditional concepts of science. The failure of Freud and many of his followers to accept this fact partially accounts for their inability to explain a central phenomenon of the analytic situation—transference—and thus the therapeutic efficacy of psychoanalysis. Their retention of an empiricist (and in the United States a medical) model of psychoanalytic theory and practice serves defensive functions as well, including a denial of the essentially interrelated and intersubjective character of the analytic process. This defensiveness cripples psychoanalytic theorists, rendering them unable to make full use of the rich clinical detail uncovered in the analytic situation and equally unable to develop an epistemology that could serve as the basis for a more adequate account of the nature of analytic knowledge and its implications for other "human sciences."

To see why psychoanalysis cannot and should not try to be an empirical or natural science and to better understand what sort of knowledge it *can* generate, we must more closely consider the analytic process itself. Freud's writings on the psychoanalytic situation reveal underlying contradictions within his theories and epistemology. In order fully to bring to light the gaps and omissions in his writings on knowledge and the analytic situation, we must supplement a postmodernist sensitivity to the effects of Enlightenment dreams of science with a feminist consciousness of the pervasive power of gender relations. Freud's own work is certainly not free from the obscuring effects of "the great riddle of sex." Anxieties about gender deeply affect his supposedly gender-neutral concepts of knowledge and the nature of psychoanalytic practice.

What did Freud think he was doing during all those hours in his consulting room? It is easier to say what Freud thought psychoanalysis is not because his writings on this subject are often intended to correct misconceptions of analysis. These misconceptions recur in contemporary writings on the subject as well. For example, contrary to the views of some contemporary commentators such Habermas, Freud did not believe psychoanalysis is primarily a cognitive, linguistic, or narrative process.[47] The pathological factor in neurosis is not ignorance, but "inner resistances." The task of therapy is to combat these resistances. In such combat, discourse is the preferred medium, but it cannot be the primary weapon. In fact, "if knowledge about his unconscious were as important for the patient as the inexperienced in psychoanalysis imagine, it would be sufficient to cure him for him to go to lectures or read books. Such measures, however, have as little effects on the symptoms of nervous disease as distributing menu cards in time of famine has on people's hunger."[48]

Contrary to the ideas Grünbaum attributes to him, Freud does not claim that either vertical insight or an increased capacity for self-reflection is the determining factor in the therapeutic success of psychoanalysis.[49] The meaning and significance of "insight" cannot be understood outside the context that gives it its distinctive connotations and status—the transference relation as experienced within the analytic situation. The capacity for veridical insight and self-reflection *should* increase within and by accurate interpretation of the transference relation. However, improving the capacity for insight and an analyst's interpretations of resistance to both it and transference are only aspects of a very complex process.

Transference and resistance, rather than veridical insight or the "tally argument," are the most definitive aspects of psychoanalysis. However it is precisely on the crucial subject of transference relations that Freud's ambivalence becomes most acute. His account of the nature of this relationship and the epistemological status of the "data" it produces is extremely contradictory and unclear.[50] Almost simultaneously, Freud discusses the need for the analyst to remain cold and distant and for there to exist a genuine positive alliance between analyst and patient, not merely a transference relation. Sometimes the analytic process is described in the language of natural science or medicine, as if the analyst were a scientist confronting a piece of data or a surgeon who must ensure that the operating theater is not contaminated. The analytic situation is also described in martial language as an ongoing battle in which the analyst and patient are sometimes allies, sometimes enemies in a shifting constellation of forces.[51] Frequently, Freud admits ruefully, the "big battalions" seem to be on the patient's side.

Freud also insists on the special character of the relationship between analyst and patient, which must be based on the "love of truth, that is on the acknowledgement of reality . . . it precludes any kind of sham or deception."[52] The practical form this love of truth takes is adherence by both analyst and patient to the "analytic rule." For the patient this means trying to say whatever comes to mind without prior censorship (free association); for the analyst it means listening with "evenly hovering attention" without prior assumptions about the relative importance of meaning for the patient of any of her or his associations.

Freud is also ambiguous on the role of suggestion in the analytic process and about the kind of truth that emerges in and through analysis. These issues are interrelated because, according to empiricist criteria of truth, admissible "data" cannot be "contaminated" in or by the process of discovery through which it is obtained. Freud both admits and denies that the therapeutic efficacy of analysis depends on the power of suggestion. What is recovered in analysis is alternately called the "truth" of what "really," empirically happened (the archaeological model) and a "construction" of what happened.[53]

Ultimately, Freud falls back on a certain view of transference to "resolve" the problem of contamination through suggestion. Even if analysis depends on suggestion, its effects can be controlled. During the course of an analysis, suggestion will be traced back to its source in transference phenomena. In a successful analysis transference, and with it the analyst's power of suggestion, will be dissolved. Transference is a necessary but reversible illness stimulated by the analytic situation but caused by the patient's own unconscious dynamics. As the transference is resolved, the "contaminating" influences of suggestion will also fall away; the "data" produced in the analytic situation will get "cleaned up" as the process proceeds.

This attempt to solve the problem of suggestion rests upon certain assumptions about the origins of its power and the nature of the analytic relationship. It is meant to rescue or preserve psychoanalysis as an empirically grounded form of knowledge. Ultimately it fails to do so. It also fails as an account of the analytic situation itself. The power of suggestion is said to arise from unconscious sources. A current relationship becomes infused with the authority of and feeling about a past, usually parental one. The continuing but unconscious power of the past renders an individual vulnerable to the present authority's judgment and susceptible to its influence.

Transference material may emerge in a wide variety of relationships, including teacher-student, religious leader-follower, wife-husband, and physician-patient. However only in analysis is transference made the object of investigation. The purpose of this investigation is twofold: to dissect transference in all the shapes in which it appears and ultimately to dissolve it. During the course of an analysis, resistances are transformed into or expressed through negative transference. It is primarily by this means that inner conflict can become available for "working through." After all, no one can be hanged *in absentia*.

Previous acts of repression can be undone if the patient cannot repeat them unwittingly in the analytic process. The role of interpretation in this process is to help the patient make sense (literally) out of transference experiences as well as out of dreams and slips of the tongue. As the analytic process proceeds, the ego is transformed; it gains more autonomy and becomes less rigid in response to unconscious demands. The unconscious compulsion to repeat is gradually replaced by a greater degree of conscious choice. Whether or not any interpretation or insight was veridical can be determined only after transference is dissolved: In a successful analysis the past gradually loses its power over the patient, and so "whatever in the doctor's conjectures is inaccurate drops out . . . it has to be withdrawn and replaced by something more correct."[54]

The "objectivity" of clinical interpretations and veridical insight depends on the capacity of both patient and analyst to become aware of the effects of the unconscious within themselves and on the relationship between them. The patient's neurosis and the analyst's countertransference material impede both the development of insight and a relationship in and through which such impediments can be experienced as problematic. Presumably, the closer any analysis approaches the ideal, the greater the probability that the "truth" about the patient's past, ego defenses, and fantasies will emerge.

Yet what is this "truth"? What is its epistemological grounding and status? Why ought we or the patient accept any claims about the meaning of particular experiences, knowledge, or human nature based on material produced or evoked by the psychoanalytic process? Freud's answers to these questions are complex and ultimately unsatisfactory. Pursuing the question of truth can bring to the surface some of the constructive omissions regulating psychoanalytic discourse. Freud's treatment of this question depends on several interconnected concepts, particularly the "objectivity" of the analyst and the "purity" of the transference relation. Underlying and grounding these concepts are the theories of narcissism and drives, science and truth. Each of these concepts is structured by Freud's desire to maintain his dream of science and by his anxieties about gender.

Freud continually denies that analyst and patient are engaged together in a unique and intimate relation. Analysis uses but cannot transform the patient's narcissism. Primary narcissism is the original human condition. Each person is born with a fixed amount of libido. At first all this energy is fixated upon the self. The goal of the human, like any organism, is maintaining internal (homeostatic) equilibrium. Given the human infant's initial physical helplessness and the id's inability to engage in reality testing, self-sufficiency is not possible. We must turn to others to satisfy our needs. However others seem to be like "things in themselves" in Kant's philosophy.[55] We know they must exist because without them certain psychic structures and life itself would not be possible. However other persons can be known only as we ourselves construct them, never as they are in themselves apart from our fantasies and libidinal investments.

Because human relationships are merely mutual projection, if one of the partners could be abstinent (e.g., refrain from projection and from using the other as a means for self-gratification), the abstinent person would become a blank facade or an empty movie screen. This is the ideal situation in analysis. The analyst abstains from projection and becomes a "mirror" for the patient. The patient's projections bounce off the mirror like light rays on glass. These projections shine so brightly in the mirror of the analytic process that the patient is forced to acknowledge their existence as projections. Because the patient is inherently a narcissist and the analyst is a mirror, what the patient sees is herself (i.e., her own repressed wishes, fantasies, etc.) as wishes produced by her and not by the analyst as a person acting upon or interacting with her. After all it is her movie—acted, directed, produced, and projected by her alone. What she projects is derived solely from her own past repressed experience. Like all neurotics, she knows only that script.

These repressed wishes are the grounds of possibility for a transference relation, and they will be reexperienced in it. Analysis compels the patient to recognize the existence, real content, and power of these wishes. Once brought into the light of consciousness, the wishes and the symptoms that partially satisfy them can be traced back to earlier psychosexual stages or object relations. In this way the spell of the past can be broken.

The analytic process will work and the accuracy of the patient's reflection in the mirror carr be guaranteed only if the analyst remains neutral (i.e., abstains from projecting her or his own wishes, fantasies, etc. onto the patient). "The physician should be impenetrable to the patient, and like a mirror, reflect nothing but what is shown to him."[56] The analyst must be as absent and unrelated as the child experiences the m/other in the initial stages of primary narcissism. The analyst's neutrality or absence-abstinence in turn depends upon the success of her or his own training analysis and capacity for continual ruthless introspection, including a willingness to reenter analysis or supervision as necessary.

In this account the analytic situation is like an empiricist's laboratory: It allows naturally occurring phenomena to be replicated in a controlled setting. If enough patients reenact more or less the same drama, we can begin to have some confidence in the theories we construct to account for the "twistings and turnings" of the psychoanalytic process. Because neurosis is only an exaggeration of the psychical process of "normal" people, as can be seen by the fact we all dream, make slips of the tongue, and so forth, clinical experience can be used to substantiate general claims about human nature, mental illness, and universally shared psychological processes. Clinical data can be used to substantiate fundamental psychoanalytic hypotheses such as the claim that the etiology of neurosis lies in the vicissitudes of the instincts, especially in the repression of wishes and excitations arising from or associated with the "component instincts of sexual life." The "data" will also determine whether or not the instincts that manifest themselves "physiologically" as sexuality play a prominent or an "exclusive" role in the "causation of neurosis."[57]

An empiricist model of the psychoanalytic situation, however, is inadequate. Such an account directly contradicts other aspects of the process. Freud does liken psychoanalysis to an archaeological process and claims "it depends only upon analytic techniques whether we shall succeed in bringing what is concealed completely to light." However he also admits that "quite often" an assured conviction of the truth of the construction achieves the same therapeutic result as a recaptured memory.[58] Unfortunately, "the problem of what the circumstances are in which this occurs and of how it is possible that what appears to be an incomplete substitute should nevertheless produce a complete result" is left for a "later" and never completed inquiry.[59]

It seems reasonable to assume that how an "assured conviction of the truth" can have the "same therapeutic result as a recaptured [actual] memory" may have something to do with the relationship between analyst and patient. But here we come up against one of the paradoxes of Freud's theories: How can someone who is fundamentally a narcissist have anything other than transferencelike relationships? Presumably in the case of analysis, patients eventually tire of trying to enlist the abstinent analyst into their delusory system and decide such a pursuit is a waste of libidinal energy. Presumably also patients discover through analysis which of their preexisting fantasies are beneficial and invest libidinal energy in maximizing gratification of the more promising ones. What does not seem possible, either in the analytic situation or in Freud's theory more generally, is that a drive-governed narcissist can also experience "object love," much less the aspect of "positive" transference that arises neither from aggressive feelings nor from erotic wishes. Nonetheless Freud claims that in analysis it is possible to do exactly this. A "working alliance" or "positive" transference with the analyst is thus established. The positive transference "brings about the successful result in psychoanalysis as in all other remedial methods."[60]

What enables patients to enter into a *therapeutic* alliance with the analyst? Why is this alliance the crucial factor in the remedial effects of psychoanalysis? Why and how does it work? What aspect(s) of the mind's structure or its dynamic processes make such an alliance possible at all, much less therapeutic? Freud is unable to answer these questions. He provides no adequate solution to the "riddle" of transference, despite its centrality in his theory and practice.

Knowledge: Science, Gender, and Politics

Part of the solution both to the riddle of transference and to Freud's inability to solve it lies in understanding the interpersonal relations of analyst and patient. Freud persistently denies such interrelatedness exists. He retains a view of the analytic situation in which the analyst is the patient's object, the patient is the analyst's object, and each person can be a subject only separately from the object. His frequent use of the imagery of war to describe the analytic process is not without significance. Surely war is one of the most objectifying and aggressive of all human practices.

Freud's persistent use of such metaphors for the analyst's role as surgeon, mirror, or general is especially puzzling because his actual clinical practice did not conform to his "technical" recommendations for the practice of psychoanalysis. According to his patients' accounts, Freud had and expressed an active concern for their well-being. He maintained warm and extensive correspondence with some former patients. He loaned money to them while they were in analysis with him. At least once he fed a patient (the "Rat Man") when he was hungry. Freud was also far from silent or abstinent in the analytic situation. He advised his patients on such questions as whether they should be divorced or attend medical school. He even lectured them during the analytic hour on the possible origins of artifacts in his consulting room and on the history of archaeology, ancient Egypt, and other topics.[61]

Although there are undoubtedly many reasons for Freud's denial of the intersubjective qualities of the relation between analyst and patient, two seem especially important, to an understanding both of his own work and its possibilities and limitations as a transitional form of knowledge. Part of the tension and ambiguities in Freud's concepts of analysis and knowledge can be accounted for by his continual attempts to fit the analytic process, clinical material, and the knowledge they generate into inappropriate categories. Freud's clinical id continually and fortunately undermines his "scientific" superego; yet he persistently pursues his dream of science.

He does so in part because of the continuing power of the Enlightenment narrative. In Freud's time and to a large degree in our own, truth claims must meet empiricist or rationalist tests. "Science" and "reliable knowledge" are still confounded, as they are in Freud's own writings on the subject of truth and the *Weltanschauung* of psychoanalysis. The compelling power of this narrative can also be seen in the interminable debate among analysts and others about whether or not psychoanalysis is or can be a science.[62] If science and rational (real) knowledge were not confounded, the question of whether or not psychoanalysis "deserves" or does not "deserve" scientific "status" would simply be irrelevant. Yet Freud himself believes that if psychoanalysis is not a science, its claims to truth can and should not be taken seriously. This belief remains a powerful, even coercive influence within the contemporary "discursive practice" of psychoanalysis. Perhaps Freud also felt he needed the legitimizing "objectivity" of science to counter the dismissal of psychoanalysis as a "Jewish" science.[63]

Nonetheless psychoanalysis simply does not and cannot fit within Enlightenment narratives of knowledge. In trying to make psychoanalysis conform to preexisting criteria for truth claims, especially as these are posited or "rationally reconstructed" by philosophers of science, analysts undercut the radicalness and power of their own potential contributions to the philosophy of knowledge.

Although Freud tries to deny or "control for" the "contaminated" and intersubjective nature of psychoanalytic knowledge, these qualities are what make it most valuable as a postmodern practice and as an alternative to existing power/knowledge discourses. Psychoanalysis is better understood as a form of "relational work" than as an empirical or natural science. Even from Freud's own account of the analytic process, it is clear that the "data" and methods of psychoanalysis are relational and intersubjective. The "logic of discovery" of psychoanalysis as it is practiced in the analytic situation immediately and directly conflicts with the empiricist's view of the self as distinct and separate from the object. It is inappropriate to dismiss the data generated within this situation as merely "intuitive," "irrational," or "epistemologically contaminated" because such a judgment presupposes exactly what psychoanalysis can call into question. Psychoanalytic practice challenges the meaningfulness, possibility, or desirability of an absolute split between the subject and object in the search for reliable knowledge.

Psychoanalysis also calls into question the assumption that rational thought and the accumulation of reliable knowledge require suppression or control of "subjective" feeling and that "reason" is the only or best source of knowledge. Analysts must be aware of and able to use their own feelings. They must be able to experience the patient's feeling states empathically. The feeling states of both patient and analyst provide important information about and insight into the patient's inner world as well as the relationship between the two members of the therapeutic alliance. The patient sometimes needs to use or be "contained by" the analyst's feeling states.[64] Rational insight alone is not an adequate basis for producing either analytic knowledge or therapeutic success. Ultimately, reciprocity between the analyst and patient, not separation of subject and object, is the goal of analysis. Its goal is also to change its object (patient-subject) and its "laws of causality," not simply to use or discover them, as in empiricist natural science.

To give an account of the analytic subject or to evaluate the knowledge generated in analysis requires an epistemology that is simultaneously empirical, intersubjective, and process oriented. Such an epistemology does not exist, although some of its elements are present in the work of philosophers such as Wittgenstein, Gadamer, Hegel, Habermas, and Kuhn as well as in a more accurate consideration of the analytic situation itself.[65] The material generated in the clinical situation will never be fully incorporated or done justice to unless the many different aspects of its subject-object are grasped. This subject is an embodied, historical, social, thinking, speaking, and desiring being in continual relation with other such (internal and external) beings, including the analyst. Existing attempts to reconceptualize the process of and knowledge generated by analysis fail partially because they ignore or sacrifice one or more of these aspects. In order to use this rich material fully, we must analyze and reject Freud's own dream of science.

Although Freud fails to overcome the limitations of rationalist or empiricist concepts of knowledge, he does have a much broader vision of the requirements for the successful practice of this "impossible profession." Instruction in a "college of psychoanalysis" should include "branches of knowledge which are remote from medicine and which the doctor does not come across in his practice: the history of civilization, mythology, the psychology of religion and the science of literature. Unless he is well at home in these subjects, an analyst can make nothing of a large amount of his material."[66]

Analytic training, especially in the United States, has failed to meet these standards. A consequence of restricting the scope of analysis— whether in the name of "orthodoxy," science, or progress—has been impoverishment of both its theory and its practice. In the training of analysts and the breadth of knowledge and research required, Freud set out rules for the discursive practice of psychoanalysis to which contemporary analysts should adhere. The character of this training also provides further evidence for the fact that psychoanalysis cannot fit within the discursive rules of Enlightenment science.

Freud's denial of the interrelatedness of patient and analyst is also rooted in his anxieties about gender relations. Feminist theorists offer ambivalent and conflicting evaluations of psychoanalysis. Some simply reject it because of Freud's patently masculinist biases. Other feminists have found the paradoxes in psychoanalytic theory a useful and revealing object of analysis. Some writers attempt to divide Freud's work into those parts affected by his anxieties and biases about women (e.g., the essays on "femininity") and those that are not.[67] The second approach is more fruitful. Unexamined anxieties about gender and gender relations do pervade, structure, and constrict the entire body of Freud's work.

The limitations of Freud's own self-consciousness are symptomatic of pervasive Western beliefs. They have been repeated in much subsequent psychoanalytic work. A principal legacy of Freud's own "unhappy consciousness" can be found in an enduring set of interlocking and gendered antimonies pervading virtually all psychoanalytic discourse, beginning with his own. Among the most important recurring antimonies are the following:

1. nature versus culture
2. other versus self
3. libido economics versus object relations theory
4. body versus mind
5. patient versus analyst

Each of these antimonies is gendered. All of the concepts on the right are "inscribed" on the side of masculinity; those on left are associated with the feminine. Analysis can never be successfully analyzed and freed from its past limitations without closer attention to feminist analyses of the dynamics and effects of gender relations. Yet many analysts, at least in their published work, continue to ignore feminist writings on gender and psychoanalysis.[68] Postmodernists also have paid insufficient attention to many of the obscuring effects of the riddle of sex on and within psychoanalytic discourse. Thus in order to acquire a fuller understanding of the meanings and prevalence of these antimonies, a feminist as well as postmodernist analysis of analysis is necessary. Elements essential to such an analysis include more attention to the gendered dualisms discussed below. In turn the evidence that even Freud's supposedly gender-neutral concepts are affected by gender relations ought to encourage more psychoanalysts and postmodernists to attend more seriously to feminist theories.

Nature/Culture: Female/Male.   The process of acculturation is simultaneously and necessarily a process in which people are gendered. The polymorphous perverse infant becomes, or at any rate is supposed to become, the heterosexual, genitally oriented male or female adult. In this process part of "natural" sexuality is sacrificed. Similarly on the social level, as societies develop, more and more instinctual renunciation is required. Family ties must be sacrificed to demands of the larger group. The incest taboo is both the culmination of this process and its symbol. Women represent the family and its "natural ties." Their demands begin to oppose those of culture, just as the son's "natural" desire for the mother conflicts with the demands of the father/culture.

The gender-based division of labor pervasive in our society is uncritically replicated in Freud's theory. Women in Western culture have the primary responsibility for the care of young children. Western society is also predicated on a split between the realm of production, in which "instrumental" relations are said to be the norm, and the realm of the family, in which "affective" relations are to prevail. The affective realm is associated with the "natural" relations between parent and child, husband and wife, with sexuality and the satisfaction of bodily needs. These affective ties are supposed to be excluded from the instrumental realm, which is also the world of men. To succeed in this world, it is necessary to behave in nonfamilial ways. Others must be treated as objects, as means to an end, as competitors for scarce resources and rewards.

The differing demands of nature and culture are not the only source of conflict here. There is also conflict between the culturally constituted demands of family life and those of work. These cultural roots are obscured by the effects of gender on Freud's thinking. Familial relations are "naturalized" by equating them with the interests and activities of women. Because women can become pregnant and give birth, it seems natural for the child bearer also to be the child rearer. The family thus appears to be the woman's world. As production becomes more frequently located outside the family, someone must leave it—the man. He must withdraw his energy from women, children, and sexuality and associate with men, who make very different and often conflicting demands on him.[69]

In associating women and what they do with nature, Freud transforms a concrete product of social activity into an inevitable consequence of the evolution of civilization, as inescapable as "modernity" itself. Freud's pessimism about the possibility of overcoming or transforming civilization's discontents is rooted in his assumption of the inevitability of the conflict between nature (drives) and culture. Once the at least partially social roots of this conflict are revealed, new questions emerge. How "inevitable" *are* these discontents? To what extent does Freud, while exposing aspects of bourgeois culture, provide new justifying myth or ideology for a more modern yet still patriarchal one?

From a feminist point of view, Freud appears less interested in divulging the secrets of the fathers than in participating in them.[70] Even more problematic is his desire to repeat rather than work through the fathers' wish: to protect themselves and their sons against the eruption of maternal secrets into consciousness. After all, as Freud himself tells us, part of the oedipal drama lies in the conflict between the son's desires to identify with the father and to overthrow him. The successful resolution of the boy's oedipal complex includes identifying with the father and abandoning his wish to overthrow or displace him. In a culture in which gender is an exclusionary category, the son can enter the masculine world only by rejecting and devaluing the female world, including his own prior identification with and internalization of his relations with his mother.

Other/Self: Preoedipal/Oedipal: Female/Male. Freud admits that the first "other" or object for the male or female child is the mother. He is eventually willing to acknowledge the importance of preoedipal experience for the *girl's* development. However Freud still insists on the centrality of the oedipal period for the boy, for psychoanalytic theory as a whole, and for the history and analysis of culture itself. Despite his own admission that his theories do not include and cannot account for many of the most important aspects of women's experience, Freud nonetheless continues to claim authorship of a radically new understanding of human rather than male psychology. He remains consistently unwilling to consider the possibility that his most fundamental concepts are not universal but rather are gender specific and gender bound and hence must be delimited socially and historically. This masculinist bias recurs in the work of many subsequent analysts, both "orthodox" and Lacanian.

Freud also fails to explore the extent to which the preoedipal mother-child relationship affects not only women's psychological development but the very structure of masculinity itself. For example, Freud discusses the boy's earliest identification with his mother primarily in terms of its effect on the child's subsequent "choice of object." Thus even the earliest boy-mother relation is reconstructed backwards from its "inevitable" terminus in the oedipal phase. The effects of this early relation on the constitution of the boy's sense of self, ego defenses, and so forth are rarely examined.

Freud even reverses the actual power relation between the mother and small child. Conceptualizing the woman/mother as "castrated" and in need of a son in order to acquire the longed-for penis renders the mother dependent on her *son* for psychological fulfillment. Such a fantasy reveals a rather high level of grandiosity about the son's significance to his mother, serving, at least in part, as a defense against acknowledging both his powerlessness vis-à-vis the mother and his fear of abandonment or injury by her. Perhaps Freud reveals more about his own fantasies than about women's when he asserts, "even marriage is not made secure until the wife has succeeded in making her husband her child as well as in acting as mother to him."[71]

"Infantile helplessness" is discussed mostly in terms of the child's "longing for the father." Freud says, "I cannot think of any need in childhood as strong as the need for a father's protection."[72] Here again oedipal wishes are evoked in part as a defense against deeper terrors. Not only are deeper terrors repressed, but so are primary infantile longings, especially for fusion with the first caretaker (mother). Freud is very resistant to discussing this aspect of infantile experience, as can be seen by his treatment of "oceanic" feelings in the opening chapter of *Civilization and Its Discontents*. First he says, "I cannot discover this 'oceanic' feeling in myself." Then he tries to explain it as a consequence of primary narcissism. This feeling becomes the "shrunken residue" of a "much more inclusive—indeed, an all embracing—feeling which corresponded to a more intimate bond between the ego and the world about it."[73] Who was in the world about the ego? With whom was the "ego" enjoying a particularly intimate bond? Freud himself claims the mother is the first love object of boy and girl. Thus this "oceanic feeling" is likely a "residue" of early mother-child relations.

Freud's claim to have uncovered the most fundamental and hidden human terror—the dread of castration, arising, of course, in the oedipal phase—conceals the deeper defensive gains of his own "naming" of the cornerstone of human psychology. In the light of subsequent object relations psychoanalytic work, the dread of castration appears to be in part a displacement of more primitive and deeply buried anxieties—the fears of annihilation, loss of love, our aggression and rage at the mother for her autonomy and power over us, and our desire to take that power for ourselves.[74]

Ironically, as is so often the case, Freud himself points the way to this reinterpretation when he discusses the "masculine protest." He acknowledges that "the 'masculine protest' is in fact nothing other than fear of castration."[75] What is feared in "castration" is to lack or lose a penis—that is, to be or become a female because in Freud's system what defines women is precisely this "lack." Such a lack necessarily entails exclusion from the more privileged masculine world, from "constant association with men," upon whom one is "dependent" to achieve any "cultural aims." Access to power and social esteem would be denied once the "magic organ" disappeared. Of course to the extent that the work of (patriarchal) civilization really is "increasingly the business of men," the boy's fears and fantasies of returning to the "mother world" will be reinforced and intensified.[76]

In the oedipal struggle father and son become allies. The son's identification with the father becomes part of his fortification against the return of the repressed mother world. By privileging the oedipal phase and denying the power of the first object relation, Freud participates in and rationalizes an act of repression both typical of and necessary to the replication of patriarchal culture.

Economics of the Libido (Drive Theory)/Object Relations Theory: Female/ Male.   One way to bury the preoedipal mother's power is simply to deny the possibility of real human interrelationships. The mother cannot "get" us because all feelings are derived from internally generated fantasy. She and our relations to her are not really inside and an inextricable part of us.

It is therefore not surprising that Freud's "object relations" theory centers on the internalization of the *father* while preoedipal psychosexual development basically remains conceptualized as endogenous and objectless. The split between object relations theory and the economic drive model is necessarily related to the other and self antimony. The irresolvability of this split is grounded partially in Freud's own anxieties about female sexuality and his inability to imagine the mother as an actively sexual being. Preoedipal objects are female, and *their* desire must be repressed. Once the object's sexuality is repressed, Freud's child remains as a solitary monad, not part of an interrelated pair. The monad's sexuality then seems to unfold in a pregiven, drive-governed way.

Furthermore this innate sexuality is conceptualized as male, not as gender neutral. Freud's concept of desire is deeply affected by the equation of "active" and "phallic" sexuality. It is significant that he names the phase of sexual exploration and desire in which fantasies about an object first come into play the phallic period. The expression of desire in its more mature phases depends on possession of a penis—or in the girl's case the fantasy of having this "magic organ." Only "little men" can actively desire the mother. Active sexuality and femaleness can be reconciled only by calling the masturbating little girl a "little man." [77] Here a dualistic two is reduced to a gender-biased one. The little boy is never conceptualized as a little woman, despite the fact that his first object relation and identification are with a woman (mother).

Gender and gender shifts are utilized to obscure potentially disturbing ideas in another way. The fact that the girl's first desired object is a female implies that female homosexuality might be a psychosexual norm. Heterosexuality is rescued by changing the gender of one of the mother/child dyad. Because Freud takes heterosexuality for granted at least as a culturally enforced norm, if not a natural one, he also assumes the girl must do more than renounce her phallic desire for the mother. In the oedipal period the "little man" must become a "little girl" and develop the kind of desire appropriate to girls and women—a passive (vaginal) receptivity to or indirectly expressed longing for an active male (penis). Because this transformed, now properly female, desire is more passive, girls do not have to renounce their oedipal object (the father) completely. Of course such desire is not a threat to, indeed it may please, the father or the patriarchal order. Girls remain partially attached to both their oedipal and preoedipal objects. Hence the girl never completely resolves her oedipal complex.

Body/Mind: Female/Male.   Despite their (sexual) passivity, women are more determined by and subject to the body and its drives. Women represent the "interests of sexual life" (and nature); they are associated with unreason, feeling, and primary process. They favor family over culture, love over duty, feeling over thought. In addition the powerful sense of "lack" produced by women's bodies (castration) determines the course of their lives to a much greater extent than men's "castration anxiety" determines theirs. Men can "master their castration anxiety"; women can merely learn to "submit without bitterness" to the "*fact*" of their castration. [78]

The incomplete dissolution of the girl's oedipal complex means her superego is never as fully developed or powerful as the boy's. Girls lack the mature conscience of postoedipal boys because the superego is a "precipitate" and consequence of the resolution of the oedipal struggle, including the (boy's) identification with the father. By identifying with the father, the (boy) child also internalizes and makes his own the morality of his culture. Without a powerful superego women will be "little capable" of carrying out the "instinctual sublimations" that civilization increasingly demands.[79]

Furthermore, because of the complex interrelations between the id, ego, and superego, the girls' (and women's) ego and hence their capacity for rational thought will also be less powerful than that of boys. The ego is a "secondary" formation, a precipitate of the id that develops as a result of the child's frustration at trying to satisfy his or her drives, to sustain an internal equilibrium, or to preserve life. Although initially a precipitate of the id, the ego requires a certain autonomy from the id and the drives in order to develop. For example, through sublimation the ego can "capture" some of the id's libidinal energy for its own purposes. Although its demands may weaken the ego, the superego can also reinforce the ego's autonomy by requiring acts of (drive) sublimation or repression. Because women's superego is weaker than men's, it will be a less reliable or powerful ally against the id. The capacity for rational thought arises at least in part from a sublimation of sexuality, so to the extent that women are less capable of sublimation, they will also be less able to reason.

In Freud's account women also suffer from a fundamental, irreversible wound to their narcissism. Women are castrated not just in fantasy, but in fact, and the inevitable consequence of this castration is penis envy. All but one of women's subsequent attempts to compensate for this narcissistic wound (e.g., their strivings for a career) are bound to fail. The only but still partial salve for the wound of castration is pregnancy and, more particularly, the birth of a son. By giving birth to a son, a woman can utilize her "defect" (vagina/hole) to obtain at least temporarily the desired organ (the penis). Hence "a mother is only brought unlimited satisfaction by her relation to a son; this is altogether the most perfect, the most free from ambivalence of all human relationships."[80]

In Freud's discussion of women's bodily self and how he imagines we experience it, an important displacement occurs: The social construction of gender is fused and confused with biological sex, especially anatomical differences. Once again, as in the antimony between nature and culture, biology is brought in to protect and more deeply conceal the riddle of sex. Anatomical differences immediately and without any social mediation become absolute determinants of women's lives. Anatomy does become destiny, but although the boy may rescue his penis and his self-esteem by entering culture, that same entrance into culture only ratifies women's (anatomical) inferiority, from which there is no escape. Biology remains "the bedrock" of all psychological strata, and the "repudiation of femininity must surely be a biological fact, part of the great riddle of sex."[81]

With the split from one (precultural, "phallic" sexuality) to two (gender differentiation), the child recognizes not just difference in bodies but a social hierarchy. The move from one to two for the child and Freud entails a realization that the two is less than the one; differentiation for the girl brings with it a feeling of loss and lack. From the "very first" glimpse of a penis, the girl knows the boy's organ is "superior" to hers. It can give the boy more pleasure than she could ever have from her "stunted" one. As good economists of the libido, both boy and girl have a *"biological"* reason for repudiating femininity—only the girl is stuck with it anyway. The girl quickly "extends her judgment of inferiority from her stunted penis to her whole self."[82] Here again the girl's experience of her body determines the subsequent course of her psychological development. Freud assumes that her biological equipment really *is* inferior. Therefore it is not necessary to explore possible social roots for her low self-esteem or to treat a girl's judgment of her self as problematic.

Freud also assumes (as Lacan does subsequently) that the penis is superior in its ability to "carry" meaning. The little girl in Freud's account immediately treats the penis as the "universal signifier." Upon seeing the little boy's organ, she reconceptualizes her clitoris as stunted penis, rather than considering the boy's penis as an enlarged and rather unwieldy clitoris. The little girl shares the boy's narcissistic investment in and evaluation of the penis. She assumes there is a one, and that one is the penis. Difference is automatically conceptualized as negative variation from the (male) norm.

The avoidance and obscurantism integral to Freud's reductionistic moments are especially striking because he criticizes others for adopting similar ideas. For example, Wilhelm Fleiss is criticized for his inclination to "sexualize" repression, "that is to say, in explaining it on a biological instead of purely psychological basis."[83] The move from "purely biological" (sex/body) to "purely psychological" (mind/mental) is not a solution either. One element of the pair is still privileged over the other, sustaining both dualism and the idea that one is always better than two. By conceptualizing differences as antimonies, Freud implies there could or should be an undifferentiated whole, that wholeness or homeo-static equilibrium is the desirable norm. Here the repressed and denied fantasy of symbiotic unity returns, joins with, and reinforces the Enlightenment dream of a unified science.

Whether Freud "really" favors the psychological/mental or biological/physical as the ultimate one is less important than his continual alternation between splitting mind and body into two and the wish for a final one. When attempting to understand gender, Freud fails to meet his own criteria for an adequate concept of the subject. He is not able to sustain an idea of the bodily and mental facets of human experience as simultaneously different, related, and autonomous.

This alternation between dualistic and unitary views of the relationships between body and mind seems especially odd. Freud's own notion of the unconscious points a way beyond it. The nature of the unconscious shows there is something between one and two. In the unconscious and in unconscious actions, the boundaries between mind and body blur. One reason for Freud's failure to make full use of the implications of the unconscious is his own anxieties about gender. He was unconsciously fearful that in undermining the dualities of mind and body, or reason and unreason, he would not expand our understanding of the relationships between them, but rather fall under the power of the repressed one. This repressed material includes the child's fantasy and fear of an undifferentiated oceanic whole, the association of bodies and women, and the son's wish and fear of reidentifying and merging with the mother/body. Freud fears that the son's ego or mind—those "secondary" qualities uneasily existing between the dark ocean of the (primary) id and the sometimes harsh and punitive superego—would be undone by the always threatening return of the repressed. The son's oppositional gender identity feels like one of his major defenses against the undermining of reason by the "enemy" within.

Patient/Analyst: Female/Male.   Freud's anxieties about gender enter both overtly and subtly into his accounts of the analytic process and the sorts of knowledge that can be gleaned from it. The overt influence of gender on Freud's thinking about the analytic process is easier to see. He insists that accepting his construction of the meaning of castration anxiety is one of the factors that determine the "success" of an analysis. Freud identifies five factors that influence the outcome of any analysis: (1) constitutional factors such as the relative strength of libido, its mobility, the individual's ability to change, and the power of the aggressive drive; (2) the strength of the roots of the defensive mechanism and how much the ego has been modified in the course of a person's life; (3) the quantity and quality of traumatic factors inflicted by the external world; (4) the analyst's personal characteristics, including the success of her or his own analysis; and (5) the "repudiation of femininity and how successfully each person comes to terms with it."[84]

By the end of his life, Freud had become much more pessimistic about the difficulties of the therapeutic relationship and the possibility of overcoming them. Given the extraordinary demands the analytic process makes on both analyst and patient and the obdurate character of the unconscious, analysis acquires some of the simultaneously heroic and tragic nature of the *Odyssey*.

Yet to what extent are these difficulties self-imposed, as in any tragedy? How many analyses "fail" because the patient cannot accept Freud's construction of the meanings of biological differences? Had Freud been able to acknowledge the more complex interpersonal aspects of transference and countertransference, perhaps he could have understood more about both his clinical successes and failures.[85] Had he been able to conceptualize the kinds of knowledge that arise in and through relations with others, he could have utilized his clinical experiences to further develop his theoretical insights, such as those about the vicissitudes of "object love" and the importance of "internal objects." Had he been able to respect the therapeutic value and power of the analytic relationship, he could have thought about analysis as a means of charting and recovering not only the *repressed* but the healing power of "caretaking" itself, for a central insight of analysis is that our relationships with others can make us ill, and hence such illness can be overcome by entering into relationships that offer the possibility of experiences that are different from the past, pathogenic ones.

Yet to Freud, and still to many persons today, this insight appears trivial or unimportant. This deeply felt lack of significance is rooted in part in gender relations, especially the pervasive devaluation of "women's" work such as caretaking in contemporary Western culture. The connections Freud unconsciously felt between gender, culture, and knowledge are still predominant today.

The denial of relatedness and its importance is connected to gender in another way. The possibility of such relatedness depends on what Freud calls human "prehistory," especially the capacity to be attached to another person who is similarly attached to yet separate from us. Freud's resistance to discussing or reviving this aspect of infantile experience is evident in his writings. These experiences, including the primary identification with a woman (mother or her substitute), are potentially profoundly unsettling to a stereotypical masculine sense of self. Here too Freud reflects and reveals the "successfully articulated" experience and reactions of his time and still to a large degree of ours.

The reconceptualization of psychoanalysis as "relational work" would threaten both the social and scientific status of Freud's discursive practice. In a culture in which affective relations are considered "natural" and "female" and "work" is considered instrumental, serious, and male, the very concept of relational work is an oxymoron. If the process of psychoanalysis is reconceptualized as "just" establishing a relationship and then working it through, would such work be taken seriously or even be considered work at all? Anyone could "mother" or relate. There is nothing "scientific" or "skilled" about such practices. It is far more congruent with the values and knowledge/power relations of Western culture to represent the analyst as a heartless surgeon, an intrepid general, an emotionally unengaged scientist in the lab, or even a heroic and ruthless "deconstructor" of the illusions of bourgeois culture.

The strongly felt need for fathers and sons and, to a lesser degree, daughters to bond against the return of the repressed mother world has not disappeared. Our postmodern culture is still pervaded by the gendered splits between nature and culture, mind and body, subject and object, self and other, reason and unreason, and male and female. For example, the split between reason and mind and empirical or contingent body is still prevalent within contemporary philosophy. The concept of deconstruction, or of philosophers as destroyers of "foundational illusions," presupposes the possibility of philosophers breaking through and escaping the web of social relations and ideas into which they were born and through which they come to be persons. Other philosophers still claim to investigate and present the logic of a disembodied, ahistoric reason or "speech act." Or philosophy is presented as "rationality's" privileged protector, representative, and judge, as if each of these claims were relatively unproblematic or even self-evidently true.

Anxieties about gender and the split between nature and culture also are far from absent in contemporary science. Some researchers collapse gender into sex in positing that the origin of such "natural differences" (male/female) lies in the "brain" or in our genes. Hence gender differences are inevitable and their consequences unamenable to transformation by human action. Alternatively, in fear that any discovery of difference would be utilized to justify hierarchy, other researchers insist that having a male or female body makes no difference at all, or that such questions should not be investigated until gender-based domination is less prevalent.

In contemporary psychoanalysis anxieties about and inadequate treatments of gender and relatedness abound. Examination of two apparently opposed and conflicting theories within contemporary psychoanalysis will show how powerful the influence of the father remains. Freud continues to determine the discursive practice of psychoanalysis. Although some of his sons have questioned his dreams of science, few sons, although more daughters, have situated, analyzed, or redressed his "constructive omissions" concerning gender.

Four

Lacan and Winnicott

Splitting and Regression
in Psychoanalytic Theory

Lacanian and object relations psychoanalytic theories are mirror opposites in their premises about the nature of self, knowledge, and social relations. There are many important issues at stake in the fundamental disagreements between these two types of psychoanalytic theorists, including how a self is constituted, the possible nature of relations between people, the basis and origin(s) of knowledge and its characteristics, what kind of knowledge psychoanalysis is and can be, the relative importance of preoedipal and oedipal experience in psychological development, how and why gender is constituted, the possibilities for the existence of human cultures relatively unmarked by relations of domination and alienation, and the nature of the psychoanalytic process, its purposes, and possible outcomes. I find object relations theorists' answers to these questions more satisfactory than Lacan's and would like to persuade others that this is so. However the lack of epistemologies appropriate to psychoanalytic discourse leaves me in the uncomfortable position of dissatisfaction with both the postmodernist position of "indeterminacy" and my own inability to give adequate reasons for my beliefs. Hence although I will often state objections to or agreements with aspects of each theory, I will not claim to have resolved any of these issues or rendered further debate unnecessary.

These analysts differ in many ways, but there are also important similarities between them. From a feminist perspective post-Freudian

89

psychoanalysis is still constituted in part by the bonding of fathers and sons against the full return of the repressed mother world. These followers of Freud, otherwise so different, still participate in and replicate some of the founder's most important acts of repression, especially those related to the objects they all share and deny—mothers and women. Hence even contemporary psychoanalysts can benefit from feminist questioning of their ideas. Subsequent psychoanalytic theorists also incorporate a regressive denial of the tensions so palpably and fruitfully present in Freud's own work. Contemporary psychoanalytic theorists tend to split and deny the relations between many aspects of Freud's antimonies (especially those related to the constitution of a self) or to "resolve" them by repressing one side. Thus the productive tension between the antimonies within Freud's work tends to be lost within subsequent psychoanalytic theories. That tension, that ability to sustain ambivalence and ambiguity, and the willingness not to claim more than he knows are some of Freud's most radical attributes. A postmodernist sensitivity to the repression of ambivalence and to maneuvers designed to disguise or reduce complexity can reopen these gaps or splits within the followers' works.

Object relations and Lacanian theories have each been posited as the desirable successor to "classical" analysis. Therefore I will also consider problems in the internal adequacy of each theory and contributions each can make to the development of postmodernist and feminist thinking.

Jacques Lacan: Narcissism and the Fetishism of Language and the Phallus

For it is still not enough to say that the concept is the thing itself. . . . It is the world of words that creates the world of things. . . . Man speaks, but it is because the symbol has made him man.

                        Jacques Lacan, *Ecrits: A Selection*

You will scarcely be able to reject a judgment that the philosophy of today has retained some essential features of the animistic mode of thought—the overvaluation of the magic of words and the belief that the real events in the world take the course which our thinking seeks to impose on them. It would seem . . . to be an animism without magic actions.

Sigmund Freud,
"The Question of a
Weltanschauung"

The Ontology of Narcissism

Lacan's exploration of the non-object-related and noncultural aspects of desire is a valuable contribution to the development of both feminist and postmodernist theories. He provides useful reasons for critiquing the adaptive and conformist tendencies that have been especially predominant in American psychoanalysis. However I cannot agree with Lacan's claim that his work represents a "true" return to Freud. Nor, unlike some writers, do I consider his work to be a very promising supplement or contribution to the development of feminist theorizing. In fact, as I will argue in this chapter, in regard to gender questions, his work is profoundly misleading and even more pervaded by masculinist assumptions than Freud's.

Lacan's work is a logical extension of certain concepts that Freud develops—an extension that requires and results in a denial and an obliteration of other aspects of his ideas. He transforms Freud's concept of narcissism into an ontological and incontestable theory of human nature. In the process the object-related aspects of Freud's concept of the development of the self disappear. The complex relations Freud at least suggests between mind and body and nature and culture tend to be replaced by much simpler and radically disjunctive oppositions. Freud's recourse to biological determination is replaced by an appeal to the supposedly universal structure of language. Lacan's "linguistic turn" may appear to allow for more consideration of contingent forces (including gender relations) within psychoanalysis and culture. In fact it shuts off many promising questions about the "inevitability" of civilization's discontents that Freud suggests. It is almost impossible to identify historically variable and changeable aspects of relations of domination once these are posited as effects of a universal logic of language.

Postmodernists' techniques are helpful in (re)reading Lacan, especially their suspicion and rejection of any universal or foundationalist claims. Postmodernists assume such claims work to obscure attempts to reduce the complex multiplicity inherent in all writing to an unalterable, "natural," and unquestionable unity. Lacan's narcissistic premise and his concept of language operate in exactly this way. A deconstructive reading of Lacan's writings is also revealing precisely because of his emphasis on narcissism and his own narcissistic style. Like any narcissist's universe Lacan's writings often seem to be a series of self-referential and opaque images. Unless Lacan's concepts of narcissism and language are removed from their ontological status and functions within the theory, there is no way to escape being drawn into and imprisoned within his texts.[1] Therefore on both feminist and postmodernist grounds I will bracket four of Lacan's most important claims: that narcissism is an "irreducible" aspect of human "nature"; that language has an invariant, universal structure and always functions to split or castrate all "subjects"; that language (the Other) operates as an independent force, and its effects on the subject have no dependence on or interaction with the child's relations with actual "others," especially the mother; and that the "phallus" is in no way related to or meant to signify the "penis."

In fact even within the operation of Lacan's texts, these four claims are problematic. The narcissistic premise clearly serves defensive purposes, and evidence for its ontological status is lacking. The relationship between (m/other and Other [language]) is more complex than Lacan would allow. Many of the functions or effects he attributes to language are possible or intelligible (within his theory and for the child's development) only if placed within the context of mother-child relationships. Finally, there is also a complex relationship between "phallus" and penis. Although Lacan claims they are theoretically distinct, they are not always so in his texts. In fact the meaning of some of his claims concerning the phallus depends on the impossibility within our existing language games and forms of life of a fundamental disjunction between these terms. Despite his narcissistic grandiosity, Lacan cannot escape one of his own injunctions: None of us can create a new language; words have meanings and operate in ways that escape our (conscious) intents. My reading of Lacan's texts is thus shaped by a refusal to see things exactly his way. Instead I will explore how these claims are manifested and function within Lacan's texts and the reasons for making and the consequences of holding such positions. I offer an alternative account of his texts to persuade the reader that Lacan's images are meant to obscure certain conditions of their own intelligibility.

Contrary to his premises Lacan's texts are best read as a *phenomenology* of what it is like to be confined within the narcissist's universe. Although Lacan seeks to persuade us that narcissism is the natural state of the human being, like Winnicott, I believe it is an aspect of human development but not its only or inevitable end point. Lacan does provide a powerful evocation of the narcissistic position. But he also reveals some of the defensive purposes that remaining within this position (and insisting on its inevitability) can serve. Narcissistic fantasies and perspectives pervade Lacan's work, and assuming that no other viewpoint can be true or real is a characteristic of narcissism. One's own condition is inescapable; one's own experience represents the truth of the whole. Accordingly, Lacan insists that "one cannot stress too strongly the irreducible character of the narcissistic structure . . . the narcissistic moment in the subject is to be found in all the genetic phases of the individual, in all the degrees of human accomplishment in the person."[2]

The narcissistic premise structures Lacan's conceptualization of the first and highly significant phase of human development—the "mirror" state—and his treatment of language. Lacan imagines this phase to be constituted by a series of encounters between an "infant" and a reflecting surface, a mirror. This mirror is a reflective object, not the loving gaze of a person who "anticipates" the infant's wholeness as in the stories of Winnicott or Kohut.[3] Infants "identify" with the image in the mirror; they are "predestined" to do so. The image (*imago*) in the mirror is a grandiose counter to infants' "prematurity," "sunk" as they are in "motor incapacity and nursing dependence." "Insufficient" infants assume this "specular" image "jubilantly." The image is a "symbolic matrix" in which the "I is precipitated in a primordial form." Significantly, for Lacan this I comes into being *alone*, "before it is objectified in the dialectic of identification with the other, and before language restores to it, in the universal, its function as subject."[4]

This I already has a paradoxical quality, being both fictional and the most real and permanent aspect of mental life. Lacking an other who *is* truly outside for comparison and reliable control, any narcissist faces a painful, persistent dilemma of the relation of image and reality. The I is fictional because it is composed of a "succession of phan-

tasies that extends from a fragmented body image to a form of totality."[5] The totality is built out of a series of such fantasy images. This I
is "real" because it is its only moment of existence before the inevitable "alienation" of its subsequent "social determination" begins.
After this moment the subject will be engaged in a perpetual series of
"dialectical syntheses by which he must resolve as *I* his discordance
with his own reality."[6] But despite what Lacan seems to say, there
must be enough of the "real" in this first I to register what follows *as*
discordance or estrangement from itself.

As for any narcissist, the relation between the primary I and anyone it cannot recognize in the mirror precipitates a "struggle to the
death." Such an I projects its need for the selfsame onto the other and
supposes that what the other wants is its complete capitulation—or
annihilation. Thus Lacan argues that the entrance of the other into
the field of the I causes the primary I to assume "the armour of an
alienating identity, which will mark with its rigid structure the subject's entire mental development."[7]

Lacan associates relations with others with the release of aggres-
sivity, "existential negativity," and paranoia. A narcissistic concept of
the self "turns the I into that apparatus for which every instinctual
thrust constitutes a danger, even though it should correspond to a
natural maturation." It also follows that the "very normalization of
this maturation" is seen by Lacan as "henceforth dependent, in man,
on a cultural mediation."[8] Nothing in the primary I pulls it toward
cooperative or reciprocal relations with others outside the self. Such
relations must be imposed from without.

Following Freud's instinct theory to the exclusion of all else in
Freud's work that contradicts it, Lacan assumes that the preoedipal
period is precultural and not social or interactive. Mothers exist for
infants only as extensions of their own bodies, as sources of frustration or satisfaction of their needs. In keeping with the narcissistic
premise, Lacan presumes that infants want total, instant, and perfectly timed responses to their wishes or needs and experience any
deviation from such response as painful frustration.

"Demand" is unconditional. What is demanded is an effortless and
invisible (objectless) steady state. The very need to ask for something
(e.g., any experience of "lack" or absence) rends this seamless symbiotic unity and sends the infant into an existential crisis. The experience of lack punctures narcissistic grandiosity; the infant is not self-

sufficient and cannot exist in a universe without others; the image in the mirror is not all. Although Lacan attributes this experience of lack to the intervention of language, it first occurs prior to the development of the infant's capacity to speak. Hence here, as in many other aspects of Lacan's theory, the m/other and Other are confounded. But his move has a double edge: While displacing interrelational issues onto language, it also reduces the narcissistic wound. A narcissist would rather be split by the impersonal operation of language than by his or her dependence on an actual other.

In the narcissistic universe any failure by the other to anticipate and respond in advance is experienced as betrayal or loss. Less than perfect "mirroring" by the other forces the infant to recognize his or her dependence on her and induces a crisis of self-esteem or a loss of narcissistic perfection. The very need to ask for what one wants destroys one's ability to enjoy what one receives and invalidates the other's gifts. Asking is associated with the lack of perfection in the self and the giving of power to the other.

Lacan actually provides a poignant *description* of the narcissist's dilemma—"demand cancels out . . . the particularity of anything which might be granted by transmuting it into a proof of love, and the very satisfactions of need with it obtains are degraded . . . as being no more than a crushing of the demand for love."[9] Narcissists are unable to tolerate their dependence on an other outside the self, experiencing such dependence as a loss of omnipotence and a threat to the perfect unity of self (annihilation). At the same time narcissists deeply wish for an other who can be a perfect mirror for and completion of the self. These intense ambivalences and contradictory wishes render narcissists unable to experience interpersonal relations as a reciprocal rather than a zero sum game in which one person's gain is invariably the other's loss. Human relations are "to be articulated, of course, as circular between the subject and the other—from the subject called to the Other, to the subject of that which he has himself seen appear in the field of the Other, from the other coming back. This process is circular, but, of its nature, without reciprocity. *Because* it is circular, it is disymmetrical."[10]

Lacan posits these dilemmas as ontological "truths" about human nature, not as consequences of his conception of the nature of demand. Humans are essentially split and alienated precisely because needs must be articulated (in language), must be addressed to an

Other who exists independent of us. Alienation is the effect "precisely of the putting into signifying form as such and of the fact that it
is from the place of the other that his message is emitted."[11] He
wishes to deny that splitting has anything to do with "effects" of "real
dependency." Although this move may sooth wounds to the narcissist's sense of self-esteem, it also has important theoretical consequences. The narcissistic position cannot be treated as a moment in
the process of human development that can be worked through.
Rather, once conceptualized as an effect of the structure of language,
the split becomes as immutable as the gap between signifier and signified itself.

Subjects and Subjugation

In the "putting into signifying form" of needs, people become "subjects" and are subjected to two purely external Others: the "desire" of
the other and the universal structure of language itself. Although Lacan treats these two as identical, I do not believe language is the only
force operating in his story. The other side of the fantasy of infantile
omnipotence is a sense of utter powerlessness and subjugation. Demand is transmuted into desire. The subject henceforth desires to be
desired by the Other. Because the subject projects its own narcissism
onto the Other, she or he assumes that only if the subject becomes the
object of the other's desire can the subject attain *its* desire (to be
loved). Narcissists believe everyone else must be exactly like them,
deficient, or hopelessly superior. A fundamental narcissistic premise
is that no one loves someone else unless such loving gratifies one's
own needs. Gratification is possible only if the object fills an empti-
ness (lack) within the self. The narcissist believes "there would be no
emergence of objects if there were no objects of use to me."[12] The
child must discover the "lack" in the m/other and attempt to fill it in
order to be desired and loved by her.

Because they must put their needs into signifying form, children
also become subject to and constituted by the structure of language.
Lacan claims language is governed by a logic extrinsic to each subject.
Speaking is an activity extrinsic to the nature of the subject because
no one creates his or her own language.[13] But the narcissistic premise
seems to shape Lacan's treatment of language. He assumes that if
something is not self-created, it must be alien and alienating. Lan-

guage and its laws are seen as imposed on the subject from the "outside"—by a culture that is "alien" to her or him.

Lacan's notion of language is also highly formal and nominalistic. Language is constituted by a chain of "materially unstable elements" and "effects determined by the double play of combination and substitution in the signifier, along the two axes of metaphor and metonymy which generate the signified."[14] Central to his theory are the opposition and gap between "signifier" and "signified." The signifier is the word or concept that somewhat arbitrarily names or represents the "thing." However, like the other, the signifier is not a passive label affixed to an object that remains as it was before. "The signifier has an active function in determining the effects in which the signifiable appears as submitting to its mark, becoming through that passion the signified."[15]

The structure of language and the child's need to be the desire of the Other produce her or him as signified, alienated, split, and a subject who is defined by these qualities. The Other is defined as "the very place called upon by a recourse to speech in any relation where it intervenes." "It is there that the subject, according to a logic prior to any awakening of the signified, finds his signifying place."[16]

The concepts of desire and of language intersect in and produce Lacan's notion of the unconscious. The "signifying place" *is* the unconscious. Unlike Freud, Lacan believes that "there is nothing in the unconscious which accords with the body."[17] The unconscious is purely what can be discovered and articulated or cannot be articulated in the field of the Other. "The unconscious is structured like a language."[18] The "it" (*ça*) is language and the unconscious. Both are constituted by the invariant rules that govern the play or dialectic of signifier and signified. It is part of the "human condition" "that it is not only man who speaks, but in man and through man that it (*ça*) speaks, that his nature is woven by effects in which we can find the structure of language, whose material he becomes."[19]

Universals and (W)holes: Fathers and Mothers
Within the Libidinal Economy

In the double determination of the subject by the other and by language, sexuality, gender, and the special role of the "phallus" as universal signifier emerge and converge. "The relation of privation or lack-in-being symbolized by the phallus, is established by derivation from the lack-in-having engendered by any particular or global frustration of demand."[20] Children want to be loved for themselves (e.g., they want total, objectless, tensionless gratification of desires). This demand, however, is a "mirage." Children discover or believe that the Other will respond only if they become the desire of the Other. What the mother desires, however, "*is* the phallus," which the mother "lacks." "The child wishes to be the phallus so as to satisfy this desire." Because the child cannot actually be the phallus, the desire of the Other "stops the subject from being satisfied with presenting to the Other anything real it might *have*."[21]

The subject thus experiences alienation and splitting in the "dialectic of demand for love and the test of desire."[22] The signifier of the mother's desire (phallus) is alien (other) to the child. The child's demand for love produces a split within the self. The wish for love is transformed into the desire to be something that one is not and cannot be in order to satisfy the desire of the Other. It is clear from this account that the Other *is* the mother as well as language because language can neither desire nor lack the phallus. In the dialectic of demand and desire, the child learns that the mother herself is lacking. She also has no phallus and cannot satisfy her own desire. The mother "lacks" narcissistic perfection and hence is an imperfect or "castrated" object. The child discovers to her or his disappointment that the Other is merely another "subject divided by the signifying Spaltung (split)."[23] The mother has a "lack" in having that causes a "lack" of being in the child.

Of course Lacan (like the child?) assumes that the mother herself is a narcissist who can be satisfied only by being restored to narcissistic perfection. Like Freud, Lacan believes a woman/mother seeks only to undo her "castration." She wants to fill in her "lack" or hole. Unlike Freud, however, Lacan believes that even having a son will not bring a woman satisfaction or relief from narcissistic injury. The mother cannot possibly be satisfied by anything "real" a baby has to offer. The equation baby (boy) = penis cannot work its magic because the phallus exists purely on a symbolic level. It grounds and circulates through a chain of signification that has no "real" biological referent. Hence one cannot gain access to the phallus by biological means (e.g., possessing a penis or having a baby boy). Castration is an effect of language and desire, not anatomy or physical injury.

Here we may pause for a moment and ask *why* the mother lacks the phallus if it is purely a linguistic artifact. Lacan insists the phallus signifies a set of linguistic/cultural structures that precede the subject and that in fact "determine us as subjects."[24] These structures include not only the binary logic of language but also its isomorphic equivalent—the "elementary structures of kinship."[25] A primary determinant of these kinship structures is the incest taboo, the "law of the father" that regulates the circulation of women among and between men. Like Freud and Lévi-Strauss, Lacan believes the internalization of the incest taboo is the founding act of culture. Some external force is required to rend the powerful, precultural, and dyadic mother-child relation. Similarly, the son's erotic tie to the mother must be broken so he will be forced to seek a wife outside the family. Families become allied with one another by exchanging women/wives among themselves. They begin to merge into larger social groups governed by rules based in kinship.

Preoedipal ties are so strong that nothing "internal" in the mother or child could cause them to break away (or split) from each other. The law introduced by the father must intervene from the "outside." The incest taboo, backed by the threat of castration, forces the child out of the bodily, seamless, wordless world of narcissistic symbiosis into existence as a cultural, universal, and specifically gendered subject. The phallus signifies the "Name-of-the-Father." It puts its mark on the child/subject. One's place in the world, sexuality, and gender are determined in being marked by and having or not having access to the phallus. The Name/Law of the Father is equivalent to culture itself.

All speaking beings "inscribe themselves" on the masculine side, no matter what their physical attributes might be. To speak one must enter into and become constituted by the realm of the symbolic—the play of signifiers and the signified and the "universal signifier" (the phallus). Those who lack access to the phallus and hence to the world of culture and language (the symbolic) are called "woman": "There is woman only as excluded by the nature of things which is the nature of words, and it has to be said that if there is one thing they themselves are complaining about enough at the moment, it is well and truly that—only they don't know what they are saying, which is all the difference between them and me."[26]

"Woman" is "not all"; she is the "empty set." Woman herself "does not exist and . . . signifies nothing."[27] Woman is the necessary binary opposite of the phallus. Her "lack" signifies "the not all" without which signification would be neither possible nor necessary. The child's discovery of the mother's lack forces the child to recognize the "gaps" that invariably exist between persons. Speaking both bridges and signifies this gap.

Woman's "essence" as not all profoundly affects her sexuality. "She has, in relation to what the phallic function designates of *jouissance,* a supplementary *jouissance.*" However, because this *jouissance* is "beyond" or outside the world of the symbolic (the phallic), woman may know or tell nothing of it. Woman can know only "that she experiences it. . . . She knows it when it happens. It does not happen to all of them."[28] The "vaginal orgasm," which Lacan associates with this supplementary *jouissance,* "has kept the darkness of its nature inviolate."[29] Presumably woman can experience it and secure it only by remaining "outside" the phallic function and in the dark.

Not a Ladies' Man:
Gender, Knowledge, Language, and Castration

Lacan's work cannot contribute very much to feminist reconceptualizations of gender. He does argue that gender identity is a purely cultural construct. Gender identity emerges as a consequence of the oedipal struggle or, more precisely, from the unconscious castration complex. Both genders *appear* to be constituted in and marked by castration. One is gendered in and through one's relation to the phallus. As a signified (subject), one is inscribed within and/or outside the phallic function. The castration complex installs in the subject "an unconscious position without which he would be unable to identify with the ideal type of his sex, or to respond without grave risk to the needs of his partner in the sexual relation, or even to receive adequately the needs of the child thus procreated."[30]

However, Lacan's work is profoundly antifeminist in its content and implications. It seems ironic that some writers have claimed that Lacanian analysis is the most useful psychoanalytic approach for feminist theorizing.[31] Lacan's work does point to the repression of women within Western discourse and hence, for Lacan, within culture and consciousness itself. His apparent emphasis on gender as a cultural construct would seem to be congruent with the ideas of many feminists. On a deeper level, however, Lacan's theory, even more than Freud's, conceals essential aspects of male-dominant culture. Thus its deconstruction can contribute to an analysis of patriarchal culture. Lacan's linguistic approach renders such cultures equivalent to culture as such. Male dominance becomes unanalyzable in theory and inescapable in practice. Lacan displaces the focus of analysis from social relations and relations of power to the supposedly universal/ahistoric structure and effects of the logic of language. Just as Freud turned to "biology" and biologistic reasoning to avoid "penetrating" further into the "great riddle of sex" that he himself initially uncovered, so Lacan deploys "language" in a similar, defensive way.

A postmodernist perspective alerts us to the fact that both Freud and Lacan call upon the same "secondary defense" for their initial acts of displacement and repression—the supposedly impersonal authority of science. Both argue that psychoanalysis is and should be a "science." They both claim psychoanalysis is grounded in and seeks to explain something "real" (e.g., outside human agency or control). In Lacan's case this real is the structure and effects of language. Lacan conceptualizes psychoanalysis as "the science of the unconscious. From this I have deduced a topology intended to account for the constitution of the subject."[32] Because science is supposedly "neutral" and objective, further questions about what might be masked by or foreclosed in this move are forestalled. The structure of Lacan's theory confirms the postmodernist claim that universalist concepts conceal acts of domination and that binary oppositions are inseparable from implicit or explicit hierarchies. However the consequences of and reasons for such acts in Lacan's work are best understood not as instances and effects of the "tyranny of metaphysics," but rather in relation to older political meanings of tyranny.

An explicitly political and gender-sensitive theory is required to deconstruct Lacan's theories of narcissism and language. From a feminist perspective it appears that much of the material concealed behind Lacan's scientizing mask is related to or concerns questions of gender. Especially predominant in Lacan's work (like Freud's) is an obscuring of female desire and the fear, denial, and displacement of the power of women in early infantile experience. To see that this is so, let us return to the questions I raised earlier. Why does the mother lack the phallus? If the phallus exists purely in the symbolic, why can it not at least circulate through her? Why does the mother or anyone desire it in the first place? Why is the phallus such a powerful but obscure object of desire in Lacan's theory? Why does it signify the "Name of the *Father*" and *his* law? Could this all have something to do with the *desire* of the father (of which Lacan almost never speaks)? Could the desire of actual, embodied, historically constituted, and not merely symbolic fathers, as well as the child and the mother, "mark" Lacan's theory?

Within the "phallic order" the mother/woman must come to desire a phallus that she must believe she and all women lack. Although Lacan claims men as well as women lack the phallus and are castrated (by language), the consequences of this lack and desire do not seem to be the same for both genders. Part of women's desire is constituted in and reflects her induction into the kinship structures of culture, especially those of heterosexual marriage. This induction requires that the woman shift her "libido" from her first object (the mother) to a male one (father/husband).

Because Lacan argues that sexuality takes its form purely in the subjectivity of the Other and its law, not from "nature," heterosexuality must be understood as culturally produced. Thus the woman's desire for an Other who is inscribed on the side of masculinity must be a consequence and product of the law signified by the phallus and a subjection to the desire of the (masculine) other. Once again this Other is not simply language. This law seems to require that the woman desire not just a phallus, but to be the "object" of desire of a being with an anatomically male body. "All" women must confront a fundamental "truth" about or behind the "mystery of femininity": "As is true for all woman, and for reasons that are at the very basis of the most elementary forms of social exchange . . . the problem of her condition is fundamentally that of accepting herself as an object of desire for the man."[33] Woman thus cannot remain content with her mother's body or her own. "Social exchange" (not language) stipulates that, unlike the man's, her desire cannot remain in the field of a female other. She is not to be the object of desire for the woman. Woman must also come to desire that her child bear the name of the father and not her own name (e.g., that the child have a "lawful" father). This is one of the meanings of her wish for the child to *be* the phallus, for it to bear the mark of the father's name. "Woman" and "man" here are the only positions in language that a person of either gender can occupy. In order for Lacan's claims to make sense, we have to assume that the "mystery of femininity" refers to a condition shared by anatomically female persons (women).

Lacan has no satisfactory explanation for all these remarkable displacements of female desire. He simply attributes them to the nature of desire as such. In turn he utilizes his account of female desire as an instance and proof of the "truth" of his theory of desire itself. Lacan makes a series of interdependent and circular claims: Culture is a symbolic system; kinship is a symbolic system; language is a symbolic system; hence all symbolic systems must have the same binary structure. If there is a series of binary oppositions, there must be some binary opposition (phallus/castration) that structures all the others. If there is a series of oppositions, some prior unity or dialectical synthesis must have broken into parts. There is a narcissistic I broken by the Other; there is an I split by (into) desire and demand. What is split asunder cannot be put back together. There is a dyad broken by the father. The dyad is precultural/linguistic; therefore the Law of the Father must intervene from the outside. This "outside" is culture, language, kinship, the Ur-signifier that makes all others possible and split—the phallus. We are back in the world of mirrors and fragmented images that are somehow to cohere into an inevitable and "universal" truth. But we are not to notice that Lacan's voice is making such claims and asking us to accede to his authority. The "fictional" dimension is to disappear behind the screen of "science's" claim to truth.

Lacan's Lack: Language and Power

Outside the hall of mirrors, Lacan's arguments look "other" to me. Ironically, their resonance with something "real"—a real other than his "all" (the universal logic of language)—allows them more persuasive force than they would otherwise have. This real is bound up with the fact that culture *is* masculine, not as the effect of language but as the consequence of actual power relations to which men have far more access than women. Here the founder (Freud) is much more honest about "reality" than is Lacan. He does not ask us to believe the sons are castrated in the same way or to the same extent as the daughters or that the oedipal struggle and induction into culture have the same consequences for boys and girls. In Freud's theory anatomy is destiny; real fathers want their sons and not their daughters to inherit

and administer their law and the power(s) behind it. Sons are prom-
ised access to and power over women (wives) when they grow up.
Freud masks power behind biology; Lacan claims we are all prisoners
of language. But the founder's thinking is more transparent and
points toward more useful dynamics for feminist theorizing than Lacan's.

Lacan's theory of language itself is also inaccurate. Language is as
much signified as it is a signifier. It depends for its actual effects as
much on the forms of life it reflects as on those it constitutes. For example, the coherence and compelling power of Lacan's notion of the
phallus as universal signifier draw upon preexisting social relations
(e.g., a gender system) that operate to create binary opposites with
unbridgeable "gaps" between the two terms. Lacan's concept of universal "binary logic" supposedly governing language itself may reflect the preexisting importance of the number "two" in our culture.
We are accustomed to dividing things in two from the moment of
birth. Often the first question asked about a newborn is whether it is
a girl or a boy. Within this gender system two opposite but not equal
types of being are constituted. Dividing things in two and the gender
system as a whole appear to rest on "natural" differences or "external" logics. However such differences or ways of counting attain their
special salience and capacity to convey meaning as an effect of the
gender system, not because of a logic independent of social relations.

Nominalistic approaches to language (including Lacan's) are inherently flawed. No signifier (not even the phallus) exists outside a "language game" in which its meaning and functions depend on historical practices and past usages of the word. For example, the term
phallus depends for its rhetorical or truth-claiming effects in part on its
uses within preexisting language games and forms of social life that
are unacknowledged within but necessary conditions for the plausibility of Lacan's theory. The notion of a phallus as universal signifier
calls upon and depends for its rhetorical effect upon the ineluctable
equivalence of phallus and penis in ordinary language. Lacan's claims
that the phallus exists purely upon a symbolic plane, that it does not
signify penis, and that any relationship between signifier and signified is arbitrary are disingenuous. Would we be persuaded by Lacan
if he claimed that the mother lacks, say, "a mouse" or that her desire
for the child is to be the "waxpaper"?

At least Freud is more transparent and accurate in his rhetoric.

Contrary to Lacan's claims, Freud is quite clear that he uses penis and phallus interchangeably and that he believes the boy's narcissistic investment in his penis as a "superior" organ is warranted in fact as well as in fantasy. What Freud (like Lacan) does not do, however, is locate his claim within a particular social context. Within a *male-dominated* society possession of a penis or access to a phallus *is* particularly valuable, and anyone interested in certain sorts of power or privilege would worry about its loss or lack. In societies free of male domination, possession of a penis/phallus would lose such incredibly charged salience.

The whole notion of a universal signifier depends on and reflects our experience that someone or something and not others has the power to order our world. The phallus signifies not culture itself, but rather a culture in which "what is called" civilization has been primarily the work of men (*qua* embodied penis-possessing beings). However, if like Lacan, we treat culture/language/Law of the Father as universal structures and equivalents, there is no way to reverse the play of signifier and signified. The phallus is never signified. We cannot ask what determines the place of the phallus as "universal signifier" within Lacan's theory or in culture. Lacan leaves us with the alternatives of phallic culture or no culture at all. He thus repeats rather than analyzes the "normal" oedipal boy's development, his "narcissistic investment" in the penis/phallus, and his choice to accede to and reify the father's law rather than to question or defy it.

Lacan's theory also reflects rather than analyzes the father's *desire:* that women see themselves and experience their sexuality as the "object" of man's desire. Women are not to question men's right to have access to, to "exchange," or to define them. Although Freud's notions of female penis envy and castration are deeply flawed, Lacan consigns woman *qua* female, embodied being to an absolute nonexistence in culture rather than to an imperfect, inferior one. By shifting the ground of psychoanalysis from the psychosexual development of concrete persons to a supposedly "neutral" and universalistic theory of language and symbolic systems, Lacan further obscures the social origins of gender and gender-based asymmetries of power. Once again the father's authority is asserted and concealed; his desire is privileged and protected.

Woman is not only identified with but relegated to the realm of the Other, the bearer of difference, the body, instinct, lacking a phallus,

castrated. If we are in or enjoying our bodies, we are perpetually outside of this and all possible cultures. Woman in Lacan's theory is
placed in a familiar double bind. She is charged with introducing "difference" into human experience. Yet as woman we literally cannot
speak, we do not know what we experience, and we can say nothing
to the men (signifiers?) who constitute culture.

Lacan's theory also reveals a further capitulation to the law of the
father (in this case Freud himself). Freud's emphasis on the centrality
of the oedipus complex can be partially understood as a denial and
defense against the return of the earlier relatedness to and identification with the mother. In Lacan's texts a similar repression is at work.
Inasmuch as women are associated with the presymbolic, they appear as the repressed within Lacan's theory. Yet like all repressed material they continue to affect the dynamics of the whole self, for to be
repressed is *not* to be absent. The repressed is omnipresent as an unconscious force within the psyche and therefore in culture itself. This
repressed material cannot be made conscious by Lacan's theory because he relegates it to the presymbolic and therefore to the unspeak-
able and unknowable. The presymbolic nevertheless haunts both
symbolic systems and the subject.

The antimony within Lacan's theory between the symbolic and the
presymbolic and his denial of the meaningfulness or possibility of the
reciprocal social relations in the presymbolic are rooted partially in
the repression of the infant's experience of the loved and feared
mother. The infant's (and the infant within the adult's) longing for
fusion is defensively turned into Lacan's notion of the lack. Even more
than in Freud's work, the powerful mother of infancy is reconceived
as the "castrated," unknowable, and unreachable Other. Once the possibility that the infant self was in a relationship with another is denied, the forming of the self can occur only through acts of alienation.
The self is necessarily always a false self in Winnicott's sense, but unlike Winnicott, Lacan believes that no other "true" self is possible.

However, as I have argued, it is better to read Lacan's work as a
description of the child who is stuck in its separation phase or the
narcissistic position and is unable to see himself in the other. His notion of the lack can then be understood as a denial of prior relatedness
rather than as an inherent and unresolvable dilemma within the human condition or as intrinsic to the nature of desire. The social history
of the subject is transformed into a universal, abstract, existential di-

lemma. Certain aspects of the subject's existence are concealed rather than radically deconstructed as Lacan claims. The subject is turned into a linguistic cipher partially to obscure its own prehistory.

In the end Lacan recreates the myth of a solipsistic disembodied self. Despite his heroic self-image as a brave Nietzschean negator of bourgeois culture, elucidating our primal alienation and fractured selves, Lacan replicates rather than dismantles a dominant strain of modern Western thought extending from Descartes through Sartre. The subject is not "decentered." An incomplete and stereotypically masculine form of self is posited as the unalterable linchpin in the chain of signifiers said to constitute culture. It is not surprising that the phallus assumes the role of "universal signifier" within Lacan's theory or that he wishes to consign women to presymbolic silence.

A Transitional Space: Object Relations and That Obscure Object of Desire

The derivation of religious needs from the infant's helplessness and the longing for the father aroused by it seems to me incontrovertible, especially since the feeling is not simply prolonged from childhood days, but is permanently sustained by fear of the superior power of fate. I cannot think of any need in childhood as strong as the need for a father's protection. Thus the part played by the oceanic feeling, which might seek something like restoration of limitless narcissism is ousted from a place in the foreground. The origin of the religious attitude can be traced back in clear outlines as far as the feeling of infantile helplessness. There may be something further back behind that, but for the present it is wrapped in obscurity.

Sigmund Freud,
Civilization and Its Discontents

In psycho-analytic and allied work it is found that all individuals (men and women) have in reserve a certain fear of woman. Some individuals have this fear to a greater extent than others, but it can be said to be universal. This is quite different from saying that an individual fears a particular woman. This fear of woman is a powerful agent in society structure, and it is responsible for the fact that in very few societies does a woman hold the political reins. It is also

responsible for the immense amount of cruelty to women,
which can be found in customs that are accepted by almost
all civilizations. The root of this fear of woman *is known.*
It is related to the fact that in the early history of every
individual who develops well, and who is sane, and who
has been able to find himself, there is a debt to a woman—
a woman who was devoted to that individual as an infant,
and whose devotion was absolutely essential for the individ-
ual's development. The original dependence is not remem-
bered, and therefore the debt is not acknowledged, except in
so far as the fear of woman *represents the first stage of this*
acknowledgement.

> D. W. Winnicott,
> The Family and Individual
> Development

The Relations of Object Relations Theory to
Its (Possible) Others

There are many flaws in object relations theory, especially in the treatment of gender, sexuality, and power. Nonetheless the work of object
relations theorists has much to contribute to the development of better theories of the self, gender, knowledge, and justice. Furthermore
certain aspects of object relations theory, especially the rejection of
Enlightenment notions of reason and knowledge and the emphasis
on the importance of mothering in the constitution of a self, are particularly compatible with the complementary to postmodernist projects and feminist theorizing.[34]

Perhaps as befits a psychoanalytic perspective in which sociality
and interpersonal interaction are stressed, there is no one founder of
object relations theory. Nonetheless I will draw particularly and extensively on the work of D. W. Winnicott. Winnicott's work precedes,
informs, and in many ways is more rich and complex than the writings of American object relations analysts such as Kernberg or Masterson and self psychologists such as Kohut. Unlike many other analysts Winnicott reflects consistently about the relationships between
symbolization, culture, and *preoedipal* experience. His concept of the
"transitional space" (which is also the space out and from which culture may arise) is especially intriguing and underutilized by other analysts and philosophers. His emphasis on play and the extrarational

sources of thinking and creativity complements and could deepen and improve the postmodernist critiques of Enlightenment approaches to these issues.

Winnicott occasionally seems sensitive to questions of gender, although his writings lack a sustained, critical account of its formation and significance within individual identity, psychoanalytic theory (especially in his own concept of the "good enough mother"), and culture as a whole. However the stress on the centrality of the mother-child relation within Winnicott's and other object relations theorists' work at least enables us to recognize and to begin to undo the repression and distortion of preoedipal experience that so pervade the theories of Freud and Lacan.

Winnicott also has a wonderful feel for infantile experience and for clinical work.[35] He is able to move easily back and forth from such experiences to thinking about their implications for disputes within psychoanalytic theory. His work thus exemplifies the extent to which psychoanalysis *is* a form of relational work in which theory and practice constantly inform, correct, and depend on each other. Winnicott shows us what kinds of knowledge are or can be generated in and through the interplay between analyst and patient or mother and child if this interplay is combined with disciplined, intersubjective reflection upon it. In this regard also I find Winnicott's work more useful than Lacan's because he almost never discusses the specific content of his work with patients. Indeed Lacan posits an irreducible gap between the analyst as the one who "ought to know" and the desire of the patient. In analysis, as elsewhere, genuine intersubjectivity is impossible. Knowledge and desire cannot be integrated or reconciled.[36]

Like Lacan, however, object relations theorists emphasize only one aspect of Freud's complex theories of the development of the self and the relations of self and others(s). This restricted emphasis is useful in some ways, in that it allows object relations theorists to explore more deeply Freud's discovery of the tenacious grip that objects, even dead ones, have on the "ego." As Freud noted in 1917, "it can be universally observed that man never willingly abandons a libido-position, not even when a substitute is already beckoning to him."[37] He even occasionally argues that "the first determinant of anxiety, which the ego itself introduces, is loss of perception of the object (which is equated with loss of the object itself)."[38] The "object" referred to here is the infant's *mother*. Although object relations theorists differ somewhat among themselves, their overall project is similar: to understand the "individual" as the product of social relations with real persons in interaction with the unfolding development of his or her unique "psyche-soma."[39] In contrast to Lacan, object relations theorists claim the child eventually comes to recognize, accept, and enjoy the independent existence of the persons who care for him or her.[40] However this emphasis on object relatedness entails certain losses as well, particularly an obscuring of the non-object-related aspects of sexuality and desire and a desexualization of the mother and the mother-child relation.

Object relations theory is more compatible with postmodernism than Freudian or Lacanian analysis because it does not require a fixed or essentialist view of "human nature." The logic of object relations theory suggests that human nature may have many forms. As social relations and family structures change, so would human nature. As the kinds of objects and relations between them a child internalizes change, so too would "the child" and the nature of "childhood" itself. But contrary to the views of many postmodernists, object relations theorists offer strong arguments for the importance of a stable, "core self." Winnicott's account of psychological development is especially important. He distinguishes between a "false" self that *is* overly rigid, intellectualized, and controlling and an alternate, "true" one that has many of the characteristics of the postmodernist "decentered" one but fewer of the deficiencies. From the perspective of Winnicott's theories, almost all postmodernist critiques of the self would in fact describe and target a false one. The ideas of object relations theorists encourage and support the suspicions of feminist (and other) theorists about the postmodernist project of abandoning all language of or desire for a self. However Winnicott's true self is remarkably degendered and asexual. Hence feminist and Lacanian theories can be deployed to identify and interrogate some of the gaps in the work of object relations theorists.

The Development of a Self
in Object Relations Con-text(s)

"There is no such thing as a baby."[41] Object relations theorists' stories of the development of a self are among their most valuable contributions to transitional theorizing. Winnicott and other theorists offer more satisfactory accounts of the origin of a self in and out of relations with others, of the nature of the baby's "need," of the origin of conscience, and of aggression and its uses. These theorists do posit at least one essentialist claim. The most basic tenet of object relations theorists is that human beings by nature are "object seeking." We need real and not merely projected or narcissistic relations with others. We seek objects for the intrinsic satisfaction of such relating, not merely to reduce drive tension. If objects in the child's environment are "good enough," humans will develop into beings who both seek and find such relations. The tortures Lacan portrays as intrinsic aspects of desire—illusion, invariable and unbridgeable gaps, alienation, and self-estrangement—are treated by object relations theorists as expressions of a pathological false self formation that can be analyzed and overcome.

In and through relationships with other persons, whether bad or good enough, a relatively unformed but potentially competent neonate develops into a human being. The child's bodily experiences (oral, anal, etc.) cannot be separated from and are always shaped and given meaning by and within the child's object relations. There is no drive without an object. Hence "instinctual" impulses cannot be distinguished or treated apart from their relational aspects.

The "psychological birth of the human infant" does not occur simultaneously with his or her physical birth.[42] Physical birth is a distinct event occurring within a finite and easily determined period of time; psychological birth is a complex process stretching over roughly the first three years of life. Psychological birth emerges out of the interaction of physical, relational, and mental processes. "Gradually the psyche and soma aspects of the growing person become involved in a process of mutual interrelation. At a later stage the live body, with its limits, and with an inside and outside, is *felt by the individual* to form the core of the imaginative self."[43]

Because psyche and soma are so interrelated, disturbances in object relations can be expressed both physically and mentally. For example, deficits in early relations may be expressed in and through infantile or adult eating disorders, psychosomatic illness, or the splitting off of mental functioning from soma and the totality of the psyche's experience.[44] In the latter instance we "find *mental functioning becoming a thing in itself,* practically replacing the good mother and making her unnecessary. . . . This is a most uncomfortable state of affairs, especially because the psyche of the individual gets 'seduced' away into this mind from the intimate relationship which the psyche originally had with the soma. The result is a mind-psyche, which is pathological."[45]

Children's psychological, somatic, and cognitive development is a process played out in and through a changing relationship between mother and child. There do appear to be certain innate potentials, dispositions, or "constitutions" and character traits within human beings (e.g., the ability to walk and talk, differing levels of capacity to tolerate stress, and vulnerability to depression).[46] However even these potentials are most adequately achieved or compensated for within good enough object relations. Sufficiently bad object relations can retard or distort the developmental process, including such "physical" achievements as walking or cognitive ones like use of language and symbolization.

The child's relation to his or her mother undergoes a developmental process as well. Although at first the mother must do most of the adapting to her infant, eventually both members of the dyad learn to be sensitive to the needs and feelings of the other. Each eventually attempts to have his or her own needs at least recognized, if not met. The child's most important tasks during the first three years of life are establishing a close relation with the caretaker, usually the mother, and then moving from that relationship through the process of separation-individuation.[47] Separation means establishing a firm sense of differentiation from the mother, of being a me/self different from but in relation to an other. Separation also entails a deepening sense of possessing one's own physical and mental boundaries, including a body with an inside and outside and a self with access to three realities—inner, transitional, and outer. Individuation entails establishing a range of characteristics, bodily experiences, skills, personality traits, and an inner world that are uniquely one's own "true self" or a creative core of being and aliveness.

Separation and individuation are two "tracts" of development; they are not identical, but can reinforce or impede each other. For example, one can separate from the mother in order to escape her inappropriate responses. The self that results from such separation is likely to be a "false" one built out of *reactions* to impingements from the outside rather than a cohering of one's own creative impulses, movement toward separation, and the mother's facilitating responses to such movement and impulses. Such a separation is also likely to require a severing or denial of ties to the other. The false self feels that relationships invariably pose a threat to its separate existence. Such a false self is likely to be plagued by feelings of deadness, futility, unreality, rigidity, and an inability to enter into and enjoy reciprocal relations with others. The false self is marked by a "dissociation between intellectual activity and psychosomatic existence."[48] Persons with a false self are also likely to be pervaded by feelings of being a "fake" or "pretender"—split between an external "performing" self and an inner world of very different qualities, feelings, and yearnings.

There is an important moment in the baby's experience preceding his or her first object relation with the mother. In this stage, lasting approximately the first six months of life,

> the unit is not the individual, the unit is an environmental-individual set-up. The centre of gravity of the being does not start off in the individual. It is in the total set-up. By good-enough childcare technique, holding and general management the shell becomes gradually taken over and the kernel (which has looked all the time like a human baby to us) can begin to be an individual . . . with good-enough technique the centre of gravity of being in the environment-individual set-up can afford to lodge in the centre, in the kernel rather than the shell. The human being now developing an entity from the centre can become localized in the baby's body and so can begin to create an external world at the same time as acquiring a limiting membrane and an inside.[49]

Neonates do not yet have a firm sense of their own body boundaries. I and not I are not yet fully differentiated, and inside and outside the self are only gradually distinguished. The baby is extremely sensitive to and affected by the mother's moods, feelings, and responses because these occur within the "environmental-individual set up" that is now the baby's primary reality. Object relations theorists claim this phase is "the primal soil from which all subsequent human relations form."[50] Without a healthy environment at the beginning, it is difficult for the infant to achieve the sense of "continuity of being" that makes further growth toward a true self possible. Frustration is necessarily wounding only for a short time. The infant needs a near "perfect" response only at the beginning.

In order for this phase to be adequate for the child, the mother must enter a remarkable state of her own—what Winnicott calls "primary maternal preoccupation."[51] This is a state of heightened sensitivity to the child that gradually recedes after the first few weeks of the child's life. In order for the mother to enter into or give herself over to such a state, she must be emotionally available to the child in a consistent, reasonably conflict-free way. She should be able to enjoy the sensual and emotional closeness of the relationship without losing her own sense of separateness. She should be concerned for the child's well-being without developing a narcissistic overinvestment in the child as a mere extension of her own self so she can also begin to let the child separate. Her infantile wishes for a merged relationship should have been adequately gratified in childhood. If this was not the case, the infant's needs may arouse resentment and hostility or envy in her. The mother requires adequate support, both emotional and material, during this period from adults who are able both to nurture her and to reinforce her own sense of autonomy.

Separation-individuation begins at about six months and continues to about the end of the third year. Unlike Freud or Lacan, Winnicott and other object relations theorists believe that the movement toward separation is generated by the child's own internal impulses. It is not primarily a defensive response to the mother's failures to reduce the child's inner tension levels (frustration). According to Winnicott frustration is completely irrelevant to the earliest phase of the infant's development. The mother's failure to adapt at the beginning produces not frustration but rather "annihilation of the infant's self," that is, a radical interruption of the baby's sense of being and security.[52]

After the earliest phase the need for a good environment becomes "relative." In fact the infant comes to need "a carefully graduated failure of adaption."[53] This failure, if matched to the infant's growing capacities, enables these capacities to develop and flourish. The baby can grow away from but still in relation to the mother. If the mother is good enough, "the mental activity of the infant turns a *good enough* environment into a perfect environment, that is to say, turns relative failure of adaption into adaptive success. What releases the mother from her need to be near-perfect is the infant's understanding."[54]

The infant's understanding of the mother and the relatedness between them enables the infant to "build the idea of a person in the mother. From this angle the recognition of the mother as a person comes in a positive way, normally, and not out of the experience of the mother as the symbol of frustration."[55]

Babies also benefit in other ways from the mother's appropriate failures, which provide a space for infants to express their aggression and to discover that both baby and mother can survive it: "The aggressive impulses do not give any satisfactory experience unless there is opposition. The opposition must come from the Not-me which gradually comes to be distinguished from the Me." Aggression does not necessarily endanger the object or conflict with Eros. To the contrary, "it is the aggressive component that more surely drives the individual to a need for a Not-me or an object that is felt to be external."[56]

The discovery of the Other through its graduated failures enables the baby to accept the existence of external reality. For Winnicott, unlike Freud or Lacan, the acknowledgment of external reality is not primarily painful or the product of the infant's reluctant accommodation to external impingement. The infant's growing sense of external reality entails more than a blow to the infant's narcissism or illusion of omnipotence. Narcissistic illusion is not always or only blissful. It is also terrifying and cripples the infant's capacity to engage in and enjoy both fantasy and objectivity. Fantasy "is only tolerable at full blast when objective reality is appreciated well. The subjective has tremendous value but is so alarming and magical that it cannot be enjoyed except as a parallel to the objective."[57]

The child's aggression, increasingly integrated and capable ego, confidence in the continuing existence of a mother who can be not-me and in me, and the mother's graduated failures all provide motivations for separation. In addition the child's locomotor skills are developing in this period, so the child can physically distance him- or herself from the mother. These physical developments reinforce the child's sense of separateness. It is hard for the child to feel separate until she or he can literally walk away from the mother. A purely external and coercive "law of the father" is not required to enforce and consolidate the child's process of separation.

The child explores and continually develops separateness, then returns to the mother for "refueling." The potential presence of the relationship between child and mother allows the child to leave it and to tolerate the mother's absences as well. The child can be alone without feeling lonely or abandoned.[58] Gradually the child internalizes the dyadic relationship with the mother, and it becomes part of the child's internal psychic reality. Both members of the dyad must learn to let go of the early bond without rejecting the other. The ambivalence present throughout this process gradually intensifies. The child both wants to return to a less differentiated state and fears being engulfed by it. The child wants to use the mother ruthlessly for his or her own purposes but also feels a growing concern for her as a separate person and guilt at the potential destructiveness of such impulses.

Unlike Freud and Lacan, Winnicott argues, "the healthy child has a personal source of sense of guilt, and need not be taught to feel guilty or concerned." This capacity for guilt arises out of the early interactions between the child and mother. It is not a consequence of the imposition of paternal law/culture, the resolution of the oedipus complex, and superego formation: "For a long while the small child needs someone who is not only loved but who will accept potency (whether it be boy or girl) in terms of reparative and restitutive giving. In other words the small child must go on having a chance to give in relation to guilt belonging to instinctual experience, because this is the way of growth."[59]

Only if the child's gifts are persistently refused will this sense of guilt and the conflicts between "instinctual experience" and object love become unmanageable. Then the child *will* develop an overly punitive superego and murderous rages or repress the capacity for concern and become estranged from self and the object. This estrangement can best be explained by the mother's inability to receive what the child really has to offer, not by the nature of desire itself and the inevitable disjunction of the baby's and mother's desires.

The Third World: Playing as Reality

Winnicott's notion of the "transitional space" is one of his most important contributions to (possible) post-Enlightenment thinking. He further undermines the distinction Freud and Lacan try to maintain between primary process (id) and secondary process (ego). He breaks decisively with Enlightenment values in identifying the capacities to play and to "make use of" and "relate to" objects, rather than reason, as the qualities most characteristic of human "being." Winnicott's notion of the transitional space shares some of the qualities postmodernists attribute to "writing," but because this space is defined by less grandiose boundaries, it provides a more useful way to think about certain aspects of experience. Furthermore, because Winnicott locates the development of the capacity to reason within the unfolding relationship of mother and child, his account is more compatible with and useful to feminist theorizing. Reason no longer appears as a fragile, tentative acquisition dependent upon the existence of patriarchal authority or the child's submission to the alien logic of language and the father's law. Transitional space and related phenomena begin to emerge during the separation-individuation phase (six months to two years). In this period the child's initial euphoria arising out of the discovery of his or her own powers and skills diminishes as the child discovers the limitations as well as possibilities of what she or he can do. The child painfully, as well as joyously, learns that she or he is not omnipotent, and that the mother, too, is not all powerful.

One dimension of transitional phenomena is that they make "it possible for the individual to cope with the immense shock of loss of omnipotence" of the mother and the self.[60] The successful creation and use of transitional space and objects enable the child to separate and appreciate the mother as a real person. Separation does not inevitably require the child to transform the previously omnipotent or phallic mother into the opposite of narcissistic disappointment: a castrated, lacking "empty set."

The transitional space is an "intermediate" area between the infant's illusion of omnipotence and "objective perception based on reality testing."[61] At first, with good enough mothering, the infant's experience is almost entirely illusory. The mother's nearly perfect adaptation to the child enables the child to have the illusion of omnipotence, that the world is under her or his magical control. Unlike Freud, Winnicott sees such magical thinking as dependent upon the mother's response to the child, rather than as an invariable characteristic of "primary process." If the mother does not respond adequately to the child in the earliest months of life, the child will not be able to use illusion and it will then lack the capacity to employ transitional phenomena and hence to bear the experience of disillusion that is to follow. "The mother's eventual task is gradually to disillusion the infant, but she has no hope of success unless at first she has been able to give sufficient opportunity for illusion."[62]

Paradoxically, adequate illusion provides the basis for the child's first belief in an external world. For Winnicott, unlike Lacan, there is no absolute distinction between the illusory, symbolic, and real dimensions of experience: "The mother's adaptation to the infant's needs, when good enough, gives the infant the illusion that there is an external reality that corresponds to the infant's own capacity to create. . . . To the observer, the child perceives what the mother actually presents, but this is not the whole truth. The infant perceives the breast only in so far as a breast could be created just there and then."[63]

Children move into transitional space when they begin to place the object outside their omnipotent control. They can do this only if they have had good enough mothering and if the reality of their object is not called into question:

The transitional object and the transitional phenomena start each human being off with what will always be important for them, i.e., a neutral area of experience which will not be challenged. Of the transitional object it can be said that it is a matter of agreement between us and the baby that we will never ask the question: "Did you conceive of this or was it presented to you from without?" The important point is that no decision on this point is expected. The question is not to be formulated.[64]

In the transitional space the baby begins to perceive the object as an "external phenomena, not as a projective entity." Here again there is a paradox: The transitional object is simultaneously illusory and real. "The baby creates the object, but the object was there waiting to be created and to become a cathected object."[65] The baby is moving from solipsistic "object relating," in which projective mechanisms and identifications are operating, to "object use" in which the object is part of a shared reality. For the baby to "use" an object, the object must exist independent of the self. The baby gradually discovers that this object he or she created was a mother with her own properties, who was there all along outside the baby. Transitional phenomena help the baby manage "the strain of relating inner and outer reality."[66]

In moving from object relating to use, another paradox arises: The baby must "destroy" the object before being able to use it. The baby destroys the object in fantasy, but the object (hopefully) survives (e.g., the mother does not retaliate for the baby's rage and reject her or him). This survival of the object enables the baby to perceive it as having an existence *outside* and autonomous of the child's inner world. The baby's prior relatedness to the object makes the destruction of the object both possible and meaningful. "In this way a world of shared reality is created in which the subject can use and which can feed back other-than-me substance into the subject." [67]

Thus the child can have relations with an other that are real (i.e., the child's object relations can be built in and out of actual experience with an other). Humans are not condemned to a world in which there are only gaps that can never be bridged between self and other. The narcissistic position in which there are only purely internally constructed "representations" or "ideas" of objects who are alive because and only so long as libidinal energy is invested in them is only one aspect of our experience with others.

The transitional space bridges the gaps—between self and other and inner and outer reality. This is the space of play and of attachment to special "not-me" possessions (a blanket, toy, etc.) that must always be accessible to the baby. The child's ability to choose and utilize a transitional object also signals that the child has begun to engage in the process of symbolization. "The object is a symbol of the baby and the mother (or part of the mother). The use of an object symbolizes the union of two now separate things, baby and mother, *at the point of time* of the initiation of their separateness." [68]

The capacity to play and the process of symbolization associated with it eventually expand "into creative living and into the whole cultural life of man." [69] Culture, like play, exists in this third area, the potential space between the individual's inner life and objective reality. Without something to make use of (tradition out there), no creativity or culture is possible. The individual's creative transformation of what exists independently in shared reality is what distinguishes art from dreams or individual delusion. But the individual *can* creatively transform what is given in part by bringing something of inner reality into the process. The subject is not only "signified" but can also disrupt or transform the pregiven chain.

Thus unlike Lacan or Freud, Winnicott does not see symbolization and culture itself as something alien to the individual, imposed over and against the inner self. Nor is culture built out of the repression and sublimation of instinctual impulses or from a logic purely external to those "subjected" to it. Culture arises out of that third space remaining within us, giving us pleasure and a sense of aliveness and continuity. In this space each relatively healthy individual carries on the lifelong process of creatively managing the strain of reconciling inner and outer realities: "It is assumed here that the task of reality acceptance is never completed, that no human being is free from the strain of relating inner and outer reality, and that relief from this strain is provided by an intermediate area of experience . . . which is not challenged (arts, religion, etc.). This intermediate area is in direct continuity with the play area of the small child who is 'lost' in play."[70]

Unlike the postmodernists, however, Winnicott does not ask us to believe this space is *all* there is, that nothing exists outside the (con)text of play. Such a claim represents a collapsing of all realities into one (the third or intermediate area). Winnicott stresses that we can enjoy and utilize this space only if it remains "neutral." To ask someone else to accept our creative object as equivalent to or inclusive of external reality is to court madness for self and other. This claim also leaves no place for the purely subjective and idiosyncratic qualities of inner reality. But to challenge someone to make her or his creative object conform to external reality, as in "socialist realism," would also destroy the integrity and meaningfulness of the third space.

A Feminist Intervention: On the Disappearance of Power, Gender (and Sex)

From a feminist viewpoint a central constituent and determinant of the self in formation is missing from Winnicott's and other object relations theorists' accounts of human development.[71] Object relations theory lacks a critical, sustained account of gender formation and its costs to self and culture as a whole. Object relations theorists claim that, by the end of the third year, a "core identity" or a distorted one will have been established. We know now that gender is a central element of this core identity. Contrary to Freud's oedipal-centered theory, the child's sense of gender is established by one and one-half to two years of age and has little to do with an understanding of sexuality or reproduction.[72]

Unlike object relations theorists, however, at least Freud and Lacan (intentionally or not) help us see that in male-dominant societies this sense of gender is not neutral. Becoming aware of gender means recognizing that men and women are not valued equally, that men are more esteemed and powerful than women. Becoming gendered therefore entails a coming to awareness of and to some extent internalizing asymmetries of power and esteem.

Indeed the *observations* of object relations theorists support this same conclusion. For example, in her study of healthy young children, Mahler noted that by the age of twenty-one months there are significant developmental differences between girls and boys. The girls seemed more "depressed" and "were more persistently enmeshed in the ambivalent aspects of the mother-child relationship"; the boys "showed a tendency to disengage themselves from mother and to enjoy functioning in the widening world."[73] Perhaps the boys could "enjoy functioning" more than the girls because both genders had already sensed that the world is open far wider for males than females.

Part of the gender blindness in object relations theory can be accounted for by the fact that the theorists take for granted the existing social division of labor in which the mother or other women do primary caretaking. Unlike feminist theorists these analysts do not usually explore the negative consequences of this arrangement. Nor do they consider the possibility that such arrangements arise not from biological necessities but from a series of social relations and structures, the replication of which is essential for the existence and maintenance of male dominance.

As I will discuss in more detail in Chapter 5, feminist theorists have emphasized at least one of the consequences of this child-rearing arrangement. The ideal goal of the "maturational process" for object relations theorists is "reciprocity." Although this is never fully achieved, ideally in good enough social relations a resolution is reached by age three in which both members of the mother-child dyad come to accept their bond (mutuality) and their separateness. This resolution is the basis of a truly reciprocal relationship between the pair, creating the possibility for the child then to establish reciprocal relations with subsequent others.

However therapists' offices are full of persons who are unable to create or sustain such relations. Contemporary Western culture more generally is full of complaints about the lack of intimacy, and pop psychology manuals discuss how to achieve it. A recurrent tendency in contemporary Western culture is to blame relational and developmental difficulties on mothering that is not good enough. Unfortunately, psychoanalytic theories can and have been utilized to reinforce and legitimate such blaming.[74] Much of this blame would be better directed at the social arrangements in which mothering must be done, including the gender system. Much more attention should be paid to the effects of the asymmetries of gender and to the fact and its consequences that only one gender is present in and must take responsibility for such a formative period in human development. Why should fathers, who after all are members of the dominant gender group, be exempt from blame for the consequences of our social arrangements?

Feminist theorists have begun to map out some of these consequences. They argue that under existing arrangements, even with individually good enough mothers, it is not possible fully to achieve reciprocity in human relations.[75] The social context of development includes not only the immediate child-caretaker(s) relation but also more general social relations that affect the child through his or her interaction with the caretaker. The caretaker brings to the relationship a complex series of experiences including not only personal history and feelings about being a particular gender, but also the whole range of social experience—work, friends, interaction with political and economic institutions, and so on. The seemingly abstract and suprapersonal relations of class, race, and male dominance enter into the construction of "individual" human development.

The correlation between these more general social relations and individual development is never simple and direct. The relationship is mediated not only by the particular qualities of each child-caretaker relationship but also by what the child brings to the world, her or his own innate constitution, the inevitable permutations and distortions that occur in the incorporations of experience in the preverbal state of infancy and later in the ongoing unconscious process, the particular characteristics of each child's family (e.g., the number of family members present), and cultural, religious, class, and ethnic norms as they affect child-rearing patterns.

Despite the many variations in human development, there also seem to be widely shared tendencies. Some of these, as Freud reveals, by example as much as by theory, have to do with gender. In contemporary Western culture, as feminist theorists have stressed, the boy by age five will likely have repressed the "female" parts of himself, his memories of his earliest experience, and many relational capacities. He will have developed the "normal contempt" for women that is a fundamental part of male identity within male-dominant cultures.[76] The girl, precisely because of her continuing ambivalent tie to the mother (which remains in part because of their shared gender identity), cannot so thoroughly repress her preoedipal experience and relational capacities. The boy deals with the ambivalence inherent in the separation-individuation process by denial of having been related, by projection (women are bad; they cause these problems), and by domination (mastering fears and wishes for regression or re-identification with the mother by controlling, depowering, and/or devaluing his original object).

These defenses become part of ordinary male behavior toward adult women and to anything that seems similar to them or under their (potential) control—the body, feelings, nature. The ability to control and be in control becomes both a need and a symbol of masculinity. Relations are turned into contests for power. Aggression is mobilized to distance oneself from the object and then to overpower it. The girl seeks relationships even at the expense of her own autonomy. The two genders thus come to complement each other in a rather grotesque symmetry.

By focusing on the mother-child dyad, object relations theorists make possible a reconsideration of the mother's power in the unconscious lives of men and women. This is an important step in the process of doing justice to the subjectivity of women and undoing the repression of experiences of ourselves as mothers and as persons who have been mothered. However, despite the claim of object relations theorists that the mother-child relation is a mutually constituting, reciprocal one, the mother appears within the theory primarily as the child's object. The mother disappears as a separate person. She does not exist as someone who has her own desires and whose reality is not fully or accurately captured in the child's experience of her and their relations.[77]

Within object relations theory the story of human development is told from the child's viewpoint. The separate aspects of the developmental processes of the mother *qua* mother and the child are not adequately considered. The extent to which each member of the dyad has processes unique and internal to her are not fully investigated. Mother and child are presented as misleadingly isomorphic. In fact there are developmental processes specific to each partner in the dyad as well as fusion, mutuality, and interaction between them. The mother goes through a process of merger, separation, and reciprocity as the child does, but her experience of this developmental sequence and the meanings it has for her cannot be identical to or confounded with an account of the child's process.

Furthermore, despite the object relations theorist's emphasis on humans' innate sociability, the mother-child dyad is frequently abstracted from all the other social relations. These relations enter into and help shape the qualities of the dyadic one and of each of its members. These social relations include the mother and child's other object relations with the father, siblings, and other significant kin/affectionate ties. Perhaps this abstraction is in part a logical consequence of telling the story from the child's viewpoint. Naturally a child will be less aware (or aware in different ways) than a parent of the effects of these other social relations. Nonetheless dyads generally exist within families, and these are also enmeshed in a larger web of social relations of class, race, and so forth. These social relations can themselves impede or facilitate good enough child care. The family members' location in the political economy, for example, has direct effects on what sorts of resources are available or what kind of impingements are inflicted upon their families.

Although part of the child's self is constituted through her or his internalization of the caretakers, in the process the child incorporates more than his or her experience of specific persons. As aspects of Freud's theory of the superego suggest, the child also internalizes the mother's, father's, and other caretakers' past and present object relations. To some extent the parents' entire social histories become part of the child's self. An adequate theory of human development from an object relations perspective would have to include an account of all these different levels and types of social relations and their interactions, mutual determinations, and possible antagonisms. It would have to include an expanded concept of families—families not merely as a set of immediate relations among individuals but also as permeable structures located within and partially determined by other social structures, including those of production, culture, and race, class, and gender systems. Theorists would also have to recover and expand Freud's radical insight that these structures can be and often are sources of mutually contradictory and antagonistic ways of organizing self and relations to others. Culture is a source of conflict and relations of domination as well as a space for creativity and play.

Object relations theory is similar to Freud's work in several ways.

From a feminist perspective one of the most important of these similarities is that object relations theorists replicate Freud's denial and repression of the sexual aspects of maternity and aggressive female sexuality more generally. The absence of any extensive discussion of these issues in the object relations theorists' account of the developmental process is striking. Thus despite the claim of possibility of a coherent self, splits remain within object relations theory, including those between the embodied, sexual, desiring, aggressive mother and the good enough, nurturing, facilitating one.

Object relations theory represents an advance over Freud's theories inasmuch as at least part of women's work and experience is presented as "facilitating" to human development. Nonetheless the concept of the good enough mother, although meant to capture and validate what women do as child rearers, also reflects deeply ingrained social fantasies about women. For example, the culturally prevalent splits between the "good," pure, self-effacing and the bad, sexual, selfish, self-determining woman are replicated within this concept. The good enough mother seems to have no life apart from her relation with the baby—no other work or pleasurable activity, no independent sexuality, no relations to other adults or even to the baby's siblings. She is utterly and exclusively devoted to one child.

These gaps within object relations theory indicate that, despite the theorists' justifiable reasons for doing so, Freud's libido theory cannot be simply abandoned or rejected. In positing a libido theory or a concept of *jouissance* Freud and Lacan do point to the existence of an autonomous and powerful sexuality that women can experience, however repressed it may be in male-dominant societies and in these theorists' own work. Thinking about the power and inadequacies of Freud's and Lacan's theories reminds us of the need for more adequate accounts of sexuality and gender and of the manifold interactions and mutual determinations of psychological and somatic processes. Object relations theorists themselves have not fully addressed these questions.

Freud and Lacan also present the unresolved questions of the relationship, necessary or possible, between gender and sexuality and between desire and object love. They suggest questions such as the following: Does the fact that I have a female body necessarily entail that my experience of sexuality and myself as an embodied being will always differ from that of men? How and in what ways? Is it possible to experience non-object-related desire? Are such desire and its expression important dimensions of human experience that ought not be suppressed or denied?

A Postmodernist Analyst's Dilemma: When Undecidability Is Not Good Enough

Disjunction and Dissemination.   Winnicott and Lacan posit radically different claims about the nature of the human being, the development of the mind, and the relation of individuals to others and to culture. We might say somewhat ironically that Winnicott and Lacan share one crucial assumption: that the subject comes to be(ing) in the field of the Other. However almost everything else diverges from this shared premise. The major differences between the two theorists include the following:

1. Although for Lacan the fact of this constitution by the Other invariably leads to alienation, self-estrangement, and splitting, for Winnicott such consequences can occur only if the child "lacks" good enough mothering.

2. Lacan believes the child can engage only in "object relating." The child relates to objects through projection; the object exists merely as a means of gratification/tension reduction. Winnicott argues that, given a reasonably responsive mother, the child can develop from this mode into object *use*. In this mode the object must be real and external and not merely the child's projection. Failure to develop the capacity to "use" objects indicates a deficit in the child's environment; it is not necessitated by or an invariable consequence of the nature of desire.

3. For Lacan symbolization is phallic; it is imposed from the "outside" by and only after a "masculine" culture disrupts the mother-child dyad. Winnicott believes the capacity for symbolization arises out of and simultaneously with the capacity to use an object. Placing the object outside the infant's omnipotent control and "substituting" something for it and one's relation to it (e.g., a toy or a blanket) is the first instance of symbolization. Symbolization arises out of and in the transitional space; it is not imposed by "external," objective reality or the "universal" impersonal logic of language.

4. Lacan believes there is a permanent "gap" between subject and

Other, self and culture. For Winnicott this gap is a "space" in and because of which play and culture are both possible and necessary. The child's inability to bridge and manage this gap indicates a failure of environmental response. It does not have an ontological and inevitable root in the nature of the human being as such.

5. For Lacan anything external (objects, culture, language) is necessarily imposed on and alien to us. Winnicott believes that, although from the adult point of view the external is preexisting, this is not the case for the baby. The baby *finds* external reality. If the conditions to allow the baby to use external reality are present, this finding presents a chance for and an experience of creativity, not alienation.

6. Lacan, like Freud, assumes there is no internal impulse to separate and become an autonomous being. Winnicott argues that separation is not the result of frustration, but of a mixture of the baby's internal impulses and the mother's optimal responses to these impulses.

7. Lacan, like Freud, believes there is no internal desire, capacity, or motive to perceive or experience the other as an independently existing being. In Winnicott's view aggression impels us to place the object outside our omnipotent control. Under the right conditions this loss of omnipotence does not have to entail only narcissistic injury or loss. There are many benefits to be gained by allowing an object to exist independent of us, including a capacity to destroy the object, to have it survive, and to feel concern for it. Within a good enough environment the child comes to desire and can recognize and appreciate an object that exists independent of him- or herself.

8. In Winnicott's theory there are three realities to which a healthy person always has access: inner, outer, and transitional. Lacan argues that inasmuch as we are (cultural) persons, there is *only* an external reality—the desire of the Other, language, the Father's Law.

9. According to Winnicott graduated frustration is necessary for the baby; it is not always or only painful. Such frustration can make objects real if it is experienced against the background of the mother's adequate adaptation and response to the child at the beginning of life. Lacan and Freud believe that frustration is always painful and intolerable and causes injury to the self for which there must be some compensation or defense.

10. Winnicott's theory of human development is an interactive one

involving an individual, environment/object, and environment/culture. Lacan's theory, like the predominant tendency in Freud's work, is an individualistic one involving a monadic individual in perpetual struggle with alien Others (desire, culture, etc.).

11. Winnicott and Lacan have very different concepts of the infant. Winnicott's baby is far more competent that Lacan's or Freud's. The infant in Winnicott's theory is not so helpless or formless as Lacan's. The infant is capable of development and change in what she or he needs or wants. Desire too is not fixed but undergoes its own complex development. In Lacan's or Freud's work desire and the child within us always remain the same: impossible to satisfy, with insatiable desires and an unalterable wish for tensionless satisfaction.

Lacan's concept of the psyche is primarily mentalistic and abstract. He argues that the development of the mind is equivalent to and dependent on the acquisition of the Father's *Law* and inscription within and by the binary logic of language. Lacan's psyche is radically severed from and other than the soma; even the unconscious has nothing to do with the body. Winnicott argues that normal psychic functioning cannot be reduced to its intellectual, cognitive, or linguistic aspects. Mind is only one aspect of psyche, and in a healthy person psyche and soma should form an interacting yet differentiated whole. Furthermore, Winnicott argues, the development of mind itself depends on and arises out of the mother-child relationship and its gradual conversion from a near perfect adaptation to the infant's needs to a series of graduated failures in responsiveness. In and through these failures infants develop their own mental capacities. They can undo and overcome the mother's failures, turning them into adaptive successes. Through this process, assuming and incorporating the continuity of the background good enough environment, the child develops an increasingly complex psyche-soma.

12. In Winnicott's view the child has a real need to give to the (real) mother and to have her or his gifts received. The persistent rejection of these gifts creates pathology in the child. However in Winnicott's theory, unlike Lacan's, the mother's implacable desire does not invariably cause her to reject the child's gifts. If a mother does so, it is not because the content of the gifts can never satisfy her true desire for the child to *be* the phallus. Rather the rejection represents a failure of empathy on her part. She cannot see that the child needs her to re-

ceive the gift in order to make reparation for his or her (fantasied) destruction of her.

13. Lacan and Winnicott have completely different understandings of the nature, therapeutic instruments, and purposes of the psychoanalytic situation. For Lacan interpretation, making the unconscious conscious through discourse, is the essential element in analysis. Transference phenomena come into play only when the analyst makes an error (i.e., compromises his or her neutrality and violates the correct position as an impersonal reflecting surface or mirror). The purpose of analysis is to confront patients with the impossibility of their desire through frustration and hence to induce them to accept alienation and self-estrangement as the necessary reality of "being."

For Winnicott such an analysis would entail and exemplify the analyst's complicity with patients' false self. Winnicott stresses the importance of the relational aspects of analysis. At times the analyst must provide the good enough mothering (adaptation to patients' needs) the patients lacked in infancy. At this stage of analysis, interpretation is either irrelevant or has a completely different quality. Its purpose would be to articulate the feelings patients are experiencing and that are present to them, not unconscious thoughts or wishes. The analyst helps patients name and articulate these feelings so they can contain or manage a level of experience that seems to be threatening or disorganizing to the self or its objects. Patients do not need to "make the unconscious conscious": Their problem may be *too little* capacity for repression rather than too much. Sometimes the analyst must indicate that she or he is able to respond empathically, enter into, not be destroyed by, or even take over and "digest" some of the patients' feelings, impulses, or needs. To be an impersonal deflecting mirror at this point would be to repeat the bad mothering of patients' childhoods.

Theory and Practice.   It appears that Lacan and Winnicott "read the text" (baby/child/human development) in almost completely different ways. The choice of readings is not "neutral"—in either philosophic or practical implications. For practicing analysts the choice of "reading" would make an enormous difference in how one responds to and interacts with patients or trains other analysts. At this point, where speech or reading and action intersect, "undecidability" does not seem to be a satisfactory or usable end point or guide. As analysts we work with other persons to whom our responses matter. In fact our failures or lack of understanding can sometimes be literally life threatening, as in work with very fragile, nearly psychotic, or suicidal patients.

Suppose a patient came to me complaining of a sense of unreality, an inability to reach or interact with another person, a feeling that everything is arbitrary or externally imposed and has no meaning. Should I assume this patient is suffering from a split between a false and true self and that these feelings are expressions or consequences of living with the true self hidden away and inaccessible? Or should I assume the patient's problem is that she thinks she has a problem—that in fact this is the nature of human being and that her difficulty is she is not yet reconciled to the self-estrangement of desire?

Obviously Winnicott would take the first approach, Lacan the second. How am I to decide and to choose a course of action? My patient seems unhappy with her current condition, but a Lacanian could say I have no right to delude her or myself that any other state is possible. An object relations theorist could say the Lacanians are merely acting out their own untreated false selves and their narcissism.

A decision must be made; one approach precludes the other. Is the choice undecidable because "texts" are ontologically open or because there are no adequate decision criteria offered by orthodox, Lacanian, or object relations analysts or by postmodern philosophers? I believe the second possibility is closer to the situation. In the third area between illusion and objective reality, where both count and also cannot be ignored, where my patient and I are sitting, postmodernism in any existing form fails. Epistemologies appropriate to this third area are lacking. Undecidability or dissemination is irresponsible, and "pure" objectivity (empiricist or rationalist) is inappropriate, as is a search for the "topology" of "mind." Two persons with bodies and feelings as well as speech in need of action and change are present in the analytic space. My patient and I are not or are not only two sets governed by the binary logic of language, which offers no answers to our questions either. Nor are we merely two intersecting stories or texts in search of a temporarily mutually agreeable ending. I am not a scientist in a laboratory confronting a piece or stream of "data" utterly other to and unaffected by me. Object relations theorists argue that we need a "science of persons," but what that would be is currently vague and unspecified.

We might argue that postmodernism represents an advance over traditional approaches because it forces us to acknowledge that we cannot choose among these theories of knowledge or persons with great confidence; such confidence might be partially illusory or even dangerous. However we must choose, and individual human lives, unlike texts perhaps, are not infinitely open. Closure is often reached, though not necessarily closures we would choose; my patient might commit suicide while I am pursuing my thoughts and uncertainties. At this point the desire and practice of the analyst, even an object relations one, and the postmodernist literary critic or philosopher conflict. Although in many ways object relations theory may be the most complementary to the spirit of postmodernism, postmodernism is not a good enough object for the *analyst's* development. The analyst must be responsible to others in her work in ways that the literary critic is not. Failure to see this difference represents a collapse of intersubjective "reality" into illusion.

We return, rather unwillingly, to Freud's challenge. This challenge still retains its force despite the fact that Freud could not resolve these questions either. He is also partially responsible for the misplaced but recurring desire among analysts to be scientists or develop a science. Freud reminds us:

If what we believe were really a matter of indifference, if there were no such thing as knowledge distinguished among our opinions by corresponding to reality, we might build bridges just as well out of cardboard as out of stone, we might inject our patients with a decagram of morphine instead of a centigram, and we might use tear-gas as a narcotic instead of ether. But even the intellectual anarchists would violently repudiate such practical applications of their theory.[78]

From the analyst's perspective our theoretical or interpretive choices matter. In all honesty, however, we ought to acknowledge that reliable, intersubjectively persuasive reasons for making them are currently lacking. Freud, Lacan, and Winnicott each offer us some pieces of the "text" and obscure others. Feminist theorists and postmodernists alert us to some of their gaps and obscuring moves, but

neither alone or together can they fill in all of these or bring the missing material fully to consciousness. Furthermore both feminist theory
and postmodernism are in need of the *analyst's* interpretations and
interventions. Each mode of theorizing displays and suffers from its
own forms of repression, denial, and displacement—as we will see in
the next two chapters.

Part Three

Gender(s) and Dis-contents

Five

Feminisms

Stories of Gender

A woman comprehends finiteness, she understands it from the bottom up, therefore she is beauteous (essentially regarded, every woman is beauteous), therefore she is charming (and that no man is), therefore she is happy (happy as no man is or should be), therefore one may say her life is happier than that of man; for finiteness can perhaps make a human being happy, infinitude as such can never do so. . . . Woman explains finiteness, man is in chase of infinitude. So it should be, and each has one's own pain; for woman bears children with pain, but man conceives ideas with pain, and woman does not have to know the anguish of doubt or the torment of despair. . . . But because woman thus explains finiteness she is man's deepest life, but a life which should always be concealed and hidden as the root of life always is. For this reason I hate all talk about the emancipation of woman. God forbid that ever it may come to pass. I cannot tell you with what pain this thought is able to pierce my heart, nor what passionate exasperation, what hate I feel toward everyone who gives vent to such talk . . . in case this contagion were to spread, in case it were to penetrate also to her whom I love, my wife, my joy, my refuge, my life's very root, then indeed would my courage be broken, then the passion in my soul would be quenched, then I know well what I would do, I would sit down in the marketplace and weep, weep like that artist whose work had been destroyed and who did not even remember what he himself had painted.

Søren Kierkegaard, *Either/Or*

Having a fling with the philosopher also entails safeguarding those components of the mirror that cannot reflect themselves. . . . Reproductive material and duplicating mirror, the philosopher's wife also has to underwrite

that narcissism which often extends onto a transcendental dimension. . . .

*The philosopher's wife must also, though in a secondary
way, be beautiful, and* exhibit all the attractions of femininity, *in order to distract a gaze too often carried away by
theoretical contemplations.*

*That woman—and since philosophical discourse domi-
nates history in general,* that wife/woman of every
man—*is thus pledged to the service of the philosopher's self
in all forms. And as far as the wedding celebration is concerned, she is in danger of being no more than the requisite
mediator for the philosopher's celebrations with himself, and
with his fellows.*

Luce Irigaray, "Questions"

*Woman exhausts her courage dissipating mirages and she
stands in terror at the threshold of reality.*

Simone de Beauvoir,
The Second Sex

The Emergence of a
Distinctively Feminist Question:
The "Other" Says No

In 1949 Simone de Beauvoir, one of the founding mothers of contemporary feminist theory, described the constricting and constricted
lives of the "second sex." De Beauvoir delineated the many ways in
which "woman" is defined and limited in her being as the (always
lesser) "other" to man. In male-dominant cultures no woman escapes
the consequences of such a position. Even the most "independent"
woman is still mutilated and deformed by the ideas and social relations that more deeply affect her less fortunate sisters.

De Beauvoir insists, as would subsequent feminist theorists, such
mutilation does not exclusively constitute and is not a reflection of
woman's "essence." Rather it is a consequence of historical and hence
changeable ideas and forces. Nonetheless, de Beauvoir recognizes,
such transformation will not be easy, either for individuals or for society as a whole. Woman must be the primary agent in her own transformation and that of male-dominant cultures; yet even the most priv-

ileged or gifted woman bears the marks of her experience as the lesser other: timidity, passivity, modesty, irresponsibility, "bad faith." The "independent woman" may become an excellent theoretician, can acquire real competence; but she will be forced to repudiate whatever she has in her that is "'different.'" De Beauvoir denounces "this reasonable modesty that has hitherto set the limits of feminine talent . . . none have ever trampled upon all prudence in the attempt to emerge beyond the given world."[1]

No particularly visible or active women's movements existed when de Beauvoir wrote her book. Perhaps even she could not have anticipated—although surely she hoped for—some of the remarkable (but far from sufficient) changes in gender relations that have occurred since the reemergence of feminism in the late 1960s. Feminist theorists are deeply indebted to these women's movements. For many, including myself, participating in consciousness raising sessions and other movement activities forced into awareness aspects of experience that we had too often taken for granted. Such experiences included the fear of rape and unwanted pregnancy, the absence of female professors, the masculinist bias of many academic fields, the violence exercised against women, the restrictions on and distortions and exploitations of women's sexuality, the sexual division of labor, and our exclusion from most positions of political and economic power.

Like many other women I sought to make sense of and to contribute to these transformations in my and others' consciousness and to translate our developing ideas into social and political changes. Like many academic and intellectual women I attempted to fit what I was learning about women's experiences and histories (outside the "mainstream" of academia) into preexisting theoretical frameworks (liberalism, Marxism, psychoanalysis, critical theory), only to find that these could not account for much of this material. In fact it gradually became evident that these frameworks also were not free from the effects of gender and hence ultimately inhibited our understanding. Emboldened and prodded by the existence of increasingly diverse and active women's movements and the unsatisfactory results of our attempts to simply "add women" and "stir" us into preexisting ways of thinking and being, many feminist theorists have come to believe we have no choice but to go beyond the "given world."[2]

The overcoming of our "reasonable modesty" is one of the most defining, exciting, and promising characteristics of contemporary feminist theories. The "laugh of Medusa" resounds ever more strongly throughout feminist texts.[3] Feminist theorists insist that we have uncovered a fundamental social relation—gender—and that without close attention to its almost infinitely variable nature and effects, theorizing must be deficient. Furthermore, because gender systems generally appear to entail relations of domination, anyone concerned with issues of power and justice ought to be concerned with their operations. Gender systems are also an important aspect of the context within and by which a self is constituted. Thus gender systems should be of interest to all those who study issues of selfhood, subjectivity, and knowledge.

The naming and questioning of phallocentric cultures have become more self-conscious and assured. Politeness is fading away. Not without ambivalence, anxiety, or fear, feminists have even begun to reclaim rather than repudiate "whatever 'woman' [might have] in her that is 'different.'" The stereotypically masculine is no longer accepted as the measure of excellence, virtue, or humanity. We no longer assume, as did de Beauvoir and others, that it is "through attaining the same situation as theirs [men's] that she [woman] will find emancipation."[4] Such beliefs now seem to be permeated with problematic (and gendered) assumptions about selfhood, freedom, creativity, domination, and the relative value of the everyday or tending to what is sometimes called "sensuous activity." These assumptions themselves have become the subject of increasingly critical feminist inquiry.[5]

With more and more audacity feminists have constructed new genres: stories about gender from women's point(s) of view. In these stories expectations about plotting, the central characters, and acceptable morality have radically shifted. Many feminists, including myself, would now argue that the "problem of women" or the "woman question" has been mislabeled and misconceived. In the process of removing woman from her position as man's lesser other, feminist theorists have discovered that the "problem with no name" has a different one.[6] By conceptualizing woman as the problem, we repeat rather than deconstruct or analyze the social relations that construct or represent us as a problem in the first place. If the problem is defined in this way, woman remains in her traditional position: the "guilty one," the deviant, the other.

It is more productive and accurate to locate both men and women as characters within a larger con-text: the relations of gender. From this feminist perspective men and women are both prisoners of gender, although in highly differentiated but interrelated ways. That men appear to be and in many cases are the wardens, or at least the trustees, within a society should not blind us to the extent to which they too are governed by the rules of gender. However, contrary to the views of some postmodernists, this does not mean that men and women occupy a fundamentally equivalent status—as "split" signified/subjects. One of the distinguishing features of feminist theories is the claim that gender relations, at least as they have been organized so far, are (variable) forms of domination. Feminist theorists are motivated in part by an active concern with justice and a desire to contribute to the overcoming of women's subordinations. The inequalities among men matter a great deal—to individual men, to the women and children connected to them, and to those concerned about justice. Nonetheless these do not negate and should not obviate the fact that men as a group remain privileged relative to most women in most societies and that there are systematic forces that generate, maintain, and replicate gendered relations of domination. One of the purposes of the study of gender for feminist theorists is to understand these forces as they operate in specific societies with the hope that such understanding may contribute to eliminating gender domination. However, as we will see later in this chapter, the questions of the relations between gender systems and male domination and between knowledge, power, and theory have themselves become increasingly controversial among feminist theorists.

Inserting both men and women within contexts of the social relations of gender has had a paradoxical effect on the status and self-understanding of feminist theorists. Feminists have begun to ask one another a number of important questions about the status of our stories about gender. Both psychoanalytic and postmodernist theories can be useful to (and in fact in some cases have stimulated) the further working out of these questions. If both men and women are formed in and through gender systems, then the thinking of women (or feminists) as well as that of men (or nonfeminists) must be shaped in complex and sometimes unconscious ways by gender relations. How can such stories in any sense be more true, more accurate, less distorted, or more "objective" than others? Are the stories feminists tell about gender more privileged, more deserving of our attention or respect? Or are they just different—an-other voice or a (hopefully) welcome, dissonant strain within the "conversation of mankind [*sic*]?"[7]

By the logic of even a feminist psychoanalysis, women (and feminists) cannot be free from the effects of becoming a person within a particular gender system. As we will see later in this chapter, becoming a female person within contemporary Western culture entails developing a self that is more likely to be structured in certain ways and troubled by some conflicts rather than others. Many of the dilemmas of the typically female self center around conflicts between and about sexuality, differences, power, autonomy, and attachment or sociality. These conflicts structure, influence, and are reflected in feminist theories, just as the dilemmas of a stereotypically male sense of self are reflected in nonfeminist or masculine writing. Thus a gender-sensitive psychoanalysis has much to contribute to the further development of feminist as well as nonfeminist theories.

Postmodern philosophies of knowledge can also contribute to a more accurate self-understanding of the nature and problems of feminist theorizing. Feminist notions of theory have become increasingly complex and often contradictory. Feminists have been attracted to at least two very different concepts of the project of feminist theorizing. One conception derives from Enlightenment ideas about knowledge, truth, and freedom; the other derives from postmodernist critiques of these ideas. Feminist theorists have tried to maintain two different epistemological positions. The first is that the mind, the self, and knowledge are socially constituted, and what we can know depends on our social practices and contexts. The second is that feminist theorists can uncover truths about the whole as it "really is." Those who support the second position reject many postmodern ideas and must depend upon certain assumptions about truth and the knowing subject that I find increasingly problematic. To attain such a truth (e.g., the "real" explanation for gender arrangements at any time is x . . .) would require the existence of an "archimedes point" outside of current, social, and self-comprehension and beyond our embeddedness in it. From this point we could see and represent an "objective" view of the whole. What we see and report would have to be untransformed by the activities of perception and of reporting our vision in language. The object seen (social whole or gender arrangement) would have to be apprehended by a mind sufficiently empty of the biases of its society and nearly perfectly transcribed by and into a transparent language.

This sort of "truth" is the necessary ground for a "feminist standpoint" that could be more true than previous (male) ones. The notion of a feminist standpoint, equivalent both epistemologically and ethically to the status Marx and Lukacs assign to that of the proletariat, has been very productive for and influential in the development of feminist theories, but it is highly problematic.[8] It depends on unexamined and questionable assumptions and motivations, including an optimism that people will act rationally on their "interests" and that reality has a structure that a more perfect reason can discover more perfectly. Both these assumptions in turn depend on an uncritical appropriation of the Enlightenment ideas discussed in Chapter 1. Furthermore the notion of such a "standpoint" assumes that the oppressed are not in some fundamental ways damaged by their social experience. On the contrary this position assumes that the oppressed have a privileged, unitary, and not just different relation to and ability to comprehend a reality that is "out there" waiting for our representation.

This view also presupposes gendered social relations in which there is a category of beings who are or can be fundamentally like one another by virtue of their sex—that is, it assumes the uniform otherness men assign to women. Such a standpoint requires that women, unlike men, can be free from determination by their own participation in relations of domination, for example, those rooted in the social relations of race, class, or homophobia. Somehow all these barriers to objectivity will be cleared away, leaving only an unmediated relation to truth and reality.

Sandra Harding argues that these differences are both necessary and fruitful. We cannot abandon the Enlightenment stance because our culture is a transitional one. There is at least a pretense that truth claims ought to be justified by "objective" reasoning and that truth and power ought to be connected. Thus feminist theorists should live with and exploit ambivalence and retain both discourses for political and philosophical reasons.[9] Harding's argument itself is too bound within Enlightenment premises. She still wants to leave open the possibility that rational argument will prevail, that (ultimately) truth, not power, will decide claims for knowledge or conflicts about justice.

I find very little support for Harding's optimism in the history of

Western politics. Anyone contemplating the history of the West in the twentieth century has a right to be skeptical of its self-representation as having substituted reason and law for authority or the resolution of conflict. As Weber argues, the rule of law is not totally other than, independent of, or exempt from force or violence.[10] Any culture that retains the possibility of nuclear annihilation as the last resort for its "defense" seems to me trapped more within Kafka's nightmare world than in the sunnier one of Kant's categorical imperative. Hence we remain too much within the terms of the ruling discourse or set of illusions if we hope that truth or a search for it may set us free. Furthermore this hope could be dangerous. Under its spell we may find ourselves caught up in complicity with dangerous transcendental illusion(s): of the possibility of a "real" nonconflictual entity, a "nostalgia" for the "whole or the one," or a belief that one can "seize reality" once and for all—illusions that can produce only a "return to terror," of which our century has certainly had more than enough.[11]

Although the work of feminist theorists has become increasingly varied and complex, our claims about the centrality of gender relations in the constitution of self, knowledge, and power and the asymmetries of these relations and their many consequences remain valid and worthy of further investigation. These claims have not been adequately recognized by or incorporated within the work of other theorists, including psychoanalysts and postmodernists. This continuing lack in other discourses is one of the reasons I will retell some of the most important stories about gender and continue to insist upon their place within the conversations of others.

Feminist theorists have provided useful hypotheses for the concrete study of gender relations in particular societies, but each explanatory scheme also is flawed, inadequate, and overly deterministic. I will pay attention to some of the gaps and omissions in these stories as well as to their main plot lines. I will employ some of the insights of psychoanalysis and postmodernism to reveal and partially account for particular choices of plot as well as some of the gaps and omissions in the stories. After considering some of these stories in more detail, I will return to questions of the character and possible status of feminist theorizing. I will argue that many of the indeterminacies within feminist theories are necessary and productive. Premature closure and attempts to construct theories conceptualized as successors to and analogies of the "grand theories" of Western thought will impede the further development of feminist theorizing.[12] Although they are ultimately not "good enough," postmodernist approaches provide more facilitating environments for the continuing growth of feminist theories than do Enlightenment order(s).

Feminist Stories of Gender

Feminist theorists have constructed a variety of interesting stories about how gender systems are produced, reproduced, and maintained and about how and why these systems become ones of domination. Certain themes, agreements, and disagreements recur throughout these stories. Each tends to locate one set of processes as crucial to and definitive of gender relations. Some of the most influential theorists offer strong arguments for the centrality of a "sex/gender system," the organization of production or the sexual division of labor, child-bearing practices, and the processes of representation, signification, or language. At stake within these stories and in the disagreements among feminist theorists are the meanings and nature of sexuality and its relation(s) to gendered anatomy; the meanings and values of "difference," including the relative importance and significance of differences among women as well as between women and men; the sources of power within societies, including the relative significance of relations of production, the sexual division of labor, child-rearing arrangements, kinship and family organizations, the control of sexuality and women's capacity to bear children, and processes of signification and language. Obviously, each of these stories has many implications for an understanding of self, knowledge, gender, and power. In addition, because feminist theorizing entails some commitment to social transformation, issues of practice are at stake as well. Those who adopt any one story would privilege certain areas of activity over others and argue that some practices are relatively irrelevant or even counterproductive.

The "Sex/Gender System": Nature, Culture, and Gender Relations

Gayle Rubin offered one of the first contemporary accounts of gender relations. Her challenge to socially predominant ideologies of sexuality and gender was startling and productive for many feminist readers. Rubin conceptualizes sexuality as unrelated to anatomical genitality. She locates the origin of gender systems and male dominance in the transformation of raw biological sex into gender and in the operations of kinship structures and the sexual division of labor. Her work raises important questions about the meanings of and relationships between nature, culture, embodiment, sexuality, heterosexuality, and power that are still controversial among feminist theorists.

Rubin defines the sex/gender system as "the set of arrangements by which a society transforms biological sexuality into products of human activity, and in which these transformed sexual needs are satisfied." She argues, "sex as we know it—gender identity, sexual desire and fantasies, concepts of childhood—is itself a social product." It is important to distinguish between the "human capacity and necessity to create a sexual world, and the empirically oppressive ways in which sexual worlds have been organized." The problem is not biology or the existence of the family, but particular *forms* of the social organization of biology, kinship, and child rearing. Kinship systems are, among other things, "made up of, and reproduce, concrete forms of socially organized sexuality. Kinship systems are observable and empirical forms of sex/gender systems."[13]

Any feminist theorist, then, would need to analyze kinship systems in order to understand how sexuality is organized and how gender is produced. Like Lacan, Rubin draws upon the work of Claude Lévi-Strauss. She argues that the essence of kinship is an exchange of women among men. The incest taboo is a means of regulating this trade. The exchange cements relations among groups and provides men with power. Those with "gifts" to exchange can enter the system of obligation and debt and accumulate power and loyalty. "The subordination of women can be seen as a product of the relationships by which sex and gender are organized and produced. The economic oppression of women is derivative and secondary. But there is an economics of sex and gender, and what we need is a political economy of sexual systems."[14]

A crucial factor in the political economy of sex is the division of labor according to sex. This division functions as a taboo that "exacerbates the biological differences between the sexes and thereby creates gender."[15] It also assures that men and women will desire each other and require each other's services, thus ensuring heterosexual relationships. The gender system is not the natural outgrowth of biological difference; rather sex differences are created and accentuated by repressing similarities between the sexes. Part of being engendered or initiated into the sex/gender system is the channeling of sexual desire exclusively toward members of the opposite gender. The constraint of female sexuality is necessary so that men can allocate women among men. Female homosexuality would disrupt patterns of kinship and exchange by permitting close ties among women.

Rubin contends that psychoanalysis is central to feminist theory because it "describes the residue left within individuals by their confrontation with the rules and regulations of sexuality of the societies to which they are born." Psychoanalysis enables us to understand how polymorphous, ambisexual children are transformed through social relations into specific gender identities and heterosexuality. Psychoanalysis also reveals the pain that such transformation inevitably entails. The attainment of female identity is a process of repression and restraint, "based largely on pain and humiliation."[16] The culmination of this process is the "domestication of women"; women learn to live with their oppression. The family is the source of women's oppression because under patriarchal domination it is the agency in and through which women and men are engendered—replicating men who dominate, women who submit.

The concept of the sex/gender system is a crucial element in feminist theories of the family. The concept can be used to counter the tendency toward biological determinism present in some radical feminist texts.[17] It is a useful tool for analyzing forms of the family and their variance over time. Yet even as Rubin argues that sex/gender systems are a product of human activity and always exist within a social-political context, she is not able to trace out the relations between sex/gender systems and other forms of exchange, such as the economy. This gap in her theory is due in part to the use of structuralism. The sex/gender system appears to run "parallel" to, not interact with, other forms of human activity.[18]

According to Rubin, "a next step on the agenda is a Marxian analysis of sex/gender systems": [19]

Sexual systems cannot, in the final analysis, be understood in complete isolation. A full bodied analysis of women in a single society, or throughout history, must take everything into account: the evolution of commodity forms in women, systems of land tenure, political arrangements, subsistence technology, etc. Equally important, economic and political analyses are incomplete if they do not consider women, marriage, and sexuality.[20]

Yet her structuralist method renders it difficult to answer a crucial question: What *is* the relation between the "laws" of the sex/gender system and those of economic development? Sex oppression is rooted in the sex/gender system and is not a "reflex" of economic forces. Because Rubin says the working-class (Marxist) movement and the women's movement address "different sources of human discontent," economic forces are presumably not a "reflex" of the sex/gender system.[21] On the theoretical level there is no common ground for explaining the mutual interaction of the exchange of women and the exchange of commodities. In terms of practice, the relation between the transformation of the sex/gender system and the transformation of the class system is also not specified. This lack of specificity seems to imply a split similar to one found in Juliet Mitchell's work: between women's oppression that arises from the family and exploitation that arises from the organization of production.[22] In Rubin's writing, however, the dynamics of oppression are analyzed in more detail, and she does not insist on economic factors being determinate in "the last instance."

Furthermore and more fatally, Rubin's distinction between sex and gender itself rests upon a series of oppositions that other feminists and I have found increasingly problematic and troublesome, especially the opposition of biological/natural (sexuality) and social/cultural. This split between natural (sexuality) and cultural may itself be rooted in and reflect gender arrangements. The recurrence in Rubin's work of this opposition in part reflects the influences of her sources, especially those of Lacan and Freud read in a Lacanian way. As I argue in Chapters 3 and 4, Freud's drive theory and Lacan's rereading of it reflect in part an unconscious motive: to deny and repress aspects of infantile experience that are relational (e.g., the child's dependence upon and connectedness with her or his earliest caregiver, who is almost always a woman). Hence in utilizing the concepts of Freud and Lacan, we must pay attention to what they conceal as well as reveal, especially the unacknowledged influences of anxieties about gender on their supposedly gender-neutral concepts. Rubin, like Mitchell, is insufficiently critical of her sources.

Although unmasking the antifeminist uses of the category of the "natural" and the conflation of sex and gender is important, simply turning sex (biology) and gender (social/cultural) into exclusionary oppositions is not an adequate alternative. At minimum such a solution leaves us no coherent way to discuss the fact of embodiment (e.g., we never encounter a person whose lived-through experience is not mediated by and through the body). Embodiment is simultaneously natural and cultural.

Rubin is not unique in her difficulties in conceptualizing the meaning of and relations between the natural/cultural. The trouble feminists have thinking through the meanings we assign to "the natural" extends throughout feminist discourse. Such difficulties can be found in the work of theorists whose premises are different in other respects from Rubin's. For example, Jean Bethke Elshtain provides an instructive instance of how allegedly "natural" properties (of infants) can be used to limit what a "reflective feminist" ought to think. In Elshtain's recent writings it becomes (once again) the responsibility of *women* to rescue children from an otherwise instrumental and uncaring world. Elshtain evidently believes that psychoanalytic theory is exempt from the context-dependent hermeneutics she claims characterize all other kinds of knowledge about social relations. She utilizes psychoanalysis as a warrant for absolute or foundational claims about the nature of "real human needs" or "the most basic human relationships." Elshtain's use of psychoanalytic theories about the formation of the self violates her own definition of truth as a "dynamic, social search for transformation and reconstructive knowledge."[23]

Like the feminists she critiques, Elshtain cuts off discourse into the social and historical bases of our conceptions, including those of the nature and development of the "self." Elshtain's theoretical practice thus violates her own criteria for emancipatory discourse. Such discourse must include "the repudiation of shaming, guilt-inducing moralisms, and the absence of abstracted assessments."[24] Like the father of psychoanalysis, Elshtain is not immune to the temptation to summon up "the biological bedrock" to foreclose further speech when discourse threatens to go too far. The frequent misuse of the "biological/natural" might seem like a good reason to continue distinguishing the concept of "gender" from "sex."

Nonetheless, although initially helpful and still politically important, the concept of a sex/gender system seems on subsequent reflection to call for further analysis of the meanings we attach to biology/sex/gender/nature. As we have become more sensitive to the social histories of concepts, it has become increasingly clear that the sex/gender disjunction rests upon problematic and culture-specific oppositions (e.g., those of body and mind) as well as "nature" and "culture." As some feminists begin to rethink these "oppositions," new questions emerge: Does anatomy (body) have no relation to mind? What difference does it make in the constitution of my social experiences that I have a specifically female body? I will return to these questions later in this chapter.

Despite the increasing complexity of our questions, most feminists would still insist that gender relations are not or are not only equivalent to or a consequence of anatomy. Everyone will agree there are anatomical differences between men and women. These anatomical differences seem to be primarily located in or are the consequence of the differentiated contributions men and women make to a common biological necessity: the physical reproduction of our species. However the mere existence of such anatomical differentiation is a descriptive fact, one of many observations we might make about the physical characteristics of humans. Part of the problem in deconstructing the meanings of biology/sex/gender/nature is that sex/gender has been one of the few areas in which (usually female) embodiment can be discussed at all in (nonscientific) Western discourses. Many other aspects of our embodiedness seem equally remarkable and interesting—for example, the incredible complexity of the structure and functioning of our brains, the extreme and relatively prolonged physical helplessness of the human neonate as compared to that of other even related species, and the fact that every one of us will die.

Male and female humans resemble each other physically in many more ways than we differ. Our similarities are even more striking if we compare humans to (say) toads or trees. So why ought the anatomical *differences* between male and female humans assume such significance in our sense of ourselves as persons? Why ought such complex social meanings and structures be "hung" upon or be justified by a relatively narrow range of anatomical differences?

One possible answer to these questions is that the anatomical differences between males and females are connected to and are partially a consequence of one of the most important functions of the species: its physical reproduction. Thus, we might argue, because reproduction is such an important aspect of our species life, characteristics associated with it will be much more salient to us than, say, hair color or height.

Another possible answer to these questions might be that, in order for humans physically to reproduce the species, we have to have sexual intercourse. Our anatomical differences make possible and necessary for physical reproduction certain fitting together of distinctively male and female organs. For some humans this "fitting together" is also highly desirable and pleasurable. Hence our anatomical differences seem to be inextricably connected to and in some sense even causative of sexuality.

Thus there seems to be a complex, pregiven set of interrelations: penis or clitoris, vagina, and breasts—distinctively male or female bodies; sexuality; reproduction (birth and babies); sense of self as a distinct, differentiated gender (e.g., as either and only a male or female person); gender relations as a "natural" exclusionary category. We believe there are two types of humans, and each of us can be only one of them.

A problem with all these apparently obvious and natural associations is that they may assume precisely what we are trying to explain: gender relations. We live in a world in which gender is both a constituting social relation and a relation of domination. Therefore both men's and women's understanding of anatomy, biology, embodiedness, sexuality, and reproduction is partially rooted in, reflects, and must justify or challenge preexisting gender relations. The existence of gender relations helps us order and understand the natural facts of human existence. Gender can become a metaphor for biology, just as biology can become a metaphor for gender.

Consider, for example, how we experience our own and other persons' bodies. Surely one of the first things we notice about people is whether they are male or female. Yet why ought this be so? Does this form of noticing not presuppose the salience of gender as a social relation (i.e., there are preexisting categories of man and woman and many social consequences for fitting into one or the other)?

Consider also how we in the West signal and accentuate our compliance with such categorization—through modes of dress, ways of walking and speaking—and the anxiety we experience if we cannot fit a person into one or the other of the gendered categories.[25] However, we may signal social rebellion by breaking gendered rules of dressing (e.g., antiwar men in the 1960s tended to grow their hair long and wear colorful clothing and jewelry).

One way to move feminist discourse forward is to substitute the problem of embodiment for that of the relation between sex and gender. This entails a theoretical move similar to that involved in displacing the "woman question" from the center of our attention and replacing it with the analysis of gender relations. The concept of embodiment includes and is shaped by the assumption that, as Winnicott argues, the fundamental human unit is a psyche-soma, which is simultaneously highly individual and already interrelated with others. The psyche-soma unit is interactive. The nature of this unity is never fixed or unchanging. Its aspects are simultaneously interdependent and differentiated. Anatomical sex differences might be merely one of the many dimensions along which the psyche-soma may be differentiated. However the significance of such differences would decline as we focus upon and investigate the complexity of the total unit. By always thinking of a psyche-soma, we would constantly be confronted with the problems of meaning and interpretation. How do we experience this process of differentiation? How is it registered in and affected by the psyche? How does the soma interpret psychic differentiation and other sorts of experience? How does change in one aspect of the unit alter the qualities of the unit as a whole? Such a focus would also enable us to render problematic men's as well as women's bodies. Men's bodies too are a psycho-somatic unit with changing and changeable qualities.

This strategy would also avoid the dangers of an alternative, postmodernist one. As I will discuss in more detail in Chapter 6, one postmodernist approach is to equate the "feminine" (now allegedly disconnected from biology and understood to exist purely on a "symbolic" plane) with "the body." Then the body/feminine is valorized over the mind/masculine. In this approach the oppositions of mind/body, culture/nature are maintained. All that is changed is how the members of the couple are ranked.

The Organization of Production and the Sexual Division of Labor

Socialist feminists have developed a second genre of stories about gender. They stress the importance of relations of production in determining the distribution of power in societies. Economic forces are central in their accounts of the origins and replication of male dominance. These theorists have made important contributions to our understanding of gender system, but locating feminist questions about production within Marxist frameworks obscures many aspects of gender systems and the masculinist bias of Marxist theory itself.

Ironically and perhaps despite their own intents, socialist feminist theorists ultimately provide the basis for a powerful critique of Marxism as a social theory and practice by focusing on gender.

Socialist feminists locate a fundamental cause of gender arrangements in the organization of production or the sexual division of labor.[26] Like "orthodox" Marxists, socialist feminists argue that history has *a* nature and *a* logic that unfold gradually over time. The nature of history is best understood in terms of "materialism." According to Marx an examination of productive activity—that is, the relations of owners to producers on the one hand and the "forces" of production (types of machinery, accumulation of capital, and techniques used in production) on the other—will reveal the determinants of the character of all human activity and the appropriate means to transform oppressive forces of social organization.[27]

In the most stringent form of this approach, the oppression of women would be considered a derivative of class relations. Such oppression would "wither away" after a socialist revolution, along with the exploitation of one class by another. In less orthodox forms of socialist feminism, fundamental Marxist categories such as the extraction of surplus and the division of labor are utilized to develop more distinctively feminist explanations for the oppression of women. Most socialist feminists acknowledge that these Marxist concepts, as well as those of labor and production, have not been applied to and may in fact exclude many kinds of activities traditionally performed by women (e.g., child care or unwaged housework). Neither of these activities, for instance, directly produces "surplus value." Hence they would not count as "productive" labor within the capitalist system.[28]

Socialist feminists have adopted a number of strategies to overcome these omissions in Marxist theory. One of the most straightforward is to analyze the mode of production by utilizing the classic Marxist categories but with a feminist sensitivity to gender relations. For example, socialist feminists have employed the concept of a division of labor to point out that the labor force is segmented by gender as well as by the division between owners and producers. There is a "sexual division of labor" in the organization of production. Many women are employed in occupations that are 70 percent or more female. Not coincidentally, feminists argue, these occupations are also lower paid than those requiring equivalent education and skills, but in which men predominate.[29] These writers discuss the congruence between gender stereotypes and some of the skills and behavior required in "women's work"—for example, caring for children (elementary school teachers) or organizing and cleaning up after men (secretaries). These stereotypes make it seem natural that women do some kinds of work and not others. In turn the devaluation of the stereotypically female contributes to and reinforces a devaluation of "women's work" and the wages it can command.

The Marxist ideas of a (sexual) division of labor and unequal exchange (extraction of surplus) have also been applied to family relations. Socialist feminists argue there is a sexual division of labor in the household in which women do more of the work (child care, cleaning, food preparation, etc.) than men. Men in families thus benefit from an "unequal exchange." They benefit "materially" from women's labor, for example, in the forms of extra leisure time as well as services they do not have to perform for themselves. The capitalist economy also benefits from women's unwaged labor because otherwise wages would have to rise to cover the purchase of these services in the market, and owners' profits would decline. In turn women's "double day" makes it more difficult for them to compete with men in the waged labor force because women must also leave time and energy for their domestic responsibilities.[30]

Another and more recent socialist feminist strategy to overcome the gender bias of Marxist theory has been to broaden the concept of production or labor to include almost all forms of human activity. The category of labor is now to be replaced by "sensuous activity" or "sex/affective" production.[31] In this way many of the activities typically performed by women but excluded from traditional Marxist analysis can be included within a now more "perfectly materialist" category of analysis. The creation of surplus value no longer becomes the distinguishing characteristic of "productive" (real) labor. Rather any activity that contributes to the production or reproduction of human life is to be considered "real" and "material" labor. Child care and household labor would be included within this expanded concept of productive activity.

Socialist feminist theorists have made several important contributions to feminist discourse. First, they delineate relations of domination that deeply affect the quality of women's lives in waged labor and in families. In an economy in which so much that is necessary for life must be purchased in the commodity markets, where one is located within the political economy deeply affects the quality of women's lives. Women as a group unquestionably have less privilege within the economy and less access to its control than do men. Socialist feminists have also contributed to the deconstruction of the popular but misleading representation of families as "havens in a heartless world." They show that families are also women's workplaces— where they labor to build and maintain shelters for men and children. Without women's hard labor these havens would not exist, but precisely because of women's unequal share in the labor, power relations, and benefits of family life, their interests and experiences are not always the same as those of men or children.

Furthermore, as befits a materialist theory, socialist feminism has more direct implications for practice than do some other types of feminist theory. Movements for comparable worth, the dismantling of occupational segregation by sex, the social recognition and compensation for household labor, and the reorganization of the reproduction of daily life are all deeply indebted to socialist feminist analysis and activities. In turn, the not insignificant successes of these movements have improved women's wages and encouraged other women to press for more equitable economic and family arrangements.

Ironically, however, a consideration of women's economic status and labors also reveals a fundamental omission from socialist feminist theory, an omission also present in other forms of feminist theory. It is clear that race relations as well as those of class and gender play a key, determining role in the distribution of resources in family structures. Women of color as a group are poorer and more likely to have to support a family, economically and in every other way, than white women.[32] So far there has been no satisfactory socialist explanation for these facts. In much of socialist feminist as well as other feminist discourse, the significance of race is (at best) acknowledged with a guilty sigh, and then the "main" plot line is resumed.[33] The fact that socialist feminism cannot account for the inequalities of race is not treated as a problem that calls into question the adequacy of the theory as a whole. Here it seems "the race question" is treated in a way analogous to orthodox Marxism's treatment of "the woman question," an interesting quirk, but not one to shake confidence in the correctness of the theory itself.

From a metatheoretic perspective there are other problems with socialist feminism as well. This explanatory system incorporates the historical and philosophical flaws of Marxist analysis. Marxists (including socialist feminists) uncritically apply the concepts Marx should have used to describe a particular form of the production of commodities to all areas of human life at all historical periods.[34] These concepts include the categories of labor (e.g., productive or nonproductive), the centrality of production in the organization and culture of any society, the importance of exchange, the creation of surplus value and commodity production within the "economy," and the definition of class solely in terms of the *individual's* relation to the means of production. Marx and subsequent Marxists replicate rather than deconstruct the capitalist mentality by essentializing what is in fact a product of a particular historical and variable set of social relations.[35] Such theoretical moves not only distort life in capitalist society but surely are not appropriate to all other cultures.

The more traditional socialist feminist approach replicates the Marxist privileging of production and the division of labor. Therefore those who adopt it incorporate the concomitant and problematic assumptions concerning the nature and centrality of labor itself. In Marxist theory labor (defined as the transformation of natural or other objects into things with use or exchange value) is treated as the "essence" of history and human "being." Under the influence of such assumptions, socialist feminists end up making reductive claims like the following: "The family is definable exactly as property relations between men and women, and the social relations of the family are those property relations in action."[36] Among other problems, such claims ignore the existence and sensuous activities of real people in families (e.g., children, for whom at least part of their formative and familial experiences have nothing to do with production). Few women would describe their experiences of pregnancy and child rearing solely in terms of the production of commodity labor power for the market.

Even a brief consideration of the vast (and gendered) number of human activities excluded from the orthodox definition of the "essential" human activity (labor) should impel us to ask (postmodernist) questions about the assertion that there is a human essence—of history or human being. What kind of relations of domination—of nature or women—lie behind such unitary visions? Because Marxists claim theirs is a materialist theory in which theory and practice are closely related, examining the actual policies of existing self-defined socialist states for answers to these questions also seems fair. The policies of such states do not reveal a heightened level of sensitivity to either ecological practices or women's needs.[37] Hence it seems reasonable to retain a suspicious attitude to these essentialist claims and their philosophical and political implications.

Socialist feminists' attempts to "widen" the concept of production to include most forms of human activity have not succeeded in overcoming the flaws in Marxist theory either. An example of the problems that follow from this still relatively uncritical appropriation of Marxist concepts can be found, for instance, in the proposal that a new category, "sex/affective production," should be incorporated within the more traditional concepts of labor and production. This new category is meant to include everything from genital intercourse to child care. One would describe and analyze all the activities falling within this category in the usual Marxist way (e.g., one would investigate the division of labor, distribution of surplus, etc., within and as constitutive of these activities). To "prove," for instance, that women are sexually exploited, we would have to construct an "empirical measure" of "male and female inputs, rewards from and control over these production processes." Ultimately such "proof will require a physical model of sexual satisfaction and sexual agency" so the precise amount of energy exchanged can be "objectively" measured.[38]

This sort of argument illustrates the distortion of experience under the tyranny of certain theoretical schemes. For example, fantasy or verbal exchange would have no place within this conception of sexuality. Does all pleasure really have a physical basis or measure? These kinds of arguments, however well intended, not only contort experience but also avoid an essential question: Why "widen" production instead of dislodging it or any other singularly central concept from such authoritative powers?

The most basic categories of Marxist analysis, no matter how radically extended or reworked by feminists, replicate the devaluation and invisibility of important aspects of women's experience so prevalent in male-dominant cultures and discourses. As feminist discourse has matured, the extent to which these notions are intrinsically gender bound and biased has become increasingly evident. It is difficult to avoid the question of whether a feminist appropriation of Marxism would not require such a radical transformation of the entire system that it would become simply unrecognizable to its founder. Feminist theorists may inadvertently find themselves in the position that Marx imagined the proletariat would eventually assume vis-à-vis capitalism—"seizing" its means of production would overthrow an entire historical structure and replace it with a new one.

Socialist feminists have been reluctant to acknowledge the deconstructive implications of their own endeavors. These feminists do break with or revise some of the tenets of orthodox Marxism, especially in their attempts to emphasize the importance of gender as well as class in the structure of all social relations and history. Nonetheless they continue to use the founder's vocabulary despite the gaps between Marx's discursive practice and the meanings of their own discoveries. Translating their discoveries back into this vocabulary and acquiescing to its authority undercut or transmute many of the radical insights of socialist feminism.

From a "nonallied" feminist perspective those philosophers (or philosophies) claiming to represent experiences excluded from "bourgeois thought" are not any more free from gender bias than their predecessors. Marx reveals more than he intends when he sets forth his own version of the Enlightenment credo: "And as everything natural has to have its *beginning, man* too has his act of coming-to-be—history—which, however, is for him a known history, and hence as an act of coming-to-be it is a conscious self-transcending act of coming-to-be. History is the true natural history of man." [39]

From a feminist perspective Marx's "conscious" act of "coming-to-be" is also an act of forgetting, or, less charitably, "man's" coming-to-be evidently entails or requires a simultaneous act of repression, for the first, specific act required if each man (or woman) is to have a history at all is that he or she must be born. As Adrienne Rich has so eloquently pointed out, this has meant that each of us is "of woman born." [40] Individual women, not "history," have invariably been our mothers.

This might seem like semantic quibbling. However substitutions of undifferentiated concepts like "man's coming-to-be" for more historically constituted, variable, and gender-specific ones like "mothers" or "childbirth" are neither neutral nor accidental. Our "conscious self-transcending act(s) of coming to be" are partially rooted in and poisoned by a flight from recognizing gendered and historical aspects of our "natural history." [41] This natural history includes the context in which we first find ourselves and come to be persons—our intense and soon ambivalently experienced dependence on the care of others. The division of labor in most cultures is such that the first "other" upon whom we depend will most likely be female. This aspect of our history is as neatly suppressed in Marxist theory as in its supposed opposite, liberalism. To unearth such history requires more attention to both often repressed lived experience and the theoretical tools by which we choose to comprehend it.

Rewriting Natural History: Child Rearing, Families, and the Social Relations of Gender

Only when contemporary feminists began to reconsider their initial hostility to psychoanalysis did it become apparent that the organization of child rearing within the family has fundamental and startling consequences for virtually every aspect of human existence. Utilizing a variety of psychoanalytic frameworks, some feminist theorists began to argue that child-rearing arrangements are central elements in the construction of gender identity and the self and in the origin and replication of male-dominant gender relations. Furthermore the consequences of contemporary (gender-bound) child rearing extend into almost every other aspect of social life, deeply shaping the character of power relations, knowledge, and the economy. Feminist analyses of child-rearing arrangements (especially mother-child relations) have been very important in the development of feminist theorizing. The ongoing exploration of these relations and their significance within the self and social life has been especially productive. Paradoxically, however, this same work is permeated and structured by deep confusions, ambivalences, and unresolved questions about the practices, meaning, and relative importance of families, mothering, sexuality, and power and about the adequacy of any of the existing psychoanalytic approaches for feminist and other forms of theorizing.

The work of Juliet Mitchell, Dorothy Dinnerstein, and Nancy Chodorow has been especially important in the development of feminist analyses of mothering, child rearing, and gender relations. These writers agree on certain basic premises: the centrality of the unconscious in human life, the difference between biological sexuality and the organization of gender, and the importance of child-rearing arrangements, and hence families, to the construction of gender identity. Despite these areas of agreement, the three writers differ on the influence of psychodynamic processes on social structures such as the economy and on the extent to which these structures influence psychodynamic processes. They also differ in the type of psychoanalytic theory they adopt and hence on the relative importance of preoedipal and oedipal relations in the constitution of a self and social life, in their conception of the unconscious, and in the political practices that would follow from their ideas.

Juliet Mitchell was among the first feminists to argue for the importance of Freud's ideas to the development of feminist theories of gender relations. Although her work provided a cogent defense of a particular (Lacanian) form of psychoanalysis and was influential among feminists, ultimately it did not point the way toward a successful appropriation of psychoanalysis within feminist theory. Mitchell argues that Freud's theory must be understood as an account of how each individual comes to acquire "patriarchal law" and how this acquisition determines psychic structure. Freud's analysis of the psychology of women must not be read as prescription—that is, as a justification of women's suffering and "place" under patriarchy—but rather as a description of the inevitable consequences for psychic development of patriarchal social relations. Female masochism, penis envy, and women's weak superego must be understood as results of the imposition of patriarchal law upon women. Freud's theory is revolutionary in content because it reveals more deeply and completely than any other psychological theory the misery women will suffer as long as they live under the "law of the father." [42]

The contention that Freud's theory should be read as an account of psychological development that has its roots in patriarchal relations rather than in biology is Mitchell's most important contribution to feminist analyses of psychodynamics. But her work is marred by a rigid insistence on the most orthodox and uncritical acceptance of Lacan's reconstruction of every major Freudian concept. Mitchell does not consider the systematic effects of gender bias in these theories or that even supposedly "gender-neutral" concepts could be gender bound or differentiated. She does not acknowledge the ongoing discourse among psychoanalysts concerning the adequacy of Freud's theory and Lacan's interpretation of it or alternative post-Freudian developments within psychoanalysis, such as object relations theory. [43] The unconscious exists for Mitchell (as for Lacan) as a disembodied structure outside both history and social relations. Despite her emphasis on the importance of sexuality and fantasy within psychoanalytic theory, Mitchell also reduces the unconscious to a series of structures, signs, and symbols. Following Lacan, she rationalizes the unconscious, the very aspect of the psyche that is constituted by preconscious, preverbal, and prerational experience and in which body and social, inner and outer are not yet distinguished.

In Mitchell's analysis of the family, the complexity of sexual politics and of its interplay with other forms of politics is reduced to "the acquisitions of patriarchal law" by each individual and the contradictions between this law and the "social organization of work."[44] The intensity of the wishes and fantasies present in the unconscious and the manner in which they affect and are affected by social relations are lost. In constructing this symbolic, structuralist interpretation of unconscious processes, Mitchell, like Freud and Lacan, renders the power of both the preoedipal period and the mother and their impact on women's and men's psychological development even more opaque. In Mitchell's theory sexual and other forms of politics are parallel, not interacting structures; grasping the interrelationships between the structures and the dynamics of the whole thus becomes difficult.

The work of Dorothy Dinnerstein and Nancy Chodorow supplies a concreteness that is lacking in Mitchell's analysis. They provide a deeper, more complex account of the unconscious, its power, and its centrality in human life, especially in the family and in the constitution and replication of gender relations. Unlike Mitchell they also begin to resituate mother-child relations within (and as important forces in) history. Dinnerstein attempts to explain the origin of the sexual division of labor, how it is replicated, and its influence not only on the relations of women to men but also on humans' relations to nature and the character of history itself. According to Dinnerstein the current social arrangements of child rearing, in which women alone are responsible for the care of infants, are the source of our current malaise and of the behavior that threatens to destroy all forms of life. Thus the current organization of the family is far from neutral or simply private; familial organization not only oppresses women and children but threatens the very survival of the human species and its habitat.

To a great extent Nancy Chodorow agrees with Dinnerstein's

premises, but Chodorow attempts to locate the dynamics Dinnerstein often discusses in an ahistoric manner within the specific relationships of mother to daughter or mother to son. Chodorow's work is also more limited in scope and less philosophically daring. She explicitly limits herself to an analysis of one aspect of Western capitalist social relations: the "reproduction of mothering."

Dinnerstein locates the origin of the sexual division of labor within biology. Because of the large brains of humans, children are born earlier in terms of maturity and capabilities than any other species and are dependent longer. For much of human history, a woman spent "most" of her "vigorous adult life pregnant or lactating. . . . Given these handicaps to wide ranging mobility, she has been the logical keeper of the hearth and doer of domestic tasks."[45] Despite women's shared ability with men to "make history," these prior conditions tie women primarily to child rearing.

Humans are faced with a fundamental dilemma: We have the power and necessity to create environments for ourselves. To some extent we can master and dominate nature and other persons; yet the ability to control our environment is never total, and we alone bear the responsibility for our fate. The tension between responsibility and lack of control leads to a desire to avoid full knowledge of this fundamental dilemma and to find either a scapegoat for it or a superhuman way out of it.

Women have historically served as this scapegoat, a role that is possible only because women take care of infants and because of the peculiar character of human infancy. Infants' mental and emotional development occurs much more rapidly than their physical development. Infants have needs before they are able to fulfill them for themself. Like Winnicott, Dinnerstein argues the mother is the first crucial link to the world of life. She is the mediator between the sensitive infant, the infant's own natural urges, and the outside world. With all its pleasures and frustrations, the relationship between mother and infant is our first major social encounter and our first experience of love. The experience of dependence and of powerful desires not within the infant's power to fulfill occurs before humans are able to speak but not before we are aware of such experiences. These experiences remain alive in our unconscious in the form of fantasy, feeling states, and desire. They especially affect our sexuality, impelling us to seek others who can gratify our wishes and with whom we can recapture something of the blissful infantile state. Yet this same state is terror filled because it is permeated by the memory of our helplessness and by an intensity that threatens the adult ego. Hence we seek sexual experience and intimate relations, but we also seek to make them safe by limiting their intensity and attempting to dominate and/or devalue the loved one.

Memory extends back to earliest infantile experiences. The later rational and articulated processes are suffused with these earliest experiences. We first encounter the general human dilemma (the desire for mastery and creativity versus the fear of responsibility) within the mother-child relation. We experience it in a relationship with a woman and only a woman or women. Because only women take care of infants, we repress the memory of this experience, our infantile powerlessness, and fear of the mother. Humans therefore come to blame women for their malaise and do not face the more general existential dilemma: our fate as a species.

Repressed infantile experience continues to exert a powerful, although unacknowledged, influence over our conscious thoughts and behavior. Men must deny infantile experience and claim a dominating form of rationality to make history. Historically men tend to be estranged from their own feelings and bodies and to have distanced themselves from nature in order to dominate it. Men must exclude women from history to maintain a "natural" sanctuary to which they can return after their history-making and often nature-destroying exploits. Women are our main contact with humanity and nature. They insist upon and remain anchored in early forms of relatedness and refuse to participate in, and have contempt for, history making. These unconscious activities distort the history men make and the psychological development of men and women. They result in an unhealthy form of dependent heterosexuality.

Chodorow contends that men's denial of relatedness and need to make history, and women's identification as mothers, are not the products of biology or avoidance of human fate. They are instead the consequence of certain forms of family relations that exist within a specific social context that reinforces and is reinforced by relations within the family. Drawing on object relations theory, Chodorow argues that humans are formed in and through social relations. Unlike

Winnicott and other object relations theorists, however, she stresses that family social relations cannot be understood apart from other forms of social relations, especially class and gender.

Chodorow is particularly interested in the reproduction of mothering—how and why only women "mother" (by which she means nurturing and caring for small children), how this pattern is replicated, and how it affects the psychological development of women. Chodorow, like Rubin, sees the family as a central element in the sex/gender system. The sexual and familial division of labor in which women mother and are more involved than men in interpersonal, affective relationships produces in daughters and sons a division of psychological capacities that leads them to reproduce this sexual and familial division of labor. Women as mothers produce daughters with mothering capacities and the desire to mother. These capacities and needs are built into and grow out of the mother-daughter relationship itself. By contrast women as mothers (and men as not-mothers) produce sons whose nurturant capacities and needs have been systematically curtailed and repressed. This prepares men for their less affective later family role and for primary participation in the interpersonal extrafamilial world of work and public life.

Women's primary location is the home because mothering occurs there. Indeed the sexual division of labor provides a basis for differentiating "public" and "domestic." However these spheres are not equal, and because "the public sphere dominates the domestic, . . . men dominate women."[46]

Chodorow stresses the importance of infantile experience for both psychological development and gender creation. Infants develop a self by internalizing their relations with their primary caretaker, usually the mother. By the time the father appears as a significant person in the child's life, the child's core identity has already been established. Hence relations with the father are less affectively charged.

Mothering has important but differing consequences for girls and boys. Girls, because they are of the same gender as the mother, tend not to develop firm ego boundaries; they never completely separate from the mother. The mother often treats the daughter as an extension of herself and discourages her from establishing a separate identity. Boys experience themselves and are experienced by the mother as an "other." The mother pushes the son toward differentiation, and this encouragement is motivated and reinforced by gender differentiation. Because they never resolve the primary attachment to the mother, girls remain more preoccupied with relational issues. Boys seem to be occupied with issues of differentiation and action in the external world. Boys must reject the female aspects of themselves and the primary relatedness to the mother to be male; girls can and must reject neither.

Thus there is a deep psychological basis for later sex role differentiation. Girls have a greater potential capacity for intimate relations, but men have repressed these capacities and turn their interest outward. Girls must reject the mother as primary love object to become heterosexual, despite their unresolved emotional ties to her, but boys must shift their love from mother to another female. The shift is usually not absolute in the girl; she retains an internal emotional triangle of mother/father/self. "Men tend to remain emotionally secondary" for women.[47]

Women satisfy their relational needs by becoming mothers; the baby creates a new triangular situation: husband/wife/child. Men satisfy their need for nonrelational activities and avoid their fear of returning to the infantile state by participating in the nonfamilial world of work and by controlling women. Men need women, and heterosexual women need men, to fulfill a desire for emotional and physical union. This is in part, especially for men, a replication of the symbiotic union of early infancy, although more safe and controlled. Yet men find it difficult and threatening to satisfy women's emotional needs because they had to repress their relational capacities to become male. So women turn to their children to satisfy relational needs. Thus women and men have differing but equally strong unconscious motivation to replicate the family, gender personality, and mothering by women.

The only solution to this endless cycle according to both Chodorow and Dinnerstein is the active participation of men in infant care. Under these circumstances, Dinnerstein contends, we would have to mature both as a species and as individuals. For the two writers shared child care would have the following benefits:

Masculinity would not become tied to denial of dependence and devaluation of women. Feminine personality would be less preoccupied with individuation, and children would not develop fears of maternal omnipotence and expectations of women's unique self-sacrificing qualities. This would reduce men's needs to guard their masculinity and their control of social and cultural spheres which treat and define women as secondary and powerless, and would help women to develop the autonomy which too much embeddedness in relationships has often taken from them.[48]

The work of Dinnerstein and Chodorow shares many strengths and weaknesses, although the focus of each is somewhat different. Both stress the power of the unconscious, the residues of infancy in adult life, and the consequent centrality of child-rearing arrangements to individual development and history as a whole. In Dinnerstein's work child-rearing arrangements have more power to determine history than Chodorow admits, although both agree that, without a radical change in child-rearing arrangements, women's status will not be fundamentally altered. Both Dinnerstein and Chodorow, unlike the thinkers who focus on sex roles or conditioning, enable us to understand how intertwined gender is with our core identity and accordingly how difficult it is to change our core selves. Their account of the importance of mother-child relations in the development of self and the constitution of gender and other social relations extends the insights of object relations theorists and corrects some of their limitations. Their analyses of the particular forms of gender identity created through female-dominated child rearing partially explain the phenomenon radical feminists identified—the male desire to dominate women—although they cannot explain the origin(s) of the sexual division of labor.

These two writers' concrete analyses of early childhood counter the abstractness of socialist feminists' treatments of children. They take into account the inevitable influence of early experience on children and the child's need for reliable and loving care, as well as the child's sociability and malleability within definite limits. Their work reminds us of two powerful forms of human experience: the infant's helplessness and a persistent longing for irresponsible infantile bliss. Dinnerstein's and Chodorow's work also provides the basis for a critique of the Marxist interpretation of the family as a purely dependent or ideological institution. The sex/gender system as psychodynamically internalized provides a motive and reinforcement for all forms of differentiation, including race, class, and the sex-stratified labor force. Their more interactive approach to psychological development provides a more adequate ground for integrating the concerns of Marxism, feminism, and psychoanalysis than does Rubin's and Mitchell's use of structuralism. We can begin to understand the sex/gender system as arising out of a series of interacting social relations, including those of families, rather than as one structure, lying parallel to others.

There are also problems with Dinnerstein's and Chodorow's work, some shared and some unique to each. Dinnerstein treats biology in a determinist manner, and consequently her work suffers from some of the same problems discussed previously in the section on the "natural." She also assumes all persons share some ahistoric, universal fate. Both men's and women's attachment to current social family arrangements seems to be ultimately rooted in a universal, general psychological motive: the avoidance of the human dilemma. This claim lacks specificity; it does not enable us to understand how the general motive is translated into and expressed through particular concrete forms of social relations. Although we are all born helpless and dependent, grow up, and die, how we experience these processes is socially mediated. The dilemma of responsibility versus imperfect control may emerge only under certain social conditions and is not felt by all persons at all times. The dilemma may arise from the breakdown of religion and community. It could also be the consequence of a certain form of isolated individualism and expectations about how much control people *should* have more predominant in contemporary Western than in any other cultures. Women tend to be blamed for whatever a culture perceives as its dilemmas, and Dinnerstein helps us understand why this is so. But the character of the dilemmas changes over time. The abstractness present in Dinnerstein's theory can be overcome only by integrating more specific political, economic, and psychological analysis into the dynamics she suggests.

Although Chodorow's work is more historically specific, neither she nor Dinnerstein adequately places childbearing and rearing into a political, economic, and social context. Although women universally have had primary responsibility for child care, the content of child care and other aspects of women's work and families have changed. The relationship between the division of labor within families and its effect on and relationship to other divisions of labor (e.g., class) should be explored. Although Chodorow is careful to state that her analysis arises from and applies to Western capitalist countries, she does not discuss class and race differences in child rearing and what these imply for a general theory of mothering and social psychology.

In both writers' work a truly social psychology is suggested but not fully developed. Their remarks on the relation of families to other social structures are not adequately integrated into the account of personality development. The concept of social relations that would allow such an integration is underdeveloped. In both authors' work, as in psychoanalysis more generally, the parents appear primarily as the child's objects. The fullness of the parents' experience and its influence on the children is not analyzed. Such an analysis would be one way to begin to investigate the interactions of social relations within the family with forms of social relations outside it.[49]

In both writers' analyses motherhood appears to be primarily an expression of neurosis—of women's unresolved infantile wishes and fantasies. The other aspects of motherhood, both positive and negative, its very real gratifications and costs, are not discussed. The economic, political, and social restrictions upon and barriers to good parenting and changing patterns of parenting are not fully acknowledged and integrated into the account of psychodynamics. The impression remains that such problems reside solely within the family; although this is clearly not Chodorow's position, it may be Dinnerstein's.

Feminist writings on the subject suggest certain conclusions about the nature of families:

1. The sexual division of labor, especially women's exclusive responsibility for young children, which is a persistent feature of history, is a crucial factor in women's oppression and the analysis of it.

2. Understanding families, their histories, psychodynamics, and relations to other social structures is a central task of feminist theorizing.

3. Families are complex structures comprised of many elements: the sex/gender system, varying relations to production and to other social structures, ideology, and power relations.

4. Families (at least as historically constituted) are oppressive to women and are a primary source of the maintenance and replication of both gender and identity and the pain and suffering endemic to being female.

5. Families as currently constituted must be changed. At minimum this requires the equal involvement of men and women in caring for young children.

6. Gender is created by social relations experienced first in fami-

lies; it is not determined solely by or limited to biology. Heterosexuality is also socially, not biologically, constructed, through social relations in families. These relations also re-create one familial "norm": that families by definition are "nuclear," comprised of (at minimum) a heterosexual pair.

7. The different roles women and men play both inside and outside families are not natural but grow out of and are the expression of a complex series of social relations: male dominance, heterosexuality, economic systems, legal and ideological structures, and early childhood experiences and their unconscious residues. All these relations are mutually interacting and reinforcing, although some may be more determinative than others, and the more determinant factors may also vary over time.

8. Nothing human is unchanging or absolutely unchangeable. This includes the character of childhood, sexuality, families, human "nature" (although Dinnerstein would disagree on this point), and the variations of each of these by gender. Everything human has a social history and a social root. Even biology is mediated by, or can potentially be affected or transformed by, social relations; biology is not simply a brute fact immediately and directly expressed in human life.

A careful consideration of even the best feminist accounts of child rearing, families, and gender relations makes it clear that child-rearing practices and family arrangements are not the originating or sole cause of asymmetric gender relations or identities. An analysis of child-rearing practices cannot explain why women have the primary responsibility for child rearing, only some of the *consequences* of this fact. In other words the child-rearing practices or family arrangements that some writers posit as causal presuppose the very social relations we are trying to understand: a gender-based division of human activities and hence the existence of socially constructed sets of gender relations and (the peculiar and in need of explanation) salience of *gender* itself.[50]

Feminist theories of the family also leave many important questions unanswered, and the writers reviewed here would disagree on the answers and on their relative significance. What healthy motives and needs draw people into families? How can these best be met?

How do we decide what constitutes a "healthy" need, or even a "need"? How do different types of social relations interact, reinforce, and conflict with one another, and how do they congeal into social structures? How does this process vary over time? How can we understand families in this context? How do families vary by class, race, and historical period? What consequences do these variations have for psychodynamics, gender, and the status of women? What economic and social barriers exist to good "family" relations, and how can these barriers be overcome? Do feminism and the liberation of women require the elimination of gender or differentiation according to gender? Are there positive aspects to gender differentiation? What are the consequences of different answers to these questions for the organization of family life? Does "the family" as such oppress women, or does the male-dominant (or capitalist) family oppress women? What would nonoppressive family relations look like? What do children really need to mature into healthy adults? How can these needs best be met? Does biology impose any limits on social relations? How can we know what these might be and how they could be incorporated into a nonoppressive society? Are Dinnerstein and Chodorow too naive and optimistic about the benefits and consequences of coparenting? Do they underestimate the extent to which internal conflict, splitting, and the acting out of such psychic experience are endemic to and inseparable from the "human condition," no matter what our child-rearing arrangements might be?

Re-presenting (Sexual) Difference: Texts, Bodies, and Writing Wrong(s)

One of the most controversial issues among feminist theorists (especially those in the United States and France) in the last five years has been the meanings and values of "difference." This issue is complex, and in fact many interrelated questions are incorporated within it. Such questions include the extent to which sexuality is embodied and gendered; whether anything is distinctively "feminine" and if so how this is or could be recovered, valued, and expressed; how difference itself is to be understood and valued; and which differences are most significant—gendered ones, ones between women and men, or ones among women ourselves. Theorists of difference have also been concerned with the importance of preoedipal relations in the constitution of the self (especially women's self) and with issues of language and power. The emergence of such theories signifies and demonstrates the distances feminist theorists have been able to open up between our discourses and phallocentric ones. Yet these feminist discourses too are marked by the effects of gender and other relations of domination, such as those of race. There are many traces of these relations in discourses on difference. Anxieties about mothering, differences, aggression, race, and power that tend to operate within contemporary white Western women's consciousness (and unconscious) are powerfully present and effective here.

Theorists of difference are heavily indebted to and dependent on feminist and psychoanalytic accounts of feminine development. American theorists of difference tend to rely on object relations psychoanalysis; the French are more influenced by Lacan.[51] Whichever form of psychoanalysis they incorporate, theorists of difference stress the centrality of the relation between mother and daughter as a primary and continuously determining force in women's psyche and activity. Indeed, in the writings of some theorists such as Cixous, the mother-daughter relationship seems to overwhelm in importance all other possible influences, except the "symbolic" system itself.

Although theorists of difference agree on the centrality of the mother-daughter relationship in the constitution of the feminine, they disagree on the relative importance of the "symbolic" (systems of signification or representation). One group of writers tends to emphasize the effect of such systems on (male-dominant) gender relations and identities; a second group emphasizes the effects of women's activity and the sexual division of labor.[52] This second group of writers tends to see gender relations and other social relations such as class or race as more constitutive of systems of representation, including language and philosophy, than the reverse. The second group of writers also focuses on women's *maternal* practices as at least partially constitutive of our thinking, ethics, and sense of self. The first group emphasizes the primacy of women's sexuality (or pleasure) and its repression in phallocentric culture. I will return to a discussion of these differences after considering the ideas or themes commonly held by the first group of writers.

My focus in the following discussion will be on those theorists of difference who stress the repression of women's pleasure/sexuality as essential in and for their oppression or absence and silence in Western culture. These writers' concerns and sources intersect with my own: Lacan; postmodernism, especially Derrida; the effects of phallocentrism on the structure and content of Western philosophy and Freud. The second mode of discourse on difference with its focus on the activities and consequences of mothering is equally important, but I will not do it justice here. Rather I employ the writings of this second group primarily to identify the lacks, omissions, and gaps in the first mode of discourse—especially those related to questions of power, practical activity, and the many other differentiated (and differentiating) determinants of women's experience.

As we have seen, the apparent connections between gender relations and such important natural aspects of human existence as birth, reproduction, and sexuality make possible both a conflating of the natural and the social and an overly radical distinction between the two. Gender (the division of persons and human traits and capacities into man and woman) has been read back and has entered into and enabled the construction of many other arbitrary and exclusionary categories. In modern Western culture *natural* and *social* are conflated in our understanding of *woman*. In our understanding of *man* a radical disjunction is made between the natural and the social. Women stand for and symbolize the body, "difference," the concrete. These qualities are also said to suffuse and define the activities most associated with women: nurturing, mothering, taking care of and being in relation with others, "preserving." Women's minds are also said to reflect the qualities of our stereotypically female activities and bodies. We are said to reason or write "differently" and to have different "interests" and motives than men. Men are said to have superior powers of abstract reason (mind), to be the "masters" of nature (including bodies), and to be more aggressive and militaristic.

Given the past and present ideological and political abuses of women that such claims both reflect and support, the reemergence of similar claims among feminists about women's difference has stimulated enormous controversy and anxiety.[53] Is this the beginning of a genuine transvaluation of values or a retreat into traditional gendered ways of understanding the world? In our attempts to rethink and revalue the "traditionally" feminine, will we end up participating in a reprisoning of a slightly reconceived "angel" within a somewhat more commodious and aesthetically pleasing house?

Feminists who are engaged in developing a discourse on women's difference claim the more salient danger is a cooptation of women's newly released energies into the replication or extension of the patriarch's house. These writers claim that only the exploration and valorization of women's difference or a genuinely "feminine" writing can provide the material for a space outside the confines of phallocentric culture. Any attempt to deny or repress aspects of our "being" out of fear of phallocratic (mis)appropriation, opinions, or power will ultimately replicate women's self-hatred, lack of self-knowledge, and confinement and will thus be self-defeating. According to two important French writers, Hélène Cixous and Luce Irigaray, women's difference seems to exist in at least two interrelated dimensions: the psychological (including sexuality and possibly biology as well) and the symbolic (including writing and philosophy). These issues of desire and language are necessarily connected with (and in feminist forms subversive of) relations of power.

According to Cixous and Irigaray, there are fundamental psychological differences between women and men. Women are more influenced by and less cut off from preoedipal modes of experience. Like Chodorow these writers claim the girl, unlike the boy, retains much of her initial identification and bonding with the mother. Because the preoedipal relation between mother and daughter is less repressed, women's selves remain more fluid, interrelational, and less split off from bodily experiences than men's. The continuing power of the preoedipal within women's more fluid self has direct effects on her sexuality. "No woman piles up as many defenses against instinctual drives as a man does. You don't prop things up, you don't brick things up the way he does, you don't withdraw from pleasure so 'prudently.' "[54] Woman's pleasure or sexuality is one of the major areas of her difference. Woman's sexuality (*contra* Freud) is *never* truly phallic/genital. Unlike the man's, the woman's pleasure is never centered on one organ or oriented to one aim: orgasmic (tension) release. Rather, it is plural: "Woman has sex organs more or less everywhere . . . the geography of her pleasure is far more diversified, more multiple in its differences, more complex, more subtle, than is commonly imagined."[55]

This fluid and unbounded female sexuality cannot be conceptualized within masculine parameters. Nevertheless, although "woman's desire would not be expected to speak the same language as man's," her desire has been (mis)represented within existing (phallocentric) discourses. Insofar as woman or her desire exists in these discourses, it has been as an other, mirror, or "use value" for man. Even her orgasms "are necessary as a demonstration of masculine power. . . . Women are there as witnesses. Their training is designed to subject them to an exclusively phallocratic economy."[56] What is repressed and cannot be represented in or by "the logic that has dominated the West since the time of the Greeks" is the "interplay of desire among women's bodies, women's organs/women's language."[57] In and as a consequence of this repression and lack of representation, women's sexuality becomes the "dark continent" even to herself. "Woman is disgusted by woman and fears her."[58]

Men and masculine discourse have an ambivalent relation to woman and the dark continent of her sexuality—they both fear it and need it. "Words have been able to circulate too much, to lose their information, to strip themselves of their use. At least let women stay as they were in the beginning, talking little but causing men's talk—stay as guardians, because of their mystery, of all language."[59] Woman and her sexuality remain the (necessary) outside, the boundary that defines and preserves the inside: "A woman serves (only) as a *projective map* for the purpose of guaranteeing the totality of the system. . . . A woman—paradoxically?—would thus serve in the proposition as the *copulative link*."[60]

Feminine pleasure signifies the greatest threat to masculine discourse precisely because of its fluidity and its double role as boundary and outside. Woman represents difference on a philosophical as well as psychological/sexual level. Masculine discourse is constituted by a binary logic (logocentrism) in which "a law organizes what is thinkable by oppositions."[61] Logocentrism is inextricably connected to phallocentrism. The binary and asymmetric oppositions by and in which this discourse is structured are all in some way related to the "couple" man/woman. By "bringing to light the fate dealt to woman, her burial," the truth of (masculine) discourse will be revealed: "The logocentric plan had always, inadmissibly, been to create a foundation for (to found and fund) phallocentrism, to guarantee the masculine order a rationale equal to history itself."[62]

The inner logic of logocentrism is the "selfsame." No true difference can exist within (masculine) discourse. The other is always reduced to being the other of the same, its inferior, reflection, "excess," hence still defined by and an extension of it. (Masculine) discourse presents itself as sexually "indifferent." What is concealed in this claim is the eradication of *the differences between the sexes* in systems that are in fact merely "self representations of a 'masculine subject.'"[63]

Hence the insertion of *female* specificity into these discourses would explode the claim of sexual indifference and instead particularize these discourses as masculine. Female particularity would disrupt these unitary and solid discourses. The same would fragment into multiplicity. The hom(m)osexual monopoly ("the exclusive valorization of men's needs/desire, of exchange among men") that orders all social life and culture would be destroyed.[64]

Given the power and centrality attributed to (phallocentric) systems of representation in the constitution of gender, subjectivity, and culture as a whole, the significance of woman speaking for and to herself can be understood. The theorists of difference reject the liberal feminist goal of equality as adequate to or even appropriate for women's emancipation because "women merely 'equal' to men would be 'like them,' therefore not women."[65] Instead of attaining equality with men, women should strive to "write" (literally and metaphorically) the feminine. In writing, "women will affirm woman somewhere other than in silence, the place reserved for her in and through the symbolic."[66]

It is time for the "commodities" (woman as use value to and for man) to refuse to go to market, to maintain "'another' kind of commerce, among themselves."[67] Writing the feminine is resolutely woman centered—speaking of her desire, her pleasure in her own body and those of other women. Such writing names the constitution and appropriation of woman's body as a sexual object for man as a central element in her oppression. Heterosexuality is understood as an expression of and an essential contributing factor to the repression of woman's desire. Freed from its phallocentric appropriation, woman's plural desire would flow between objects and activities of all sorts: her own body, men, women, and writing itself.

Writing provides an anticipatory experience of liberation. It is therapeutic, returning woman's repressed forbidden pleasure to her. It also helps create a collective, interpersonal space in which women can finally speak of and to themselves. "While not yet 'here,' it is there by now—in this other place that disrupts social order whose desire makes fiction exist. Not any old fiction."[68] As men have always done,

women will seize the means of representation for their own self-
(re)presentation. Men have always "written from the body"—the
"phallus' " role as primary signifier is not accidental or arbitrary. Juxtaposing feminine writing against and within phallocentric discourse
allows the system of signification and its "signified"—the subject and
its modes of consciousness—to be transformed. Such transformation
is a necessary, but not sufficient, condition for and aspect of revolution.[69]

Yet I do not believe desire, even in its "feminine" form, can be this
liberatory. Even these radical critics of phallocentric discourse are still
too much their *mother's* good daughter. Here we can usefully deploy
psychoanalysis against feminist (self) presentations. This account of
the feminine represses elements of woman's desire that are often forbidden by mothers as well as by male-dominant cultures: woman's
aggression, her desire for separation, autonomy, and mastery. Too
many forces are absent in these accounts of mother-daughter relations, feminine desire, or "maternal thinking": the mother's rage, her
envy of her daughter's (potential) freedom, her desire for her daughter to be the selfsame and not different or separate from her. These
daughters are silent about the psychological and, not infrequently,
physical violence between mothers and daughters. They rarely speak
of the mother's need for her daughter and its frequent consequence—
a fear on the daughter's part that if she separates and differentiates
from the mother, her mother will be irreparably harmed—or will
damage or abandon *her*. The competition among women and woman's desire—not to be in the endlessly fluid circle of exchange, but
rather unique, the best or recognized as other, different, distinct,
closed off, only in and for herself—remains unvoiced.[70]

The daughter's fear of differentiation, of separation, of boundaries
is expressed also in the lack of discussion among these theorists of
differences among women. To some extent it may be true that "a long
history has put all women in the same sexual, social and cultural condition. Whatever inequalities may exist among women, they all
undergo, even without clearly realizing it, the same oppression, the
same exploitation of their body, the same denial of their desire."[71]

"Whatever inequalities may exist among women" are not so minor
and inconsequential. They affect women's relations with one another
and our particular experiences of oppression, desire, or motherhood.

Such differences can seem minor only to those who are less unequal than the others.

If we listen to some of the voices of women of color in the United States, for example, it will be clear their melodies may have some shared themes, but the tunes are different from those of many white women. The social relations, for example, race, that structure and are reflected in women of color's writings cannot be of minor significance in their lives. The significance of the differences of race are at least as salient in the lives of women of color as those of gender, as Jessie Redmond Fauset illustrates in this passage from her novel: "Colour or rather the lack of it seemed to the child the one absolute prerequisite to the life of which she was always dreaming. One might break loose from a too hampering sense of duty; poverty could be overcome; physicians conquered weakness; but colour, the mere possession of a black or a white skin, that was clearly one of those fortuitous endowments of the gods."[72] Unlike women of color, white women have many reasons for repressing the significance of such relations for us as well as for women of color. Unlike women of color, white women have the "privilege" of "forgetting" or not noticing the operations of race and many socially sanctioned opportunities for doing so. These reasons include our complex relations to the privileges of racism, our complicity in its maintenance, and our guilt.

The voices of women of color also make it clear that it is wrong to assume there is or can be one experience (or discourse) of female sexuality. Black women's sexuality has been represented as primitive, powerful, "free" from cultural constraints and morality, as contrasted to the delicate, repressed hysteria of middle-class white women. This representation, in turn, has been utilized to justify and deny the continuing sexual abuse of black women and the absence of tenderness and respect in relations with them. As Barbara Smith writes:

Black women have traditionally been reluctant to talk about sex with their daughters. "Keep your dress down and your drawers up," is a homily of this reticence. At the very same time, all Black women have been viewed as sexual animals by the society as a whole and at times by Black men as well. In such a charged context, considering the dimensions of Lesbian sexuality has been totally taboo. Sexual repression, coupled with blatant sexual exploitation, has contributed to a complex psychological mix. Who knows what we think and, more importantly, feel? But it is up to us, with each other's help to find out.[73]

Nor can there be a uniform experience and discourse of mothering. The context of racism creates distinct pressures on women of color. Women of color's "maternal practice" is constituted in part by a struggle against antinatalist policies and against a misconstruing of the strength required for sheer survival as "castrating" matriarchy. Alice Walker describes some of the painful dilemmas of black women:

Black women are called, in the folklore that so aptly identifies one's status in society, "the mule of the world," because we have been handed the burdens that everyone else—*everyone* else—refused to carry. We have also been called "Matriarchs," "Superwomen," and "Mean and Evil Bitches." Not to mention "Castrators" and "Sapphire's Mama." When we have pleaded for understanding, our character has been distorted; when we have asked for simple caring, we have been handed empty inspirational appellations, then stuck in the farthest corner. When we have asked for love, we have been given children. In short, even our plainer gifts, our labors of fidelity and love, have been knocked down our throats.[74]

Thus the practice of mothering varies by race. As mothers, women of color in the West face dilemmas not shared by white women. One of the most important of these is how to raise children who can be self-respecting and have a sense of hope and competence while living in cultures that routinely undermine one's dignity and sense of being a legitimate or worthwhile person. Audre Lorde describes some of the contradictions that pervade the experiences of black mothers:

Black women give our children forth into a hatred that seared our own young days, hoping we have taught them something they can use to fashion their own new and less costly pathways to survival. . . . I sat listening to my girl talk about the bent world she was determined to reenter in spite of all she was saying, because she views a knowledge of that world as part of an arsenal which she can use to change it all. I listened, hiding my pained need to snatch her back into the web of my smaller protections. I sat watching while she worked it out bit by hurtful bit—what she really wanted—feeling her rage wax and wane, feeling her anger building against me because I could not help her do it nor do it for her, nor would she allow it.[75]

This dilemma deeply affects the character of the alliance and tensions between mothers and daughters in black and other "minority group" families, just as the existence of racism affects women of color's need from and experiences within families more generally. Paule Marshall writes about some of the complexities of black families' experiences:

Selina listened. For always the mother's voice was a net flung wide, ensnaring all within its reach. She swayed helpless now within its hold, loving its rich color, loving and hating the mother for the pain of her childhood. The image of her father swaggering through the town as a boy and bounding on the waves in some rough game slanted across that of the small girl hurrying from the dawn ghosts with the basket on her head. It seemed to Selina that her father carried those gay days in his irresponsible smile, while the mother's formidable aspect was the culmination of all that she had suffered . . . inside she was frightened by the thought of those memories always clashing within the mother. She was afraid that they would rend the mother soon and kill her finally, and she would be left without her. The world would collapse then, for wasn't the mother, despite all, its only prop?[76]

In considering difference white women must acknowledge and confront the importance of the opposition black/white that has so deeply structured the history of the West and through colonization the rest of the world. Women (of color and white) cannot be exempt from the many subtle and not so subtle consequences of this binary and asymmetric opposition. White women cannot enter into meaningful discourse with women of color wherever this "difference" remains excluded. Why would women of color listen to us when the very categories of our writing prohibit such differences from being named?[77]

The category of "discourse" or the symbolic seems as problematic and homogenized as that of "women" or the feminine. It is ironic for a discourse that so stresses multiplicity that within one of its central concepts—the symbolic—are collapsed activities and organizations as varied as the state, law, production of goods, television, advertising, and literary texts. All these disparate activities and organizations are treated as "the same" (e.g., as systems of signification or representation). A common logic is said to govern them all. One consequence of this unitary approach is that very different domains are treated as isomorphic. Displacing the "authority" of an author of a text becomes as "revolutionary" as overthrowing the authority of a state or law. Writing literary criticism becomes equivalent to any other activity in the symbolic realm, for example, political action. Hence the literary critic can make claims like the following: "Much like any other radical critic, the feminist critic can be seen as the product of a struggle mainly concerned with social and political change; her specific role is to extend such general political action to the cultural domain. This cultural/political battle is necessarily two pronged; it must work to realize its objective both through institutional changes and through the medium of literary criticism."[78] As this quote reveals, a problem with such unitary thinking is that texts, signs, or significa- tion tend to take on a life of their own or become the world. Soon it seems "nothing" exists outside of a text; everything is a comment upon or a displacement of another text, as if the modal human activity is literary criticism or writing. Such an approach obscures the projec- tion of its own activity into the world and denies the existence of the variety of concrete social practices that enter into and are reflected in the constitution of language itself. The fact that a variety of activities may or must be represented in consciousness does not make them all the same—or imply that the "best" way to analyze them is in terms of such representation.

The lack of attention to concrete social relations and the qualitative differences among them, such as the distribution of power, results, as in Lacan's work, in the obscuring of relations of domination, includ- ing those *among* women, such as race. Treated this way, relations of domination tend to acquire an aura of inevitability or become equated with language as such. Attention shifts from the many and varied sources of women's oppression to "whether or not we can in fact es- cape from the structuring imposed by language."[79]

Discourse *becomes* a closed system in which the writer becomes a prisoner of the oppositions she intended to deconstruct. For example, much of the writing on difference seems to assume and perpetuate a radical, even ontological rather than socially constructed disjunction between sign/mind/male and body/nature/female. Some feminists' prescription for the recovery (or reconstitution?) of female experi- ence—"writing from the body"—seems problematic without assum- ing and sustaining this sort of (Cartesian) disjunction. Without it how could feminine desire be emancipatory or exist "outside" or be dis- ruptive of phallocentric discourse and culture? Yet because the (preoedipal) body is said to be presocial and prelinguistic, what could it say to the speaking subjects already formed by existing systems of signification? The end point of this logic seems to be woman *qua* woman would once again be consigned to silence. Within the bound- aries of this discursive practice, perhaps Lacan is more honest than his feminist critics and appropriators.

Prisoners of Gender:
Ambivalence and Anxiety in
Feminist Theory

All the stories posited as explanations for gender relations may be more or less important, interrelated, and themselves partially constituted in and through gender arrangements in a particular context. As in any form of social analysis, the study of gender relations will necessarily reflect the social practices it attempts to understand.

From a psychoanalytic perspective the tensions and repressions often found within feminine identities appear to be reflected and played out in feminist discourse as well. Feminist discourse is marked by ambivalence, omissions, and gaps. Underlying and partially motivating these gaps are contradictory feelings about sexuality, motherhood, and autonomy that enter into the structure of feminist discourse in its present forms. Anxiety and the need to split off or deny our own ambivalences are revealed in the positing of conceptions such that only one perspective can be "correct" or properly feminist. Such intolerance and desire for premature closure also indicate the embeddedness of feminist theorists in the very social processes and psychological structures we are trying to critique and our need for more systematic and self-conscious theoretical self-reflection.

As feminist theorizing is presently practiced, we seem to lose sight of the possibility that each of our conceptions of a practice may capture an aspect of a very complex and contradictory set of social relations. Confronted with complex and changing relations, we try to reduce these to simple, unified, and undifferentiated wholes. We search for closure or the right answer or the "motor" of the history of male domination. The complexity of our questions and the variety of the approaches to them are taken as signs of weakness or failure to meet the strictures of preexisting theories rather than as symptoms of the permeability and pervasiveness of gender relations and the need for new sorts of theorizing.

Some of these reductive or oppositional moves have become evident by juxtaposing the variety of stories about gender relations. Among them I would include the following: the constriction of "embodiedness" to a glorification of the distinctively female aspects of our anatomy.[80] This reduction limits a consideration of the many other ways in which we experience our embodiedness (e.g., the many non-sexualized pleasures or the processes of aging or of pain). It also replicates the equation of women and body—as if men did not have bodies also! Alternatively, there is a tendency simply to deny or neglect the meaningfulness or significance of bodily experience within both men's and women's lives or to reduce it to a subset of "relations of production" or reproduction.

Within feminist discourse women sometimes seem to be the sole "bearers" of both embodiedness and difference. Thus we see arguments by those who call themselves feminists for the necessity to preserve a gender-based division of labor as the last barrier against de-personalizing and atomizing state power. In such arguments the family is posited as an intimate, affective realm of natural relations—of kinship ties, primarily between mothers, children, and female kin. This "family" is opposed to the impersonal realms of the state and work (the worlds of men).[81] Alternatively, feminists sometimes simply deny that there are any significant differences between men and women or that, insofar as such differences exist, women should become more like men or engage in men's activities. Or the family is understood only as the site of gender struggle and the "reproduction" of persons—a miniature political economy with its own division of labor, source of surplus (women's labor), and product (children and workers). The complex fantasies and conflicting wishes and experiences women associate with family and home often remain unexpressed and unacknowledged.[82] Lacking such self-analysis, feminists find it difficult to recognize some of the sources of our differences or to accept that not everyone shares the same past or needs in the present.[83]

Female sexuality is sometimes reduced to an expression of male dominance, as when MacKinnon claims that "gender socialization is the process through which women come to identify themselves as sexual beings, as beings that exist for men."[84] Among many other problems such a definition leaves unexplained how women could ever feel lust for another woman and the wide variety of other sensual experiences women claim to have—for example, in masturbation, breast feeding, or playing with children. Alternatively, the "essence" of female sexuality is said to be rooted in the quasi-biological primal bonds between mother and daughter.[85]

Our fantasies and internal worlds are said to have expression only in symbols, not actual social relations, as when, for example, Iris Young claims that gender differentiation as a "category" refers only to "ideas, symbols and forms of consciousness." [86] In this view fantasy, our inner worlds, and sexuality may structure "intimate" relations between men and women at home, but they are rarely seen as also entering into and shaping the structure of work and the state. Thus feminist theory re-creates its own version of the "public/private" split. Alternatively, as in some radical feminist accounts, "innate" male drives, especially aggression and the "need" to dominate others, are posited as the "motor," substance, and teleology of history. [87]

Feminist theorists have delineated many of the ways in which women's consciousness is shaped by mothering, but we often still see "fathering" as somehow extrinsic to men's and children's consciousness. [88] The importance of child-rearing modes to women's status and men's and women's sense of self is emphasized by feminist theorists; yet we still write social theory in which everyone is presumed to be an adult. For example, two recent collections of feminist theory focusing on mothering and the family contain almost no discussion of children as concrete human beings or mothering as a *relation* between persons. [89] The modal "person" in feminist theory still appears to be a self-sufficient individual adult.

Our upbringing as women in this culture often encourages us to deny the many subtle forms of aggression that our being in intimate relations with others can evoke and entail. Much of the discussion of mothering and the distinctively female tends to avoid discussing women's anger and aggression—how we internalize them and act them out on our children and our internal selves. Women may not be any less aggressive than men. We may express our aggression in different but equally culturally sanctioned and partially disguised or denied ways. Sometimes feminist theorists also tend to oppose "autonomy" and "being in relations." These theorists do not see that, for adults, forms of being in relation can be claustrophobic without autonomy, and autonomy without being in relations can easily degenerate into mastery.

In insisting upon the existence and power of such relations of domination, we should not fall into the victim's viewpoint: That is, we need to avoid seeing women as totally innocent, acted upon beings. [90] Such a view prevents us from seeing the areas of life in which women have had an effect, are not totally determined by the will of the other, and the ways in which some women have and do exert power over others (e.g., the differential privileges of race, class, sexual preference, age, and location in the world system).[91]

Some of the problems within feminist theory reflect and are rooted in our difficulties in thinking relationally about gender as well as in the ways we think about or do not think about thinking itself. The difficulties in thinking have social roots, including the existence of relations of domination as well as the psychological consequences of our current modes of child rearing. Sustaining domination requires denying the interrelation and interdependence of one group upon another. Connections can be traced only so far before they begin to be politically dangerous. For example, few white feminists have explored how our understandings of gender relations, self, and theory are partially constituted in and through the experiences of living in a culture in which asymmetric race relations are a central organizing principle of society.[92] Relations of domination are transformed into prohibitions upon thought.

The enterprise of feminist theory is fraught with temptations and pitfalls. Inasmuch as women *have been* part of all societies, our thinking cannot be free from the modes of self-understanding of the cultures in which we live. We as well as men internalize the dominant gender's conceptions of masculinity and femininity. Unless we see gender as a social relation, rather than a set of opposite and inherently different beings, we will not be able to identify women's or men's full part in and how we are affected by particular societies.

Feminist theorists are still faced with a fourfold task: We need (1) to articulate feminist viewpoints of and within the social worlds in which we live, (2) to think about how we are affected by these worlds, (3) to think about how our thinking about them may itself be implicated in existing power/knowledge relationships, and (4) to think also about the ways in which these worlds ought and can be transformed.

We still need to search into all aspects of a society for the expressions and consequences of relations of domination. Such exploration is far from complete; we have identified only the less subtle of phallocentrism's manifestations. Because so much remains unknown about the constitution and effects of gender relations, we should first assume that such relations are social, that is, not the result of the differentiated possession of natural or unequal properties among persons, until evidence to the contrary is amassed.

We also need to recover and explore the aspects of social relations that have been suppressed, unarticulated, or denied within the master's (male) viewpoints. We need to recover and write the histories of women and our activities into the accounts and stories that cultures tell about themselves. Yet we also need to think about how so-called "women's" activities are partially constituted by and through their location within the web of social relations that make up any "society." We need to know how they are affected by and also affect or enable or compensate for the consequences of "masculine" activities and their implication in class or race relations as well.

Feminist theorists have made radical discoveries and have shed new light on the dark continent of women's lives. We have also begun the task of tracking the effects of gender relations and male dominance throughout histories and cultures. Yet these same discourses are necessarily limited. Too many white feminist theorists have ignored or marginalized the voices of women of color in the West and throughout the world. Like Foucault, I do not think such omissions are accidental, unnecessary, or unrelated to the character of the "whole."[93] As we saw in the discussion of the category "mother" or "women," disciplined consideration of the multiplicity of experiences of concrete women or mothers destroys the unitary representation or truth claim of the (dominant) voice.

Hence I would argue, despite an understandable attraction to the (apparently) logical, orderly world of the Enlightenment, feminist theory more properly belongs in the terrain of postmodern philosophy. Feminist notions of self, knowledge, and truth are too contradictory to those of the Enlightenment to be contained within its categories. The way(s) to feminist future(s) cannot lie in reviving or appropriating Enlightenment concepts of the person or knowledge. Our lives and alliances belong with those who seek to decenter the world further—although as we will see in Chapter 6, feminists and psychoanalysts ought to be suspicious of their motives and visions as well. Feminist theorists, like other postmodernists, should encourage us to tolerate, invite, and interpret ambivalence, ambiguity, and multiplicity, as well as to expose the roots of our needs for imposing order and structure no matter how arbitrary and oppressive these may be. If we do our work well, "reality" will appear even more unstable, complex, and disorderly than it does now. In this sense perhaps Freud was right when he declared that women are the enemies of civilization.[94]

Part Four

Knowledge in Question

Six

Postmodernism

Thinking in Fragments

No one knows who will live in this cage in the future, or whether at the end of this tremendous development entirely new prophets will arise, or there will be a great rebirth of old ideas and ideals, or if neither, mechanized petrification embellished with a sort of convulsive self-importance. For of the last stage of this cultural development, it might be truly said: "Specialists without spirit, sensualists without heart; this nullity imagines that it has attained a level of civilization never before achieved."

> Max Weber, *The Protestant Ethic and the Spirit of Capitalism*

But cleverness becomes meaningless as soon as power ceases to obey the rules and chooses direct appropriation instead. The medium of the traditional bourgeois intelligence—that is discussion—then breaks down. Individuals can no longer talk to each other and know it: they therefore make the game into a serious and responsible institution which requires the application of all available strength to ensure that there is no proper conversation and at the same time no silence.

> Max Horkheimer and Theodor Adorno, *The Dialectic of Enlightenment*

We are wondering about the meaning of a necessity: the necessity of lodging oneself within traditional conceptuality in order to destroy it . . . does it hide . . . some indestructible and unforeseeable resource of the Greek logos? Some unlimited power of envelopment by which he who attempts to repel it would also already be overtaken?

> Jacques Derrida, "Violence and Metaphysics"

Fragments

Like the category "feminist theory," "postmodern philosophy" does not correspond to any actual or unified discourse. The persons and modes of thinking aggregated under the category of postmodernism are quite heterogeneous in regard to voice, style, content, and concerns. Jacques Derrida, Richard Rorty, Jean-François Lyotard, and Michel Foucault are four particularly influential writers associated with postmodernism. Yet each writer's focus and the salience he assigns to certain issues differ. Derrida has a special concern for ontological questions, including the "misrepresentation" of Being, "writing," and the "tyranny of metaphysics." Rorty is interested in epistemology and the history of philosophy, especially the traditional practices and concepts of philosophy and truth and alternatives to them. Lyotard and Foucault focus on relations between truth, power, legitimation, and the "subject." By even speaking of "postmodernism," I run the risk of violating some of its central values—heterogeneity, multiplicity, and difference. Postmodernists claim, however, that the "fictive" and nonunitary nature of concepts need not negate their meaningfulness or usefulness. Therefore I will assume here it is possible to speak of "postmodernism." Although internally varied, postmodernist discourses _are_ unified in identifying certain subjects of conversation as particularly appropriate to and necessary for "our" time. These crucial subjects include: (1) contemporary Western culture—its nature and the best ways to understand it; (2) knowledge—what it is, who or what constructs and generates it, and its relations to power; (3) philosophy—its crisis and history, how both are to be understood, and how (if at all) it is to be practiced; (4) power—if, where, and how domination exists and is maintained and how and if it can be overcome; (5) subjectivity and the self—how our concepts and experiences of them have come to be and what, if anything, these do or can mean; and (6) difference—how to conceptualize, preserve, or rescue it. Postmodernists are also unified in their rejections of certain positions. They all reject representational and objective or rational concepts of knowledge and truth; grand, synthetic theorizing meant to comprehend Reality as and in a unified whole; and any concept of self or subjectivity in which it is not understood as produced as an effect of discursive practices.

Furthermore postmodernists all share a common framework

within which they attempt to conceptualize contemporary Western culture. All define Western culture by its struggle with, in, and against *modernism*.[1] My primary disagreement with and disappointment in postmodernist thinking is that this struggle, and hence postmodernists' understanding of contemporary Western culture, is primarily (re)situated and understood as occurring within the history of Western *philosophy*. Postmodernist discourse is constituted by and in a series of attempts to close doors or paths back to Enlightenment modes of thinking or promises of happiness. This is precisely what I find most valuable and problematic about it. Unlike the work of other radical critics such as Habermas or Marcuse, the postmodernists question the necessity and desirability of completing the "project of modernity" or making good on the "emancipatory" promises of bourgeois culture/Enlightenment.[2] By rejecting the teleological view of history implicit in such claims, the postmodernists encourage us to create alternative modes of thinking and practice outside this project's imperative. Disrupting the equation of modernity, enlightenment, and emancipation opens a space to explore the "dark side" of reason and modernity in greater depth than Horkheimer and Adorno were able to do.[3] The postmodernists go beyond their critique to throw into doubt the ideas that reason is the necessary ground for philosophy or freedom and that an emancipatory culture will arise if and when the "negative" aspects of modernity (or "modernization" in Habermas's terms) can be *"aufheben."* To the advocates of modernity, the postmodernists say we need "something else." What this something else might be, either in philosophy or practice, is not clear. This "lack" is one of the reasons postmodernism is more successful as a critique of philosophy and modernity than as a theory of the postmodern as such.

Postmodernism is a valuable form of discipline philosophers impose on themselves. Postmodernists generate intradiscourse warnings and limitations: No, you can't do that. That way lies grandiosity, illusion, the seductive tyranny of metaphysics, truth, the real. They also articulate, reflect, and exemplify a belated shift in philosophic consciousness and some of its paradoxes and limitations. This shift is a response to fundamental changes in Western culture and the epistemological and sociopolitical consequences of these transformations. In the realm of knowledge, postmodernism represents philosophic attempts to come to grips with the displacement of philosophy from any privileged relation to truth and knowledge. In post-seventeenth-century Western culture philosophy as the enunciator, representative, or guarantor of truth has gradually been displaced, first by the natural sciences and then by the so-called "human" sciences. Despite such rearguard skirmishes as may be found in the "philosophy of science" or attempts by logical positivists to scientize philosophy, no one except a few philosophers really pays attention to philosophers' epistemological judgments. Philosophers may evaluate whether certain "truth claims" are "warranted," but the practitioners of the allegedly problematic practices continue, by and large, to be unconcerned and unaffected by the philosophers' judgments of them. Scientists would not grant philosophy a place as the "queen of the sciences." Nor would they turn to it for a more accurate understanding of their own "logic of discovery."

Philosophers' repeated attacks on psychoanalysis or "technical reason" are in part battles for terrain and dominance.[4] Despite their claims, postmodernists are not willing to abandon this terrain. Although Plato considered poetry and drama as his rivals to the claim to represent truth, today conflict exists between philosophy and the sciences of "man" and nature. But practically speaking, in contemporary Western culture the philosopher literally and figuratively can produce nothing. Hence, philosophy has already lost. Marx was perhaps more correct than he knew when he stated: "The philosophers have only *interpreted* the world, in various ways; the point, however, is to change it."[5] This, however, philosophy cannot do.

Faced with philosophy's impotence in a relentlessly materialistic and nonmetaphysical Western world, the would-be philosopher could pursue several strategies. Instead of practicing "pure" philosophy, one might enter into an alliance with science and create a new form of "practical reason," as for example in the neo-Kantian and Weberian "policy sciences." Alternatively, ceding the "material" world to the scientist or denying its existence, one might attempt to reclaim the world by "textualizing" it. Here language plays a doubly mediating role in the following series of claims. There can be no (practical) thought without language, and thought within the modern world has no practical effect without being transformed into writing or texts that are "disseminated." Hence there is no world outside the text. Philosophers can reclaim terrain; as theoreticians of writing or texts, their place is resecured. By claiming to "know" the endless heterogeneity and undecidability of texts, philosophers can displace or "set to play" any particular truth claim among others. "There is no truth" is merely the equal and opposite of "these are the conditions that all truth claims must meet." Confronted with the philosopher's failure and impotence to change the world, one can make a counterclaim: Everything *is* interpretation in various and unending ways. The reader is enticed into a (Kantian) discussion of what cannot be known, what *cannot* be done. The philosopher is necessary to show us our errors, limitations, and "excesses."

But who is this "us"? Here a suspicious but seductive compounding of the philosopher and "the others" emerges. Certainly a major contributing factor to the philosopher's displacement or crisis of confidence is the revolt of the others against any unifying authoritative voice. The voices of the others include nonphilosophical modes of formal knowledge. Equally important are what Foucault calls the "subjugated discourses." Among these are the voices of women and people of color throughout the world. These voices have enunciated a "great refusal" on a scale not even Marcuse dared to dream.

The voices of others radically undermine the philosopher's claims to representation. Such representational claims have many different components: that there is *a* truth to be represented, that there is *a* subject of history, that there is *an* emancipatory project, that there is *a* form of progress that *a* reason can discern and make real. Here too philosophers may accept displacement or try to reclaim terrain. They may attempt to dictate the form these voices ought to take (conversation), to cut off clamorous accounts of alternative experiences by proclaiming the nonexistence of subjectivity, or to forestall discomforting, heterogeneous demands for justice by disconnecting all possible interrelations between knowledge(s), truths, and emancipation(s). As we will see later in this chapter, each of these tactics appears at some point within postmodernist texts.

Like psychoanalysis and feminist theories, postmodernism is ambivalent and ambiguous as a transitional mode of thinking. In its closure vis-à-vis Enlightenment, postmodernism has much to contribute to the deconstruction of certain authoritarian forms of thought and practice, including its own. Although it cuts off certain moves "backward," the same postmodernist devices make it more difficult for the others to be heard. There is a danger of being seduced by its claims to set free the play of differences. Unfortunately, postmodernist philos-

ophers are not free from a will to power whose effects they trace elsewhere. A cooptation of the others and an effacement of the traces of
these maneuvers frequently result. This double erasing may account
for some of the obscurity in the writing of postmodernism; tracks
have to be erased or effaced as they are made.

Ultimately, I will argue, in their naming of the most fundamental
problems of contemporary Western culture, postmodernists, like critical theorists before them, succumb to the "siren's mythic song."[6] Although philosophy is supposed to become only one voice in the "conversation of mankind [*sic*]," what the philosopher "really does"—
conversation or writing—retains a privileged place within much of
postmodernist thought. Therefore I will treat postmodernist discourse as one, internally varied, necessarily imperfect, and partial set
of stories about contemporary Western culture. These stories capture
some important elements of a more complex plot but obscure others.
The incompleteness of postmodernist stories is not the problem that
concerns me. Like other postmodernists I do not believe it is possible
ever to capture the "truth" of the "whole." The problem is rather that
postmodernists repress, exclude, and erase certain voices and questions I think should be heard and included. This excluded or repressed material includes many of the ideas and social relations feminists and psychoanalytic theorists correctly believe are essential to
understanding self, knowledge, and power. Hence postmodernist
discourses must be supplemented and interrogated by the others.

Postmodernist Deconstructions of Knowledge

This is a paradox of postmodernism: If philosophy *is* so problematic
as knowledge, and if its claims as the representative of truth are so
unwarranted, then why is it worthy of anyone's attention—even as
the object of critique? Part of the answer lies in the postmodernist
equation of knowledge and philosophy.

Postmodernists paradoxically accept fundamental Enlightenment
tenets—the identification of Western culture and self-understanding
with reason and of reason with philosophy. They believe the history
of the West *is* the history of reason and philosophy. This is a negative
history, one in which domination, exclusion, and asymmetry are the
true concealed effects. Western culture is imprisoned in and by meta-

physics. An understanding of the failure of Enlightenment must therefore be achieved by an immanent critique of reason. The focus of this critique should be philosophy because it is seen as reason's primary representation and representative. Relations of domination are understood as effects of this imprisonment, not as its origin or source.

A (postmodernist) deconstruction of the history of Western philosophy reveals at least three errors at the heart of Western culture and thought: (1) a misrepresentation of the real that necessarily entails the suppression of difference (the violence of metaphysics), (2) an obsession with and misapprehension and overvaluation of the redemptive or emancipatory qualities of truth, and (3) the constitution of the "self" as the "subject" of knowledge in the double sense of subject of and subject to. These three errors are necessary in and to the construction of Western thought/philosophy. They cannot be resolved, avoided, or transcended within its context. Hence the unveiling of these errors must lead to a conviction of the necessity of the displacement of the mainstream practices of Western philosophy (and culture?). The deconstructionists do not intend to counterpose an alternative *philosophy* that would more "adequately" "solve" the problems of being, truth, or subjectivity. Rather they wish to persuade us not to ask the old questions anymore, to change the subjects of the conversation completely.

Derrida, Rorty, Foucault, and Lyotard all conceptualize philosophy fundamentally as episteme—as knowledge and as knowledge about knowledge. This concept of philosophy does reflect an aspect of philosophic practice. Since Kant, philosophy has sustained itself in part by claiming special insight into the "foundations" of human knowledge and the conditions of its possibility. Epistemology is to provide a firm grounding for the queen of sciences. Other forms of philosophy such as ethics or aesthetics are nonfoundational, hence less important.

These writers do not treat this overvaluation of epistemology as a curious quirk of some professional philosophers to be understood in relation to the sociology or history of the profession. Rather they believe it reveals something about the "essence" of philosophy itself. In turn the "dominant" Western concept of philosophy is said to reveal and mirror certain problems and fundamental qualities of Western culture. To the extent that all experience is textual or interpretative, ways of thinking cannot be separated from ways of being. Rorty argues, for example, "you won't understand the West unless you understand what it was like to be bothered by the kinds of issues that bothered Plato."[7]

Thus in postmodernist writings knowledge is still conceptualized as originating in and expressed through *thought*, even if thought is to be understood in relation to language rather than the intention or consciousness of an individual or collective subject. Except for Foucault, postmodernists define and confine knowledge by what can be linguistically expressed. Under the cover of the "displacement" of philosophy, a traditional activity continues: an inquiry into the conditions of possibility, meaning, and limitations of our *knowledge* via a critique of reason and philosophy.

The continuing privilege of philosophy in relation to *knowledge* is revealed by the fact that the inquiry is undertaken in the form of a deconstruction of epistemology and metaphysics. Alternate approaches are not explored. Alternatives do exist; for example, Melanie Klein postulates the existence of an epistemophiliac instinct arising out of and expressed through the infant's curiosity about and exploration of the mother's body.[8] The inquiry into the conditions of knowledge is then framed within an investigation of child-rearing practices, fantasy, research on infant development and neurophysiology, and so forth. Yet this is clearly not a postmodernist approach. For postmodernists knowledge and philosophy as well as knowledge and reason and knowledge and the subject are inextricably tied. Both the inquiry into the nature of knowledge and the possibility of shifting an understanding of knowing are located within the terrain of the history of philosophy.

Nonetheless for anyone trained in relatively traditional ways of philosophizing, reading postmodernist texts is a frustrating task. Intrinsic to traditional philosophy is the demand to "give reasons," to offer a set of arguments for why x is better than y. It is precisely this sort of discourse that postmodernism seeks to displace. Derrida claims the goal is not the end of philosophy, but reading it in a certain way. This way of reading generates a series of interpretations through which a story emerges. A fictive entity, for example, "philosophy," is constructed. The narrative is to lead to the conclusion that it is impossible to philosophize in the traditional way. The story of knowledge, philosophy, and thought becomes a narrative of its own deconstruction seen as such (as in Hegel's dialectics) by a consciousness that can grasp the hidden "essence" of philosophy. This essence is composed of self-reflexivity, acts of exclusion and self-generation, intertextuality, and lack of relation to the real. The impossibility and self-contradictions of "philosophy" are not demonstrated in a logical, cumulative argument. Both logic and any notion of the progression to "truth" are themselves suspect. The strategy is to construct an alternative narrative whose rhetorical force is to displace the traditional self-understanding of mainstream Western thought.

Much of the force of this counternarrative is derived, as postmodernists argue about other forms of philosophy, from its own acts of exclusion and construction. It is important to emphasize at the outset that the philosophy postmodernists seek to displace *is* a fiction, chosen (in some sense) as a maximally effective rhetorical device. The history of philosophy could be told in many different ways. By the logic of postmodernism itself, the adequacy of any of these stories can be judged only by the effects produced and by whether and to the extent that such stories open up or permit further, interesting conversation to proceed. Nor could only one (his)story of philosophy be "true." Postmodernists claim the construction and choice of one story over others is not governed by a relation to truth, but by less innocent factors. These ultimately include a will to power partially constituted by and expressing a desire *not* to hear certain other voices or stories. However from feminist or psychoanalytic viewpoints the absences postmodernists evoke and attend to in their discourses or in those of others are not necessarily the most salient ones.[9]

The postmodernist tendency to collapse the histories of Western philosophy and culture is perhaps most evident in the work of Jacques Derrida, who writes, "What has seemed necessary and urgent to me, in the historical situation which is our own, is a general determination of the conditions for the emergence and limits of philosophy, of metaphysics, of everything that carries it on and that it carried on."[10] Derrida believes the misrepresentation of Being is intrinsic to the "founding" of Western philosophy. It has been dominated by the metaphysics of presence, by the desire and claim to represent the real. The real of philosophy is not the Real of Being, but rather an artifact and consequence of certain philosophic practices. These entail both inclusion and exclusion. The exclusions are not neutral or extrinsic to the discourses or the cultures that follow the founding. Instead they actually determine and dominate their texture.

Derrida's deconstruction of the misrepresentation of the Real presupposes and depends upon his own, often covert ontological premises. For him the Real does have a (mystical) essence. It is heterogeneous, infinitely open, and governed by chance. The philosopher's
task is to invoke rather than present the Real. Any attempt at representation results in a reduction of the Real to what can be present
to consciousness and hence becomes its equivalent (the same). These
attempts do violence to Being. They enclose its otherness, chance,
and heterogeneity within the homogeneity of a consciousness whose
contents are to be transparent and not alien to itself. All of Derrida's
key moves and concepts (differance, chance, deferral, spacing, writing, supplement, trace, and other) are bound up with the attempt to
evoke a nonrational Real without transforming it into the Same of
consciousness, reason, and logic. As we will see, these concepts also
turn out to be related inextricably to another one: "woman." As in
Lacan's work "Woman" turns out to ground and represent "other" in
many complex and partially "veiled" ways.

   Derrida's primary criticism of mainstream Western philosophy is
directed at its incapacity to respect "the Being and meaning of the
other." Since Socrates, Western philosophy has been dominated "by a
Reason which receives only what it gives itself, a Reason which does
nothing but recall itself to itself." Its "ontology is tautology and egol-
ogy. . . . It has always neutralized the other, in every sense of the
word." Western philosophies have thus been philosophies of violence
or philosophies of power. In its suppression, exclusion, and transformation of the Other to the Same, "the entire philosophical tradition,
in its meaning and at bottom, would make common cause with
oppression. . . . To see and to know, to have and to will, unfold only
within the oppressive and luminous identity of the same." The equation within philosophy of the Real with what can be seen by and in
the light of reason provides an alibi "for the historical violence of
light: a displacement of technico-political oppression in the direction
of philosophic discourse."[11]

   The ontology of Western philosophy permits and requires us to
turn our glance away from "the origin of the world"—the other. This
other is "the inaccessible, the invisible, the intangible, secret, sepa-
rable, invisible." It is absence and the nonphenomenal. It is the trace,
not a Being perfectly seen and re-presented in thought. It is difference
(alterity without contradiction or end): "the infinity which no thought

can enclose and which forbids all monologue." The other's alterity is absolutely irreducible, that is, infinitely irreducible, and "the infinitely other can only be Infinity."[12]

The other can be invoked by speech but never captured by or represented in it. It moves through texts and between them in a general economy of the infinite play of meanings. It can be approached only by desire, not Reason. The proper relation to it is one of respect and separation, not consumption or mastery. Its truth cannot be grasped and represented once and for all. The other is thus the limit of Reason because it is "unthinkable and impossible." It cannot be re-presented in or through concepts or in logocentric discourse (the coherent discourse of reason). The other "interrupts all historical totalities through its freedom of speech."[13] It is under no obligation to mean, to be, to conclude; it exceeds all meaning, truth, unities, or totalities. It is *writing*, not philosophy. The repression of writing/the other/difference constitutes "the origin of philosophy and *episteme*, and of truth as the unity of *logos* and *phone*." The unity and homogeneity of thought, the system, the subject, Reason, the Real is made possible and is "haunted" by this repression. The traces of the repressed are everywhere within these apparent unities for those who know how to evoke them, for "repression as Freud says, neither repels nor flees, nor excludes an exterior force, it contains an interior representation, laying out within itself a space of repression." These traces "can no longer be represented except by the structure and functioning of writing."[14]

Unlike philosophy, writing is *not* bound up with the myth of an "originary or modified form of presence."[15] In writing, the play of differences circulates in and through texts. Texts like the other do not *mean*. There is nothing (no presence already there) they are trying to represent in or to consciousness. Texts cannot be univocal because they are constituted of and by written signs, signs that already exist, have always already existed, within a system of relations. As a (or many) system(s) of relations, signification has no single origin or author. Nor does a text. The text is not the product of the consciousness of a singular author making present some aspect of experience, history, or thought. Real writing means to perform, evoke, and operate within and be operated upon by the "scene of writing." This scene is not one of presence, intentionality, or consciousness, but rather of the trace, other, difference, and change. "The trace is the erasure of self-

hood, of one's own presence, and is constituted by the threat or anguish of its irredeemable disappearance, of the disappearance of its
disappearance." "The subject" of writing does not exist if by subject
we mean a sovereign solitude of the author. The subject of writing is
a "system of relations between strata . . . the psyche, society, the
world."[16]

Writing offers an at least partial alternative to or beyond the violence of metaphysics. To write is to open oneself up to chance, to free
oneself from the compulsive linking up of "meaning, concept, time
and truth" that has dominated Western philosophic discourse. Writing involves risk, play, loss of sense and meaning. It rescues the "poetic or ecstatic . . . in every discourse," even philosophy. But in order
to "run this risk in language, in order to save that which does not
want to be saved . . . we must redouble language and have recourse
to ruses, to stratagems, to simulcra." Writing "*exceeds* the *logos* (of
meaning, lordship, presence, etc.)." Unlike the philosopher the
writer renounces "the desire to hold on, to maintain his certainty of
himself and the security of the concept" against the sliding into the
nonmeaning or the excess of meaning, which is the "nonbasis" of an
"unknowledge."[17] This unknowledge is *not* a "moment" (in the He-
gelian sense) of knowledge—but the absolute other, difference, supplement.

To write in this sense is to "transgress the entirety of the history of
meaning and the entirety of the meaning of history, and the project of
knowledge which has always obscurely melded these two together."
It is to "absolve myself of absolute knowledge, putting it back in its
place as such, situating it and inscribing it within a space in which it
no longer dominates." Writing is dedicated to the "indefinite destruction of value." Its predicates are not there in order "to *mean* something, to announce or signify, but in order to make sense slide, to
denounce or deviate from it."[18]

Writing cannot be the completion or *Aufhebung* of philosophy.
Rather, by freeing the poetic traces within it, by desiring the Other
and evoking it, writing can undo the "violence of metaphysics."
"Nonviolent language, in the last analysis, would be a language of
pure invocation." It would do without the verb "to be" because "pred-
ication is the first violence."[19] Freed of the obligation of meaning, of
presenting being and its unity in transparent language, writing effects the destruction from within of philosophic discourse. It "multi-

plies words, precipitates them one against the other, engulfs them too, in an endless and baseless substitution whose only rule is the sovereign affirmation of the play outside meaning." [20]

The "irruptive emergence" of the scene of writing poses the unanswerable "question of speech and meaning." [21] Writing is also the space of the other—of dissemination, of an "irreducible and generative multiplicity, the supplement and the turbulence of a certain lack fracture the limit of the text, forbidding an exhaustive and closed formalization of it." [22] Only within this space can we hope to encounter the Being with no name, the (unrepresentably) Real. This is the space also of "strategies" for endless readings, not for representing the Real in an en-closed final totality. This space is to be the dis-placement of philosophy.

Derrida's concept of the Real is somewhat contradictory. On the one hand any finite, unitary concept of the Real is said to be merely an effect of a delimited set of (deconstructable) philosophic strategies or metaphysical claims about the nature of Being. On the other hand Derrida does make ontological statements about the Real. It is "really" heterogeneous, fluctuating, infinitely open, and governed by chance, not logic or an immanent *telos* unfolding inexorably in and over time. Furthermore there is one practice, writing, that seems to have a privileged relationship to this Real.

If taken seriously, this view of the Real and of "writing" undermines or renders problematic many traditional philosophic concepts of Truth and of the relation of Truth to emancipation, freedom, or justice. Although Rorty, Foucault, and Lyotard have somewhat different views of the Real, they all attack the "metaphysics of presence." They treat "philosophy, truth, goodness and rationality [as] interlocked Platonic notions." [23] The postmodernist intent is to deconnect and dislocate these notions in both philosophical and political/practical discourses. All these philosophers assume that any transcendental or representational theory of truth is necessarily false. This conclusion follows from one or both of these postmodernist tenets: metaphysical claims about the nature of reality and epistemological ones about the nature of thought/mind as intrinsically nontranscendental, historical, linguistic, and context dependent.

If reality is infinitely open and fluctuating, it, like texts, generates an infinitely large number of possible interpretations and material for interpretations. Closure is merely an effect of a philosophic strategy,

as are all systems claiming to be based on self-evident or transcendental axioms. Truth cannot be conceptualized in terms of completeness,
adequation, transcendence, or self-identity. It cannot be the representation or mirror of an eternal or universal substance ("presence") or
subject because none exists. Truth can no longer be understood in
terms of a correspondence to the Real because the Real always exceeds and escapes our thinking about it. As Derrida says, the problem
is not that there is no truth, but that there is "too much" truth.[24]

The "origin" of thought in any case is "preconceptual." It exceeds
and is other than all logic or logical systems. Postmodernists argue
that thought is irreducibly linguistic; it can be practiced only in and
through historical and context-dependent "language games" or "discourses." The effect of truth is produced only through discourse, that
is, in and through systems of signification or practice. "There are no
criterion that we have not created in the course of creating a practice,
no standard of rationality that is not an appeal to such a criterion, no
rigorous argumentation that is not obedience to our own conventions."[25] But these systems themselves are generated by interpretations of previous such systems. Hence they too are infinitely open,
heterogeneous, and subject to further interpretation and change.
There is no Reality for us outside such systems because, as Rorty argues, "there is no way to think about either the world or our purposes
except by using our language." We cannot step out of "the traditions,
linguistic and other, within which we do our thinking and self-
criticism and compare ourselves with something absolute." We
should thus "drop" the notion of truth as correspondence to reality
altogether, for we "never encounter reality except under a chosen description."[26]

The notion of truth as correspondence to the Real rests in part
upon mistaken ideas about both philosophy and ethics. Since Plato,
some philosophers have seen the idea of an absolute, transcendental
truth as a necessary foundation and condition of possibility for desired human outcomes such as justice. Somehow "asking questions
about the nature of certain normative notions (for instance, 'truth,'
'rationality,' 'goodness')" has been seen as necessarily connected to
redeeming "the hope of better obeying such norms."[27]

On the contrary "it will not help to say something true to think
about Truth, nor will it help to act well to think about goodness, nor

will it help to be rational to think about rationality."[28] Truth is merely the name of a property that all true statements share, or a kind of honorific we give to practices or ideas that accord with our cultural assumptions. It is not possible to have an interesting philosophic discussion about such notions. Nor should we expect that conflicts about the meaning of truth, goodness, and so forth can be resolved philosophically. The perennial controversies about these notions throughout the history of philosophy indicate the futility of this expectation. Instead the only test of truth is a pragmatic one: whether some ways of talking and acting are "better" or "pay off" within the context of the needs of a particular culture at a particular time.

"Knowledge is power, a tool for coping with reality." Different sorts of knowledge help us cope with different bits of reality. No kind of knowledge, even science, has a privileged relation to reality or can produce a noncontextual Truth. "Modern science does not help us to cope because it corresponds, it just plain helps us to cope."[29]

Rorty argues that a postmodern culture will also be a postphilosophic one. In postmodern culture philosophy, understood as the desire, attempt, and claim to be able to divide sentences into "an upper and lower division—the sentences that correspond to something and those that are 'true' only by courtesy or convention"—will be abandoned. Instead the philosopher will no longer claim any special relation to Truth or the Real, even *via* "writing." All postmodern philosophers can or should do is "compare and contrast cultural traditions" and languages. They will engage in a process of "playing vocabularies and cultures off against each other" with the hope of seeing how things "hang together" in the broadest sense.[30] The philosopher helps keep "the conversation of mankind" going by providing information about possible "alternative self-images" humans have had and may once again choose. In doing this philosophy can contribute to human "edification" (i.e., the project of finding new, better, more interesting, and more fruitful ways of speaking). These new ways of speaking are also ways of remaking ourselves. Edifying philosophy is to "break the crust of convention, thus preventing man from deluding himself with the notion that he knows himself, or anything else except under optional descriptions."[31] Although edifying philosophies may have an unsettling effect, choices about how to remake ourselves ultimately can be made only by a "slow and painful" social process of discussion.[32] In no case will philosophers or anyone else discover how things "really are" and settle once and for all the questions of how we should live.

To have this view of philosophy is also to forswear or at least question the philosopher's relation to legitimation. Unlike Rorty, Lyotard and Foucault explore the more sinister aspects of the relationship between knowledge and power. Unlike Derrida, neither Lyotard nor Foucault believes "writing" can provide a space beyond or outside power. According to Lyotard any attempt to seek the Truth, rather than play within a circumscribed language game, entails an obligation to "legitimate the rules" of the game. All language games generate their own rules about how to play, what counts as a successful move, and so forth. But by definition these rules are context dependent and valid only within a particular game. Games and their rules are incommensurable. Hence any more general truth claims would have to be made by constructing a "metadiscourse" that has the appearance of universality and neutrality. Such a discourse entails a claim to authority "legitimated" by a particular relation to Truth: "Narrative knowledge makes a resurgence in the West as a way of solving the problem of legitimating the new authorities. It is natural in a narrative problematic for such a question to solicit the name of a hero as its response: *who* has the right to decide for society? Who is the subject whose prescriptions are norms for those they obligate?"[33]

This attempt then "produces a discourse of legitimation with respect to its own status, a discourse called philosophy."[34] Such "metadiscourses" take the form of a "grand narrative" in which the relationship of knowledge to power and to specific language games is obscured. Lyotard argues that two such narratives have dominated the modern Western world: the Enlightenment narrative and the narrative of spirit. In the Enlightenment narrative the philosopher is the representative of universal truth and of humanity whose emancipation will occur through the learning and development of such truth. The exemplar of such a narrative is, of course, Kant. In this narrative "all peoples have a right to science. If the social subject is not already the subject of scientific knowledge, it is because that has been forbidden by priests and tyrants. The right to science must be reconquered." It can be reconquered by creating an enlightened (e.g., representative) state. The spread of new domains of knowledge to the population is the means of winning freedom and progress for the people and the nation as a whole. Only an enlightened people can create and sustain an enlightened state. The state "receives its legitimacy not from itself but from the people," who must be taught to demand and obey a state founded on reason and rational authority.[35]

In turn, claims to power must be made on the basis of claims to knowledge. "The connection of knowledge, legitimacy and power gives rise both to an idea of socially useful but neutral [universal] knowledge and to the creation of agencies and professions whose task is to spread and apply this knowledge throughout the population, thus further emancipating it." Knowledge, power, and emancipation are thus inseparable and interdependent in the Enlightenment narrative; "its epic is the story of [the people's] emancipation from everything that prevents it from governing itself."[36]

The second narrative, of the Spirit, is more philosophical. Its exemplar is Hegel. In this narrative "philosophy must restore unity to learning . . . it can only achieve this in a language game that links the sciences together as moments in the becoming of spirit." The narrator of this story is a "metasubject" whose task is "the process of formulating both the legitimacy of the discourses of the empirical sciences and that of the direct institutions of popular cultures." In contrast to the previous metanarrative, "knowledge first finds legitimacy in itself, and it is knowledge that is entitled to say what the state and society are." Such knowledge also begins to speculate on how it knows what it knows, on how other knowledges know what they know, and on the place of all other knowledges within *its* system of knowing. This narrative assumes that "there is meaning to know and thus confers legitimacy upon history (and especially the history of learning)." Its metasubject "grasps" reality as the unfolding history of a subject who is also the "ground" of learning, society, and the state. From this transcendental standpoint "true knowledge . . . is composed of reported statements that are incorporated into the metanarrative of a subject that guarantees their legitimacy."[37] Inasmuch as philosophy is bound up in "grounding" and constituting these narratives, it is also implicated in the contemporary and oppressive practices of legitimation and power. These two grand narratives condition and shape our belief that truth and justice are necessarily related. On the contrary, like Foucault, Lyotard argues, "truth is of this world."[38] Truth claims must always be understood in relation to political and social practices, not an abstract correspondence to the Real.

Lyotard defines the postmodern in terms of an "incredulity towards metanarratives." This collapse of belief in metanarratives contributes to "the crisis of metaphysical philosophy and of the university which in the past relied on it." Although he does not privilege writing, like Derrida, Lyotard equates the postmodern with that which seeks to "impart a stronger sense of the unpresentable." The postmodern philosopher's obligation is not to "supply reality" or represent humanity or the spirit, but to "invent allusions to the conceivable which cannot be presented." Truth is decoupled from the representation of the Real and instead is placed in the space of the aesthetic, the "sublime," the "event," of "working without rules in order to formulate the rules of what *will have been done*." [39]

The Limits of Postmodernist Discourse: The Subject of Knowledge

In many ways Foucault's work is radically different from that of Derrida, Rorty, and Lyotard. Foucault provides pointed and accurate critiques of some of the ideas of other postmodernists. His emphasis on power and domination and the ways these are conceptualized has been most productive and stimulating for the further development of discourses about justice. However in his treatment of the questions of self and subjectivity, he shares many of the inadequacies of other postmodernists. His inattention to gender relations and the weakness of his alternatives to biopower call for feminist and psychoanalytic critique and supplements.

As Foucault argues, the notion of an avant garde (intellectual) writer who can somehow escape the rules of the dominant "discursive formation" of his or her culture is a self-serving illusion. Through the "relentless theorization of writing," [40] the writer tries to hold on to the Enlightenment privilege of the "universal intellectual" who serves as the voice and representative of a general consciousness, free subject, or at least some transcendental "other" that escapes or is outside of the contingencies and power relations of our time. In granting a primordial status to writing, "we . . . in effect simply reinscribe in transcendental terms the theological affirmation of its sacred origin, or a critical belief in its creative nature." [41]

Unlike Rorty, Foucault is not enamored of the self-understanding and practices of "postmodern bourgeois culture." [42] For Foucault the most important feature of contemporary culture is the process by which humans become "subjects" of knowledge. The "conversation" of this culture generates ever more subtle and extensive exercises of "biopower" and self-deception, rather than more interesting sentences about ourselves. He is also much more attentive than Rorty to the conflict and polyphony of Western culture. Instead of as a relatively benign set of "moves" among fairly equal and homogeneous "partners," Foucault conceptualizes contemporary Western culture as an ongoing struggle between heterogeneous elements that cannot be assimilated. "The history which bears and determines us has the form of war rather than language."[43] There are dominant and marginal discourses, innumerable instances of the effects of power and local resistances to them. Foucault's view provides more space for the acknowledgment and analysis of relations of domination within "bourgeois" Western culture.

Like Lyotard and Rorty, Foucault conceptualizes knowledge as historical, contingent, and always generated by pragmatic questions oriented to action. Knowledge can be produced only within and is an effect of "discursive formations," which originate in historically specific, often random events. They are discontinuous both internally and across time. Internally, a discursive formation is often made up of heterogeneous activities. "What is found at the historical beginnings of things is not the inviolable identity of their origin, it is the dissention of other things, it is disparity."[44] Across time these formations are incommensurable. They are not all (better, worse, or progressive) approximations to one "unsaid thing, or an unthought, floating about the world, interlacing with all its forms and events."[45]

Unlike Rorty, Foucault stresses the role of conflict and violence within "our" practices; "we must conceive discourse as a violence that we do to things, or at all events, as a practice we impose upon them; it is in this practice that the events of discourse find the principle of their regularity."[46] Discursive shifts do not occur as a result of the introduction of a better theory or the emergence of a great, creative mind. They are an effect of changes in the unceasing struggles for power that are a constitutive element of history. Discursive shifts occur when violence is inflicted on violence, and "the resurgence of new forces . . . [is] sufficiently strong to dominate those in power."[47]

A discourse is a system of possibilities for knowledge. Discursive formations are made up in part of sets of usually tacit rules that enable us to identify some statements as true or false, to construct a map, model, or classificatory system in which these statements can be organized, and to name certain "individuals" as authors. The rules provide the necessary precondition for the formation of statements. The place, function, and character of the knowers, authors, and audiences of a discourse are also functions of discursive rules. All discursive formations simultaneously enable us to do certain things and confine us within a necessarily delimited system. "Truth" is simply an effect of the rules of discourse. Because there are no non-discourse-generated rules, there is no external standpoint from which we can claim to judge the truth, falsity, or "adequacy" of a discourse in its entirety. The relationship between words and things is always partial and rooted in discursive rules and commitments that cannot themselves be rationally justified. These tacit rules are usually exposed only when an object of discourse is modified or transformed.

The foundations of a discourse can be located only in power; "all knowledge rests upon injustice."[48] The "will to knowledge" cannot be separated from the will to power even though, as presently constituted in our culture, "the fact of power [is] invariably excluded from knowledge." Contemporary culture effects this exclusion of the fact of power in part by masking power and our subjection to it in the discourse of "humanism." Through this discourse Western man is told, "even though you don't exercise power, you can still be a ruler. Better yet, the more you deny yourself the exercise of power, the more you submit to those in power, then the more this increases your sovereignty."[49]

Like other postmodernists Foucault intends to weaken the hold of "the theory of the subject" and to destroy concepts of the subject as "pseudosovereign." To effect this deconstruction he adopts a strategy with at least two key moves. The first is to destroy any essentialist claims regarding "human nature" by demonstrating the historical origins and contingency of all such notions. Like Rorty and Derrida, Foucault denies that there is really anything "deep inside" us that is not a product of the practice and discourses in which we literally and figuratively find our "selves." The second move is to locate the constitution of the contemporary Western subject and our apparent experiences of subjectivity within two sorts of practices: disciplinary and confessional. These practices are important elements within the dominant form of power (biopower) in contemporary Western societies.

They are also connected to and effects of certain kinds of knowledge that emerge over the course of the eighteenth and nineteenth centuries in Europe—the human sciences.

Foucault studies the triangle of power, right, and truth. He questions the "how" of power. What rules of right are implemented by relations of power in the production of discourses of truth? In our culture we must produce the truth; there can be no exercise of power except through the production of truth. These "truths" reflect the "facts of human nature" as revealed by biological and human sciences. These discourses tell us what it is to be human. They "normalize" the "individual" who is constituted and named by these discourses. The individual that power has constituted becomes the vehicle of that power. Power cannot be understood in terms of repression or domination. It is a "productive" force. It does not "only weigh upon us as a force that says no but traverses and produces things, it induces pleasure, forms knowledge, produces discourse."[50]

The "individual" comes to be first through disciplinary power. New forms of knowledge that permitted time and labor to be extracted from bodies with increasing regularity emerged in the eighteenth century. The human population's health, numbers, and condition are studied in order to increase these subjected forces. The more abstract knowledges that make such studies possible are developed and improve the force and efficacy of that subjection. The purpose of disciplinary power is to assure a cohesive public body. To make the heterogeneous elements of a population cohere, concepts and practices of "normalization" are produced. These practices are supported and exercised both by the state and by new bodies of knowledge, especially medicine and the human sciences. Under the humanistic rubric of the state's interest in and obligation to the creation and protection of the "well-being" of its inhabitants, global surveillance of its members is increasingly instituted. The state needs experts to amass the knowledge it requires and to execute the policies said to effect and maximize this well-being and protection. Instances of such knowledge and associated practices include medicine, education, public health, prisons, and schools.

Concepts of deviancy, illness, maladjustment, and so forth are products of the same discourses that create the normal. These concepts also name the dangers the normal must be protected against. They justify the need both for new and better knowledge to control the problems and for the exercise of power. This knowledge is simultaneously individual and global. It entails both the study of specific "traits" possessed by individuals that cause their deviations and the search for methods that can be applied to all such individuals to effect the disciplinary results desired in the population as a whole. "Prevention" of disease or crime requires the at least potential extension of these knowledges and practices to everyone. The state's interest is in ensuring regularity of behavior, not only in punishing crimes after the fact. The more peaceful (e.g., controlled) the population, the more the state's power is legitimated and assured. Failure of disciplinary practices becomes the basis for "experts" to ask for more resources and power to pursue and exercise their knowledge in the name of the public good. A new form of power, "biopower," begins to emerge. Biopower is distinguished from other forms of power by the concrete and precise character of its knowledge of human bodies. Biopower is based in and effects a "real and effective 'incorporation' of power. It circulates through and roots itself in the concrete lives of individuals and populations through multiple and variegated means."[51]

In addition to the processes of normalization and discipline, the individual subject is also created through confessional practices. The primary exemplars of these practices are psychoanalysis and psychiatry. These discourses produce sexuality as a dangerous force within us that can be controlled only by the person exercising surveillance upon her- or himself. Such surveillance is said to lead to both "self-knowledge" and freedom from the effects of these forces. However, in order to attain such self-knowledge and self-control, the individual must consult an expert whose knowledge provides privileged access to this dangerous aspect of the person's "self."

These discourses create the idea that there is something "deep inside" us, something bodily but at least partially knowable by consciousness, a source of both pleasure and danger. By transforming pleasure into "sexuality," these confessional discourses/practices in turn give rise to further practices/knowledges of self-control and self-knowledge. They teach us we have an individual "self" about which knowledge is possible. This self is seen and experienced as deep and foundational. However such experience is not "true" in some ontological or essentialist sense. It is merely an effect of a subjectivity constituted in and through certain discourses, especially Freudian psychoanalysis. In other discourses no such notions and hence experience exist.

What is the point of Foucault's painstaking "genealogies" of power? He tells us that the will to know and the will to power cannot be separated. Presumably his own researches are motivated, at least to some degree, by desires or interests that may not be evident in the content of these studies themselves. Foucault's work does have an ethical or "positive" intention—one bound up with freedom. Foucault hopes at least to facilitate better outcomes in the ongoing if submerged struggles between heterogeneous and localized "subjected knowledge/practices" and the forces of biopower. However Foucault's notion of freedom or the possible locus of opposition shares many of the weaknesses of that of Derrida and Lyotard. It has an aesthetic or even romantic cast that by its nature excludes important social relations from further consideration. He counterposes an older Greek idea of "the *bios* as a material for an aesthetic piece of art" to the modern notion of a *techne* of the self. The ethics of this older *techne* are aesthetic; they are bound up with the effort to "make everyone's life become a work of art." Foucault argues, "from the idea that the self is not given up to us, I think there is only one practical consequence: we have to create ourselves as a work of art."[52] Freedom, ethics, and "selfhood" would be situated in the individual's creative activity, as she or he ceaselessly creates and recreates the "self." New forms of knowledge would be generated by the practices of making one's self and life into a beautiful object.

Significant Absences: Gender and Subjectivity in Postmodernist Discourses

Like many feminists and psychoanalysts I believe postmodernists make important contributions to undermining the faulty ideas about self, knowledge, and power still prevalent in the contemporary West. However there are also many important tensions and gaps between feminist and psychoanalytic discourses and those of postmodernism. First and most obviously, extended discussion of gender relations as essential to and constitutive of contemporary Western culture is absent. Postmodernism itself suggests that we ought to query the relationship between acts of exclusion and the founding and apparent coherence of any discourse. The absence of any serious consideration of feminist discourses or of gender relations profoundly affects the texture of postmodernist works. None of the metaphors for the post-modern (writing, the sublime, conversation, or aesthetic practices) seems congruent with the concerns of feminist discourses or prac-tices. It is questionable whether any of the spaces opened up by post-modernism would be comfortable to or inhabitable by those con-cerned with issues of gender and gender justice.

Second, the postmodernist narratives about subjectivity are inade-quate. As postmodernists construct subjectivity, only two alternatives appear: a "false" unitary and essentialist self or an equally nondiffer-entiated but totally historically or textually constituted "true" one. The nature of this dichotomy itself is partially determined by the ab-sence of any systematic consideration of gender or gender relations. Within postmodernist discourses there is no attempt to incorporate or do justice to the specificity of women's experiences or desires as dis-cussed by women ourselves. Women's experiences of subjectivity suggest there are alternatives to the two presented within postmod-ernist discourses.

From a psychoanalytic viewpoint postmodernist discourses on subjectivity are naive and self-deceptive. Postmodernists seem un-aware of the possible differences between a core self and a unitary one. Although claiming to see the self and concepts of it as socially and historically constituted, postmodernists do not adequately con-sider some of the most important social relations in self-formation (e.g., early mother-child relations, the sexual division of labor in child rearing). Paradoxically, although appearing to critique and reject any form of "deep" or nonsocial subjectivity, certain elements of each writer's theory in fact presuppose it. The capacity for aesthetic or mystical experience (Lyotard, Derrida, Foucault), the ability to utter new and interesting sentences (Rorty), and the will to resist totalizing discourses (Foucault) all require a "deep" subjectivity.

Gender: Its Absence and Effects
in and on Postmodernist Spaces

Postmodernist discourses, or even commentaries about them, notably lack any serious discussion of feminist theories, even when these theories overlap with, supplement, or support postmodernist writers' ideas. Rorty's work, for example, contains no references to the feminist critiques of philosophy or to the feminist discussions of science and philosophies of science that parallel and would enhance his own. The exclusion of any consideration of gender relations has political and intellectual consequences for Rorty's work. It contributes to his sense of smugness about and mystification of "our" postmodernist bourgeois culture. The identity of this our is never clear. Rorty never specifies whose practices and experiences, said to be constitutive of this culture, are included within its parameters. The problem of inequality is excluded from Rorty's pragmatism. Feminists and those concerned about relations of domination such as racism must be concerned with the possibility that incommensurable and unequal forms of life exist in any apparently singular culture. Rorty does mention that our culture includes many different communities. However he never systematically explores the possibility that some of these communities are enmeshed in systematic and pervasive relations of domination. Despite his emphasis on the historically specific and pragmatic basis of all thought, he fails to acknowledge that in one culture the experiences of some persons or groups may be radically different from those of another. In such situations a problem is how to develop a capacity to engage in empathic translation rather than "conversation." It is misleading and dangerous to assume that everyone is engaged in more or less the same "language game." It is not evident how either systematic biases or constraints within a culture may be acknowledged within, much less resolved by, conversation.[53]

Despite Rorty's emphasis on the social and historical constitution of practices and of individuals through these practices, his conversation "partners" have a strangely abstract quality. He does not question what sorts of conversation could exist among fundamentally unequal partners. His partners are never marked by asymmetric social relations. Such relations do not affect and constrain the kinds of moves people make or the kinds of conversation they may imagine, welcome, and sustain. The problems Foucault raises about marginalized and subjected discourses or the critique of consensus that Lyotard offers are ignored. A more feminist sensitivity to gender-based asymmetries would disrupt this form of happy unconsciousness.

Foucault mentions women as one of the subjected or marginalized and resisting elements within contemporary culture. He stresses the need to pay attention to the minute, local, and differentiated forms of events and power that are said to constitute "history." However he does not consider the feminist claim that in important ways the histories of men and women are themselves differentiated and heterogeneous. Foucault's histories seem totally uninformed by any awareness of feminist narratives of his major subjects (e.g., sexuality and biopower). Systematic consideration of gender relations would profoundly affect his genealogies of sexuality, subjectivity, power, and knowledge.[54] Many of his historical claims appear problematic when juxtaposed against feminist narratives. For example, his notion of biopower as a uniquely modern form of power runs contrary to many feminist accounts of history. According to these accounts, women's bodies have always, although in many different ways, been "colonized" by the intersection of knowledge and power.[55] Struggles around conceptualization and control of women's bodies have been a predominant but historically variable feature in all cultures. Perhaps what distinguishes modern culture is not the introduction of biopower per se, but rather the extensions of this power (in old and new forms) to different groups of men as well as women.

The absence of any systematic consideration of gender is especially puzzling because Foucault claims to be writing "histories of the present" that will in some way be useful to marginalized groups. From a feminist perspective no compelling history of the present could ignore the centrality of relations of gender and the struggles about them that reemerged in full force in the late 1960s.

Derrida's treatment of gender is also problematic. He claims one of the asymmetric and false dichotomies produced by the violence of metaphysics is that of man/woman. A deconstructive reading of this discourse would first reverse the asymmetry of the pair. Writing should effect a transvaluation of values. The qualities attributed to or associated with "woman" should be rescued from the ordinary phallocentric concept of them (e.g., the body would be exalted over the mind, feeling over thought, the preoedipal over the oedipal, the mother over the father, pleasure over work and production, the noncultural [other] over culture, style over truth). In these reversals one would begin to "read like a woman." "Woman" operates "outside" and disrupts the metaphysics, logic, and concepts of phallocentric culture. "Out of the depths, endless and unfathomable, she engulfs and distorts all vestige of essentiality, of identity, or property. And the philosophical discourses blinded, founders on these shoals and is hurled down these depthless depths to its ruin."[56]

Reversal, of course, is not sufficient. A "positive" deconstruction of the man/woman pair must also be effected. Woman (and man) and sexual difference itself must be disconnected from any historical, specific, or biological referent. Woman must be deessentialized and set to play among other equally nonnecessary, nondetermined, and nonreferential signs. "There is no such thing as a woman, as a truth in itself of woman in itself." There is also "no truth in itself of the sexual difference in itself."[57]

As sign, woman has the following effects and affects in addition to her generally disruptive character: She is that which will not be pinned down by truth. She is "skepticism, dissimulation, and swirl of veils."[58] She is "too clever to believe in castration or anti-castration" (its exact opposite). Thus woman wants nothing to do with feminism, for "feminism too seeks to castrate. It wants a castrated woman, gone with style." Unlike the "masculine dogmatic philosopher," woman renounces any claim to "truth, science and objectivity." She is beyond metaphysics. Her "affirmative" and dionysian power is that "she plays at dissimulation, at ornamentation, deceit, artifice, at an artist's philosophy." By affirming the beyond of metaphysics, the "question of woman suspends the decidable opposition of true and non-true. . . . Whereupon the question of style is immediately unloosed as a question of writing."[59] Beyond metaphysics woman turns out to be identical or interchangeable with writing, the other, being, the supplement, the trace.

Derrida's deconstruction of woman may seem compatible with aspects of feminist discourse. His move away from biological, essentialist, or nonhistorical concepts of gender appears congruent with the intent of many feminists. Yet his writings make me profoundly uneasy. Derrida's own concepts of woman/gender have a transcendental quality. He poses a constricted set of choices in which woman always ends up signifying "sexual difference," despite his claims to set her free. Derrida asserts that most concepts of woman are essentialist and wrong. The only alternative is concepts of woman that have no referent to any historical, specific beings constituted by and through differentiated sets of social experience. Woman as writing/other/style is "outside" all concrete history and bodily experience or determination. This set of choices excludes the possibility of considering differ-

ences as arising out of nontextual and historical as well as race and
class differentiated experiences. The specificity of being woman in lo-
catable and discrete cultures is lost. The lack of a historical and social
consideration of woman also leads to an obscuring of her constitution
in relations of domination that have not ceased to exist whether or
not she "affirms" artifice and style.

Women in modern Western culture occupy *"a specific liminal cultural
position* which is through a tangled skein of mediations somehow connected to their anatomical difference, to their femaleness." Derrida's
elimination from consideration of concrete, historical female differences in time forecloses exploration of a space that has only begun to
be explored: "the pitch black continent of what patriarchal culture has
consistently connoted as feminine and hence depreciated." Even if
cultural criticism has such power, it is too soon to tear down the
"ghetto where the feminine has been confined and demeaned, we
need to map its boundaries and excavate its foundations in order to
salvage the usable relics and refuse of patriarchy, for to do so is perhaps the only chance we have to construct a post-deconstructionist
society which will not simply reduplicate our own." [60]

There is another problem with Derrida's approach. It seems to replicate woman's place as the undifferentiated other to man rather than
to conceptualize both man and woman as constituted by and existing
within historically discrete systems of gender relations. There is no
internal deconstruction of the concept "woman" so that the many differences among women could be spoken. Instead woman is confounded with so many other complex categories (writing, style,
being, other) that such deconstruction becomes even more difficult.

Consideration of "man's" fantasies about women or the effects on
him of defining himself in relation to the other/woman is also lacking.
Despite the rhetoric of "reading like a woman" or displacing "phallocentrism," postmodernists are unaware of the deeply gendered nature of their own recounting and interpretations of the Western story
and the strategies they oppose to its master narratives. Postmodernists still honor Man as the sole author and principal character in these
stories, even if this Man is dying, his time running out. They retell
the contemporary history of the West in and through the stories of
the three deaths—of Man, (his) History, and (his) metaphysics. Whatever women have done with and in all this (becoming past) time is

"outside" by definition and according to the conventions of (their) story/line.

Postmodernists do not question whether woman "is" the "excess," the "margin," or the "supplement" only by virtue of and as an effect of (still) being placed within phallocentric discourse and culture. This "effect" is not produced by and is not a consequence of the structure of "language" (or its "binary" logic) or the inescapability of "intertextuality." It is produced by the logic and dynamics of contemporary gender systems and identities, including the repression and denial of women's acts of agency and mastery, even by the writers of postmodern "texts." One of the grounds of possibility for and consequences of phallocentrism *is* the repression and denial of such acts.

However, rather than "deconstruct" such acts of repression, Derrida builds a theory out of and on top of them. If he really wanted to effect a reversal of or to deessentialize the pair man/woman, he could assign to "man" the characteristics stereotypically associated with "woman": style, artifice, and so forth. However, as in the similar case of Lacan, the coherence and plausibility of Derrida's discourses depend on the *congruence* of the qualities he assigns to woman and the pervasive social meanings associated with her.

Stripped of its word play, its opaque, narcissistic rhetoric, Derrida's writings echo phallocentric metaphysics. Minds and bodies are two completely distinct entities. Those who engage in rational thought are inscribed on the side of masculinity and culture. Yet one can become woman without having a female body. Through writing some may elude the phallocentrism that imprisons the others. Woman's "style" is dangerous to culture because it has been outside it. Woman/writing/the other is thus the unthinkable, mystical, dionysian force outside or beyond time. She is the Real, the disorder men have sought to both subdue and possess in the course of constructing rationality, truth, and culture.

In fact there is nothing new or "postmodern" in such claims. Similar themes have recurred in Western philosophy, for example, in the work of Plato or Rousseau.[61] What is still "absent" (forbidden) is the in-corporation of "woman" *qua* embodied, desiring, and concrete and differentiated being(s) *within* culture, language, ruling, or thinking *on our own terms* and not as man's "other," "Object of desire," or linguistic construct. The "postmodernist" woman is in the same position as

Emile's Sophie. Sophie is good because she is outside politics and her "goodness" (outside) is necessary to the preservation of culture and man's selfhood.[62] The major difference I can see between Rousseau's position and that of Derrida is he wants to identify, read like, become, or (at least) openly envies woman *as he has defined her*. He still does not want her to speak for herself or, as Irigaray points out, among her or ourselves without him.[63]

Subjectivity: Feminist and Psychoanalytic Questions

The absence or disappearance of concrete women and gender relations suggests the possibility that postmodernism is not only or simply opposed to phallocentrism but may also be "its latest ruse."[64] A closer consideration of the postmodernist critique of subjectivity and its possible defensive functions and purposes provides further support for this suspicion. The writings of Derrida, Lyotard, and Foucault on subjectivity are contradictory. Although they denounce any essentialist or universalist notion of human nature, their work also incorporates a profoundly romantic/aesthetic dimension.

Both Lyotard and Derrida restore a form of transcendental subjectivity in and through its relation to the unrepresentable other. As in high modernism the writer (writing/text) reemerges as hero. Against the banalities of mass culture, he "wage[s] a war on totality [and] activate[s] the differences" that have their (nonoriginary) origin in the unpresentable other.[65] Writing transgresses the limits of language and at least evokes something beyond or outside of contemporary cultural practices. A transcendental faculty must exist in order for the artist-writer to enter or be affected by the "scene of writing" or for anyone to have an experience of the sublime as defined by Lyotard or Derrida. This faculty cannot be merely a knitting together of the "same" conventional historical and social practices in and through which "the beyond" is said to be produced, or it could not go "beyond" the given. Shifting the metaphor from the individual artist-author to "writing" or the "sublime" cannot successfully conceal the congruence of this view with the "high culture" modernist view of the work of art and the artist. In this view "true" art signifies and refers only to itself; yet at the same time it and the artist can represent a "higher" dimension of reality and being "outside the words of the tribe."[66]

In Foucault's work the aesthetic is connected with subjectivity in his idea of replacing the technologies of self with the ideal of making one's own life a work of art. Yet paradoxically, despite his criticism of Derrida's mystification of writing, Foucault does not ask himself the question "What forms of life make such a notion possible?" about his own aesthetic ideal. Such a constant remaking of the self presupposes a socially isolated and individualistic view of the self. It precludes the possibility of enduring attachments or responsibilities to another in which the other can rely on one's stability and "continuity of being." [67] Indeed, despite Foucault's criticism of Sartre's "humanism," this aesthetic self seems to have some of the same empty, projective qualities of Sartre's monad, which is driven to throw off the "slime of history" in its constant search for freedom. [68] I do not see how this highly individualistic and atomistic quest for the "beautiful life" could be reconciled with, for example, the care of children or with participation in a political community. [69] It is deeply antithetical to feminist views of self in relation to others. And despite Foucault's critique of the notion of the "universal intellectual," it betrays a romantic hope that the beautiful can rescue us from the "totalizing discourses" of modern Western culture.

Despite their aesthetics these writers continue to deny that "deep" subjectivity exists. By deep subjectivity they mean any sort of experience that is not "put into" the person by the immediate practices and discourses of that person's culture. A person is just a "tissue" of these practices. There is nothing else there. Such a view obviously implies or entails a rejection of the ways psychoanalysts have conceived the unconscious, drives, innate constitution, primary process, and fantasy. This is particularly evident in Rorty's work. He dismisses Freud's view of the unconscious as a "dark cauldron" and rejects Freud's concept of the mind as structured by intrinsic and necessary conflicts between and within its three parts (ego, id, and superego). [70] Instead we should read Freud as populating "innerspace . . . with analogues of persons—internally coherent clusters of belief and desire." The mind is not a dynamic and often conflictual interplay of somatic drive, ego, and superego forces. Rather it is a "conversation" among three partners. These "persons" all have interesting "stories" to tell about our experiences. There is no fundamental disjuncture between primary and secondary process. Instead the unconscious is defined as a "rational unconscious—one that can no more tolerate inconsistency than can consciousness." [71]

Thus no part of ourself is fundamentally strange, alien, inaccessible to or through discourse. Yet, as in Rorty's other discussions of "conversation," these "partners" have a strangely abstract and harmonious quality. They are pieces of a "self" that in its parts and thus as a whole arises out of nowhere and exists in no relation(s) to others, to desire, or to the body. These partners were evidently never children who had parents toward whom they felt complex feelings of love and hate. Freud's ideas of the ego as constituted in part by the precipitates of its object relations and of the often intra- and interpersonal conflicts between the multiple desires of a self and its "others" have simply disappeared.

Postmodernists *have* made important contributions to deconstructing the (apparently) universalizing forms of conceptions of the self. Postmodernists join feminist theorists in viewing these concepts as artifacts of (white, male) Western culture. However the postmodernist critique of subjectivity differs in important ways from both psychoanalytic and feminist views. Postmodernists seem to confuse two different and logically distinct concepts of the self: a "unitary" and a "core" one. All possible forms of self are confounded with the unitary, mentalist, deeroticized, masterful, and oppositional selves they rightfully criticize. It has been important to point out that these forms of self overlap and are congruent with definitions of "masculinity" that have recurred throughout Western culture. It is also true that in many ways Freud's own work reinforced and revalidated in scientistic disguise these traditional, Western conceptions of self and masculinity. As the founder of the discursive practice of psychoanalysis, Freud of course deeply affected the work of subsequent analysts. Hence in rethinking the question of subjectivity, we would be foolish not to interrogate and regard with skepticism psychoanalytic discourses on this issue. Nonetheless postmodernists' critiques of subjectivity remain incomplete and simplistic. These critiques do not provide persuasive grounds for abandoning all possible discourses concerning subjectivity.

I work with people suffering from "borderline syndrome." In this illness the self is in painful and disabling fragments.[72] Borderline patients lack a core self without which the registering of and pleasure in a variety of experiencing of ourselves, others, and the outer world are simply not possible. Those who celebrate or call for a "decentered" self seem self-deceptively naive and unaware of the basic cohesion within themselves that makes the fragmentation of experiences something other than a terrifying slide into psychosis. These writers seem to confirm the very claims of those they have contempt for, that a sense of continuity or "going on being" is so much a part of the core self that it becomes a taken-for-granted background. Persons who have a core self find the experiences of those who lack or have lacked it almost unimaginable.

Borderline patients' experiences vividly demonstrate the need for a core self and the damage done by its absence. Only when a core self begins to cohere can one enter into or use the transitional space in which the differences and boundaries between self and other, inner and outer, and reality and illusion are bracketed or elided. Postmodernist texts themselves belong in and use this space. It is grandiose and misleading to claim that no other space exists or that this one alone is sufficient.

Many feminists (including myself) are skeptical of the motives of those who would deny the existence of subjectivity or an "outer" reality constituted in part by nontextual relations of domination. Given the particular forms of self and repression (political and psychodynamic) that women in Western culture are likely to experience, feminist theorists have a special interest in constructing concepts of self that do justice to the full complexity of subjectivity and the spaces in which it is likely to find itself. It is possible and more desirable to construct such concepts of subjectivity than to "repress our intuitions of it" or abandon the subject altogether.[73]

It is possible to construct views of self in which it does not experience difference as irreconcilable or the existence of others as an *a priori* threat to getting what it wants. Thus it does not fall into the sense of alienation and permanent estrangement that Lacan attributes to a "decentered" or nonunitary self. Unlike the postmodernists' vision such a self would also feel no need to forswear the use of logic, rational thought, or objectivity, although it may play with them. Neither would it lose itself and imagine the I to be merely the effect of thinking or language rather than also its cause. It would also know itself to be social, to be dependent for its existence on others. Yet at the same time it could experience itself as possessing an internal world that is never exactly like any other. It appreciates the fact that others also possess such a world. It could acknowledge the desire of its sexual aspect and the autonomy of desire and its objects. It would tolerate or even enjoy the tragedy and comedy of desire: the frequent failure of objects and even our own desire to conform to our wishes or "rational" plans, the strangeness and otherness of that desiring aspect and of that aspect in others.

To glimpse such a self is also to confront a paradox: It cannot fully exist within contemporary culture. The forces of repression here are not only within the individual, metaphysics, metanarrative, or discursive formations, but in social relations as well. These social forces are too powerful, too fragmented, and too pervasive for any individual or individual analysis to comprehend or overcome. The existence of asymmetric gender relations and the asymmetries of race encourage and reinforce the splitting off and disavowal of parts of the self. Homophobia is used to enforce repression of aspects of desire, sexuality, and relations with others. These forces enter into and help structure our "inner" world. Hence consideration of this multiple self, its absence, repression, and mutilation, pushes us "outside" to take up existence as agents who can aggressively confront civilization and its discontents.

Postmodernists intend to persuade us that we should be suspicious of any notion of self or subjectivity. Any such notion may be bound up with and support dangerous and oppressive "humanist" myths. However, I am deeply suspicious of the motives of those who would counsel such a position at the same time as women have just begin to re-member their selves and to claim an agentic subjectivity available always before only to a few privileged white men. It is possible that unconsciously, rather than share such a (revised) subjectivity with the "others," the privileged would reassure us that it was "really" oppressive to them all along. As (more or less) well-trained women, we may still be too willing to abandon our own agency and ambitions. Our choice is not limited to either a "masculine," overly differentiated, and unitary self or no self at all. We should be suspicious of those who would revise history (and hence our collective memory) to construct such flawed alternatives. By retrieving or reconstructing repressed aspects of the self together—our anger, our connections with, attractions to, and fear of other women, our self-hate—women in feminism's "second wave" have begun to re-member memory—as differentiated yet collective experience (history). This "new" memory provided many women with a powerful impulse toward action (politics) and the need for more just social relations. In a respectful evaluation of these experiences, we may find alternatives to and ways to incorporate the postmodernist metaphors and spaces of writing, aesthetics, and conversation. Without an emphasis on justice, however, these postmodernist spaces threaten to become another "iron cage."

Experiences in therapy as well as in feminist consciousness raising suggest that, without access to many aspects of the self, memory in its fullness cannot emerge. Without a location and participation in collective memory and its retelling or reconstruction, a sense of "we" cannot emerge or be sustained—a we of which each I is a part and to which each I is responsible. Without a sense of an I among we's, politics as (distributive) justice is not possible.[74] Postmodernists have not offered adequate concepts of or spaces for the practice of justice. What memories or history will our daughters have if we do not find ways to speak of and practice it? Without re-membered selves how can we act? Such questions may be foreclosed within existing postmodernist discourses, but many feminists insist upon reopening them. We cannot risk such repression (again).

Seven

No Conclusions

Gender, Knowledge, Self, and Power in Transition

No Conclusions

A fundamental and unresolved question pervading this book is how to justify—or even frame—theoretical and narrative choices (including my own) without recourse to "truth" or domination. I am convinced we can and should justify our choices to ourselves and others, but what forms these justifications can meaningfully assume is not clear to me. I do not find it helpful to think about this question in terms of a search for "less false" representations because postmodernist critiques of representation are too compelling.[1] Rather I would argue it is both necessary and difficult to displace truth/falsity with problems of meaning(s). Some combination of Foucault's concept of power/knowledge and Wittgenstein's notion of language games would be helpful in sorting through questions of meaning, although I cannot pursue this intuition in detail here. Like the use of language, interpretation of meaning is not a purely private or unbounded process, but the rules may be so much a part of the game that it is hard to bring them to consciousness. Nor can the rules be understood solely within or as generated by language because language and discursive rules both reflect and are located within complex contexts of social relations and power. Any resolution or even serious response to these problems would require a book itself and far more understanding than I possess. It is also possible that such yearning for meaning itself reflects experiences in this culture and outmoded ways of thinking. Perhaps it is better only to analyze desires for meaning and to learn to live without grounds.

Nonetheless I have argued that some theories and interpretations of these theories are more helpful in understanding our transitional culture than others and have given reasons for my choices. Such arguments are not meant to "privilege" a theory—that is, to place its "truth," appropriateness, or maker beyond question. The point of making such beliefs clear and giving reasons for them is so the reader can respond and conversation continue. To pursue promising ways of understanding our experience is not necessarily to seek "truth" or power in an Enlightenment sense. Rather it entails a commitment to responsibility and a hope that there are others "out there" with whom conversation is possible. It also entails and reflects a commitment to nonnarcissistic concepts of subjectivity, to assume that there are others out there existing independent of my fantasies about them. Because these others are not (only) "in my head," if I want to converse with them, I must try to make my meanings and intentions intelligible. Such a wish can exist independent of and unmotivated by any notion of "undistorted communication" or communicative competence.[2]

The fear that inviting open-ended discourse on such questions necessarily leads to the domination of one view or group over others reflects an inflated sense of the power of writing and thought and a denial of the others' autonomy. It also reveals an inability to escape the categories of the Enlightenment such that the assertion, "this seems to make sense of x under these conditions and for these reasons, but with these problems," becomes equated with "this must be true (for you and everyone)." The search for intelligibility and meaning is not necessarily the same as the imposition of reason. It need not enmesh us within the "metaphysics of presence." One can seek meanings without assuming they are rational, context-free, or fixed "forever" or that meanings can be attained only through or depend on the use of reason. Play, aesthetics, empathy with, or being used by other's feeling states are also sources of meaning and intelligibility. Although postmodernists are correct to argue that many Western philosophers confound reason and meaning, the claim that a commitment to intelligibility or meaning necessarily traps us once again in the metaphysics of presence is not warranted. Meanings can be unconsciously and intersubjectively constructed without the constructor assuming they are "found" bits of the Real or True.

Furthermore I do not think it is possible to forswear or operate without or outside theoretical choices and assumptions. There are many important purposes and functions compounded within the processes of claiming meaning (and even in older notions of truth). We need to see how such claims function within different language games and which of these functions we might want to preserve, even if in altered forms. Because our thinking always occurs within preexisting theoretical, social, and linguistic frameworks, it is not possible to think, argue, or write without presuppositions. But the bondedness of our thought need not always lead to domination, to acts of violence upon things and others. Rather truth, domination, argument, and intelligibility are more likely to be conflated when participants in arguments do not try to make assumptions clear or pretend they do not have them or that they are not located within social contexts that shape our thinking and make some discussants more powerful than others. Thus unlike Rorty I do not think we can do without epistemological talk altogether. Rather we need to be clearer about the point(s) of such conversation. The point of such conversations has much more to do with accountability than with the purification of self-consciousness or reason or "foundational" motivations. Because even the most thorough conversations with others will necessarily leave certain unconscious or widely shared social forces in operation, we need reminders and spaces to throw knowledge into doubt. None of this talk, however, may have any effect on inequalities or relations of domination and *their* effects on conversation. Unlike Rorty I believe contemporary Western conversations are too infrequently self-correcting. Forceful political actions are often required before "more interesting" sentences are generated and the subjects are changed.

Transitional Thinking and Fragments
of Contemporary Western Culture

Throughout this book I have made arguments for the meaning and utility of certain theories and for the centrality of certain issues within the contemporary West and our understandings of it. I have argued that psychoanalysis and feminist and postmodernist theories have much to teach us about the character and importance of their particular objects of inquiry: gender, knowledge, self, power, and justice.

Each theory is also flawed in many ways. Each unwittingly provides reasons for and proof of the inadequacy of some of the ideas it posits but cannot abandon. None of these ways of thinking can stand alone as a basis for adequate social theorizing; together they are mutually self-correcting but still limited. Ironically, all three kinds of theory fail fully to account for, interpret, or deconstruct the aspects of experience, culture, and philosophy they identify as problematic. Each theory's failure to carry out its own projects and their mutually reinforcing and conflicting contributions to understanding contemporary Western culture reflect the necessary incompleteness of all conversations about questions that matter to the ways people live. Conversations about and within fragmented and transitional cultures are likely to be particularly polyphonic.

Despite the many flaws, weaknesses, and omissions within these theories and in the conversations I have constructed between them, many important and promising themes and insights have emerged about both these theories and the questions they investigate. I will summarize and raise further questions about some of these issues in the remainder of this chapter.

Gender

Psychoanalysis and postmodern theories are both overtly and subtly gender bound and biased. Despite the emphasis within psychoanalysis on the centrality of gender relations to the organization of the self and culture as a whole, the story it tells about gender excludes and obscures female sexuality and nonoedipal modes of relatedness. This repressed material also deeply affects psychoanalytic accounts of knowledge, the psychotherapeutic process, the nature of society, interpersonal relations, human embodiment, and selfhood.

Postmodernism is equally inadequate in its treatment or avoidance of gender. Some writers grapple with or attempt to integrate postmodernisms with a variety of feminisms.[3] Yet their work is often unacknowledged within the work of writers like Foucault, Lyotard, or Rorty. Despite the rhetoric of "reading like a woman" or displacing "phallocentrism," many male postmodernists seem to be unaware of the deeply gendered nature of their own recounting and interpretations of "the" Western story and the strategies they oppose to its "master narratives." "Man" retains his privileged place as the sole author and principal character in their stories. If the story or stories were told from within women's experiences, the dramatic episodes might not be the three deaths, but rather an ongoing series of struggles: to give birth or to avoid giving birth; to be represented or to avoid being as misrepresented; to be concretely in time and to have one's activities order time and conceptions of history; not to exist as the eternal, "feminine," "other," or "mysterious" life source.

In postmodern philosophies woman is often still utilized as the other or as mirror for Man; when she exists at all, it is as the repository for the qualities Man has denied to himself and now wishes to reclaim. Woman's speech is constricted by these rules—or she is (and may remain) silenced. As Irigaray so aptly puts it, woman is "for them—but always according to him—essentially an-archic and a-teleological. For the imperative that is imposed on them—but solely from the outside, and not without violence—is 'enjoy without law' . . . when that strange state of 'body' that men call women's pleasure turns up, it is gratuitous, accidental, unforeseen, 'supplementary' to the essential." [4]

"Woman" often retains her most ancient "position" within postmodernist discourses: "Women as womb, the unconscious womb of man's language; for her own part, she would have no relation to 'her' unconscious except one that would be marked by an essential dispossession. In absence, ecstasy . . . and silence. Ek-sistence falling short of, or going beyond, any subject." [5] Perhaps even the qualities some postmodernists attribute to Being (flux, lawlessness, chaos, etc.) are in part projections, condensations, or displacements of their fantasies about the Being of women onto Being as such.

Like any mode of thinking, feminist theories themselves are not free from the effects of gender. According to psychoanalytic theorists, current gender-structured social practices create men who have difficulties acknowledging interdependent relations between people. These same social practices produce women who have difficulties acknowledging differences within relations. In either gender these social practices produce a disposition to treat experience as all of one sort or another and to be intolerant of differences, ambiguity, and conflict. In feminist theories these difficulties underlie and are reflected in the treatment or lack of acknowledgment of differences among women as well as in writings about a variety of other issues including: sexuality, aggression, children, motherhood, embodiment, ethics, and the "traditionally" or "stereotypically female" virtues and attributes; the proper relations between and meanings of "public" and "private" domains; male domination; and the appropriate forms of feminist theorizing itself.

Feminist theorists have only begun critically to analyze how our own experiences predispose and enable us to think in certain ways but not others. Such experiences include coming to be a person in a society in which one's class, race, and gender are constituting social relations and in which claims to knowledge are integrally connected to power. Applying psychoanalytic theory to the process and contents of feminist theorizing can reveal distinctively female acts of repression and displacement. In bringing such acts to consciousness, feminist theorists can begin to acknowledge and overcome gender and other related blindness.

Knowledge

From a postmodernist perspective feminist theories and psychoanalysis seem to be naive and un-self-reflective about the epistemological premises upon which each depends. Both kinds of thinking appeal to notions of reason, science, and objectivity that postmodernist philosophers have thoroughly and effectively deconstructed. For example, the notion that there is *a* feminist viewpoint that is more true and not just different from previous male ones seems to rest upon many assumptions uncritically appropriated from and dependent upon Enlightenment thinking. These assumptions include an optimism that people can identify and act rationally on their "interests" and that reality has a structure that a more perfect or less "biased" reason can portray more adequately.

Many psychoanalysts remain committed to Freud's positivistic projects. They attempt to legitimate their claims to knowledge by "proving" that psychoanalysis is a "science."[6] By science they mean some system of representational or empiricist truth claims. Such an enterprise seems pointless or at least anachronistic in light of more recent philosophies of science and power/knowledge relations. It also obscures the most interesting and significant qualities of the psychoanalytic situation and its possible interpretations and epistemological implications.

Postmodernist discourses about knowledge are also problematic. The radical rhetoric about dualisms within Western philosophy conceals the extent to which postmodernism is still their prisoner. I remain suspicious of strategies that attempt to undermine metaphysics or philosophy by identifying and then juxtaposing the "suppressed" opposite to a "unitary" concept. We cannot effectively displace the metaphysics of presence by saying that everything is "really fictive" or flux. These are also ontological statements that lie within or seek to reclaim the traditional terrain of philosophy.

A psychoanalyst or feminist can also question the postmodernists' desire. The move toward interpretation, linguistics, and rhetoric conceals a different, but still dominating, form of desire within postmodernism—the desire of postmodernists to displace the philosopher as the "master artificer," speaker, or writer within the "conversation" of "mankind." Why should a radical critic of Western culture privilege anything, much less writing or conversation, as the metaphor, exemplar, or constitutor of human experience? Why not play with a variety of metaphors, including child rearing or less verbal/linguistic ones like dancing and painting?

The Self

In all three modes of thinking, the Enlightenment conception of a unitary or essentially rational self is "decentered." The psychoanalytic notion of the unconscious undermines the belief that it is possible to have privileged access to, accurate knowledge of, or control over one's mind. Both Freud's "drive" theories and his later structural views of the mind erode the distinctions between reason and unreason and mind and body essential to Enlightenment concepts of the self.

Yet in many ways, as postmodernists claim, Freud's thinking remains within the Enlightenment project. His emphasis on the liberating power of rational insight; his individualistic concept of the self; his distrust of the "irrational," including "illusions" such as religion as well as the unconscious; and his insistence on the importance to the individual and to culture of the defense of the ego and reason against the "irrational" demands of desire or authority place him firmly within the "master narratives" of the Enlightenment. Freud's and Lacan's moves to locate and conflate women, the irrational, desire, and nature "outside" and against culture are also congruent with and contribute to the persistence of these narratives.

Feminist theorists also displace unitary, essentialist, and asocial or ahistoric ideas of the self by analyzing the ways gender enters into and partially constitutes both the self and our ideas about it. They have shown that the stories philosophers or psychologists tell about "the self" tend primarily to reflect the experiences, problems, and acts of repression of a stereotypically white, Western, masculine self.[7] Ideas about "the" self are dependent upon and made plausible by the existence of specific sets of social relations, including gender. For example, Kant and other philosophers distinguish our phenomenal and embodied self from a (higher) noumenal, rational, and transcendental one. The noumenal self can be free precisely because it is removed from empirical contingency. The possibility and plausibility of such distinctions rest in part on the prior existence of a gender-based division of labor. In this division of labor, women take responsibility for and represent bodily processes, leaving the (male) philosophers "free" to contemplate the noumenal world. In turn the lack of conscious involvement with such processes and the existence of a whole class of persons who share similar social experiences render a split between the noumenal and phenomenal plausible.

Only when persons with different sets of experience enter into or question philosophic discourse do these distinctions lose their "intuitive" plausibility. Different questions then emerge (e.g., not what *is* the relation between mind and body, but rather why anyone would assume such a distinction is meaningful or central to philosophic discourse or why the contingent is seen only as a source of unfreedom). This evaluation of the contingent and the predominance of certain questions within philosophy reflect in part the prevalence of relations of domination in which only the unfree care for our contingent existence.

Feminist theorists, like object relations psychoanalysts, stress the central importance of sustained, intimate relations with other persons or the repression of such relations in the constitution, structure, and ongoing experiences of a self. In this feminist psychoanalytic account the self loses its asocial, isolated qualities and is reconceptualized as a complex "inner world" with its own system of internal relations. Each self is partially constituted in and through networks of relations, fantasies, and expectations among and about "internal objects." Unlike object relations theorists, however, feminists pay attention to the lo-

cation of persons (and families) within wider contexts of social relations. Some of these relations are structured by and through domination so that feminists conceptualize families, for example, as
constituted by far more than the dyads (or occasionally triads) of object
relations accounts.

Although feminist theorists seem to undermine essential properties of the Enlightenment self, they are also unable to abandon it fully.
The relations of feminist theorizing to the postmodernist project of
deconstructing the self and the Enlightenment are necessarily ambivalent. In many ways women never "had" an Enlightenment. Enlightenment discourse was not meant to include women, and its coherence depends partially on our continuing exclusion.[8] Concepts such
as the autonomy of reason, objective truth, and universally beneficial
progress through scientific discovery are very appealing, especially
to those who have been defined as incapable or merely the objects of
such feats. Furthermore it is comforting to believe that Reason can
and will triumph—that those who proclaim such ideals as objectivity
and truth will respond to rational arguments. If there is no objective
basis for distinguishing between truth and false beliefs, then it seems
that power alone may determine the outcome of competing truth
claims. This is a frightening prospect to those who lack or are oppressed by the power of others.

Feminists also depend partially on Enlightenment ideals in the
ways claims to and visions of gender justice have been formulated.
Concepts like natural rights, due process, and equality are grounded
in part in certain ideas about innate or essential human properties.
These properties are supposed to compel the state to act because it is
required as part of its contractual obligation to protect the rights it did
not create. Such preexisting "natural rights" are also meant to be barriers *against* state intervention, as, for example, in the use of the "right
to privacy" doctrine to legitimize abortion. Although many reasonable arguments have been made about the limitations of liberal Enlightenment concepts and practices of citizenship, no persuasive alternatives to them exist.[9] Given the enormous risks involved, it is
reasonable for feminists to be skeptical about abandoning these practices before most women have fully enjoyed their admittedly limited
and ambiguous benefits.

Postmodernist rhetoric about "the self" is simultaneously one of its
most intriguing and disappointing features. Like feminist theorists,
postmodernists intend to particularize and historicize all notions of

"self." However, unlike feminist or psychoanalytic theorists, postmodernist deconstructors of the self empty subjectivity of any possible meaning or content. The postmodernist desire is to render conversation about the self as anachronistic and irrelevant as discussions about "the ether" would be to contemporary physicists.

However this desire cannot be above suspicion. Elements of postmodernists' discourses are incoherent without some implicit notion of a self. For example, Foucault stresses the existence and importance of "suppressed discourses" and local and particular forms of knowledge. It is incomprehensible that such discourses could persist despite the "disciplinary and surveillance" aspects of power without the existence of some form of "self." Something must exist within and among persons that is not merely an effect of the dominating discourse. Otherwise how could conflict and struggle against domination continue even in the most totalistic discursive formation?

Without some notion of a self, one of Foucault's most striking propositions cannot be fully developed. Foucault stresses the interrelations and interdependence of knowledge and power, especially in the genesis of the "human sciences." Part of the power of the human sciences is based on the capacity of people to adapt their behavior and govern themselves according to the dominant truth claims of these "sciences." Power is exercised only on "free" persons; it exists only if someone has several courses of action open but chooses the one congruent with the wishes of another. The capacity to chose in any meaningful sense requires the existence of a human will that is not merely an effect of discourse. Foucault believes that power is exercised as thousands of individual choices or acts of will, not as the massive external imposition of repression on the part of a police state. It is thus hard to make sense of his theory without imputing the existence of a mental quality similar to Freud's superego. Otherwise we cannot explain how discursive formations grab onto or into people or how such formations are able to constitute people as "subjects" who then watch over and regulate themselves.

Another reason to be suspicious of postmodernist treatments of self is the complete disregard for aspects of subjectivities rooted in intimate social relations. Such social relations are displaced by the postmodernist insistence on self as a "position in language" (Derrida) or an effect of discourse (Foucault). From a feminist psychoanalytic viewpoint it is striking that a primary strategy adopted by these postmodernists to deconstruct "essentialist" concepts of self is to juxtapose and insist upon a notion of the self as "fictive." An alternative strategy would be to argue that "the self" is social and in some important ways gendered. Hence any self or concept of it must be differentiated, local, and historical. Gender can be used as a lever against essentialist or ahistoric notions of the self. A feminist deconstruction of the self, however, would point toward locating self and its experiences in concrete social relations, not only in fictive or purely textual conventions.

A social self would come to be partially in and through powerful, affective relationships with other persons. These relations with others and our feelings and fantasies about them, along with experiences of embodiedness also mediated by such relations, can come to constitute an "inner" self that is neither simply fictive nor "natural." Such a self is simultaneously embodied, gendered, social, and unique. It is capable of telling stories and of conceiving and experiencing itself in all these ways.

In most cultures the first person we are in an intimate, social relationship with is a woman—a mother or her substitutes or relations. Hence many feminists, including myself, are suspicious of theories that require denying the centrality of human relatedness or obviate the ways these relations become part of a complex inner world or distinctive subjectivity. Feminist theorists have argued that the repression, especially by men, of these primary relations and the relational aspects of our subjectivity is necessary for the replication of male-dominant cultures. A feminist theorist might well ask whether certain postmodernist deconstructors of the self are not merely the latest in a long line of philosophic strategies motivated by a need to evade, deny, or repress the importance of early childhood experiences, especially mother-child relationships, in the constitution of the self and the culture more generally. Perhaps it is less threatening to have no self than one pervaded by memories of, longing for, suppressed identification with, or terror of the powerful mother of infancy.

Power and Justice

By their own logics neither feminist theorists nor postmodernists can claim to be politically neutral or indifferent. Postmodernists claim that knowledge and power are inextricably intertwined. Foucault's work encourages us to reconceptualize power and the complexity of its workings. Yet, although I find much of what he has to say about shifts in the nature of power and state compelling, the many absences in even his and certainly in other postmodernist discourses are troubling.

Postmodernist discourses do contain at least tacit assumptions about the liberating potential of freeing differences and refusing totalities. Beyond this, however, it is not clear that postmodernism has or could offer a positive vision(s) of justice or the good life. A deconstructive project is to clear spaces in which many disorderly or local forms of life could flourish. However postmodernists have so far had little to say about how or why totalizing discourses could or would contract or cease their imperialist expansion. Nor do most postmodernists have much to say about the concrete practices and knowledges that could replace the current ones.

In some ways postmodernism makes it more difficult to discuss questions of justice and power. These fragments disrupt master narratives of the West and the language games in which terms like *freedom* and *emancipation* take on meaning. In pondering their meaning we become hesitant to speak for or prescribe our good(s) for others. It is harder to separate normative discourse from potential exercises of power or to conceptualize power as other than domination.

Writers such as Rorty argue that pragmatism or pluralism is congruent with postmodernist projects. However, as anyone familiar with the history of Western political thought is aware, pluralism or pragmatism is far from unproblematic as a theory or practice.[10] Postmodernists ignore or fail to acknowledge many of these important difficulties. The political problems intrinsic to both pluralism and pragmatism include how to resolve conflict among competing voices; how to assure that everyone has a chance to speak; how to ensure that each voice counts equally; how to assess whether equality or participation is necessary in all cases or in which cases; how to effect a transition from the present in which many voices cannot speak, are necessarily excluded, or are not heard to a more pluralist one; how to instill and guarantee a preference for speaking over the use of force; and how to compensate for the political consequences of an unequal distribution and control of resources. The absence of discourse about such questions reinforces a suspicion that deconstructive politics may be most appealing to those who are accustomed to and confident of having their voices heard in almost any conversation and therefore feel no particular need to be worried about such "details."

Feminist theorists do not and cannot enjoy such confidence. Feminist narrations of the History of Man focus on relations of domination. Feminists do not recount History primarily as the story of the tyranny of the "metaphysics of presence," but rather as the persistence of asymmetries of power between men and women; the denial of Being, equality, and justice to women by men in and through concrete social relations; and the at best partially successful struggle by women against these relations of domination. Feminist theorists look to History for explanations of women's experiences, reasons to and methods of struggle against domination, and evidence that such struggle is worthwhile.

Although Rorty may be right that talking about "justice" in the abstract may not help us to do right, there are also very good reasons why we cannot stop doing it. A purely pragmatic approach of examining our current practices is not satisfactory because justice is often most noticeable by its absence. Our practices do not necessarily compel self and social criticism or reflection. In fact, as critical theorists point out, they may operate to negate or disarm exactly these qualities. Rorty's implicit assumption that conversations may be self-correcting suggests further questions about postmodernism. Is it tied to the "triumph of the therapeutic" and thus reflects our time in another way? Do postmodernists tacitly assume that knowledge of our absences and acts or repression is itself a liberating force, and for whom?

To the extent that all political practices and visions of justice have been affected by or reflect the existence of male domination, feminist theorists also feel compelled to offer something new: concepts of justice that do not presuppose or require asymmetric gender relations for their realization. Feeling themselves oppressed *now*, feminists cannot be indifferent to questions of how transformations are to occur. Given the disappointing results of previous, allegedly radical practices, feminists also have no reason to trust that what will show up in these potential deconstructive spaces will be for our own good(s).[11]

Psychoanalysis has had an ambivalent relationship to issues of power and justice. Freud is never reluctant to point out the irrationality of existing social and political behavior. Like his Enlightenment predecessors he believes the only hope for human progress lies in the rule of reason and the replacement of superstition by science within the individual and society as a whole. Freud is also acutely aware of the pain inflicted on and experienced by individuals in the effort to conform to social norms. He tries to envision ways of reducing the costs of living in society for the individual and the level of conflict and violence within cultures. Like the other sciences, he believes, psychoanalysis could be an emancipatory form of knowledge because it contributes to the development of a more rational society.

However Freud and Lacan also believe that society must necessarily exact sacrifices from individuals. There will always be conflicts between the a- or antisocial drives and the demands of culture. Such conflicts are rooted in the intrinsic opposition of the aims of nature (drives) and culture; hence they will never disappear. Our unhappiness within society might decrease within a more rational order, but it can never end. Psychoanalysis can only teach us to bear the unhappiness arising from the renunciation of desire more stoically and with less effort.

Freud and Lacan break with the Enlightenment narrative because they do not claim that accurate knowledge and the development of society necessarily result in an increase in human happiness. However from my postmodernist and feminist viewpoints both writers join with and provide support for totalizing and phallocentric discourses. Freud in particular constructs a notion of subjectivity, especially female subjectivity, that invites and requires constant social and individual surveillance and control. His romantic notion of powerful and irrational "natural forces" (desire) within the individual is the necessary binary and asymmetric opposite to the Enlightenment ideas of the ego or Reason as representing the forces of order and the reality principle against, in this case, the chaos within. His theories provide legitimation and support for practices of surveillance, regularization, and control.

Instead of encouraging development of a more "fluid" self, Freud ultimately attempts to unify the forces of the mind under the control of the One (ego) in alliance with the Real (the reality principle). He displaces conflicts within culture onto conflicts between "nature" and culture; hence he renders their social sources, especially in gender relations and discourse dependence, opaque and inaccessible. He leaves as his legacy to psychoanalysis a set of dualisms that still govern its discourses today: bodies as nature opposed to mind and culture, reason or law opposed to an object-related self, male opposed to female, right or justice opposed to desire, the individual dependent upon but opposed to the community.

Within these dualisms the "Great Refusal" and "revolutionary aestheticism" of Marcuse, the social conformity of Hartmann and ego psychology, the hermetic authoritarianism of Lacan, and the facilitating environment of Winnicott can all be accommodated.[12] Like their founder these followers of Freud fluctuate between a painful awareness of conflict and a reconciliation to the demands of contemporary culture. What remains unspoken is a suspicion that the "demands of culture" may represent merely an accommodation of the sons within and to a discourse that is a "compromise formation" between their own desires and fears. Within this discourse whispers from other, suppressed ones may sometimes be heard: the voices of women, the "goods among themselves," and a desire for pleasure and justice beyond stoic reconciliation, the "law of the Father," the unrepresentable, writing, "polymorphous perversity"—or even polyphonic conversation.[13]

As I come to the end of this book, many questions that motivated me to write it remain unanswered, including the following: Is discussion of knowledge and promising theories still and necessarily motivated by an Enlightenment belief that knowledge can set us free? Do I and others discuss knowledge as an avoidance or denial of the deeper power relations that "really" control us? Can we treat Enlightenment beliefs as an important series of questions that still have value apart from their hopelessly contaminated answers? If justice has something to do with appropriateness (Plato), can we have fragmenting and fragmentary theories and practices of justice—and still worry about the question of doing right?[14] What *are* the relations of knowledge and power? Does all knowledge necessarily inflict violence on things, ourselves, and other persons? Is (some or all) intellectuals' work merely play with "the prettier unforced blue flowers of bourgeois culture"?[15] Although these questions remain unanswered to my satisfaction, behind them lies a recurrent nightmare. This nightmare is not unusual among those who reflect upon experiences in the contemporary West. In this nightmare there "really is" something "out there" after all—a (Hobbesian) Leviathan at work, content merely to watch while and only as long as we amuse ourselves elsewhere. I leave this dream for others to interpret—if and as they wish.

Notes

Chapter One

1. Articulations of and explanations for such dislocation vary widely. See, for example, Charles Newman, "The Post-Modern Aura: The Act of Fiction in an Age of Inflation," *Salmagundi* 63–64 (Spring–Summer 1984): 5–170; Julia Kristeva, "Women's Time," *Signs* 7, no.1 (Autumn 1981): 13–35; Christopher Lasch, *Haven in a Heartless World* (New York: Basic Books, 1977); Max Horkheimer and Theodor Adorno, *Dialectic of Enlightenment* (New York: Herder & Herder, 1972); and Sheldon Wolin, *Politics and Vision* (Boston: Little, Brown, 1960), chap. 10.

2. Expressions of this vertigo and its consequences are abundant. Examples include the essays in Jonathan Arac, ed., *Postmodernism and Politics* (Minneapolis: University of Minnesota Press, 1986); Samuel Weber, ed., *Demarcating the Disciplines: Philosophy, Literature, Art* (Minneapolis: University of Minnesota Press, 1986); Richard J. Bernstein, ed., *Habermas and Modernity* (Cambridge, Mass.: MIT Press, 1985); and Kenneth Baynes, James Bohman, and Thomas McCarthy, eds., *After Philosophy: End or Transformation?* (Cambridge, Mass.: MIT Press, 1987).

3. On the disruptive effects of feminist theories, see Seyla Benhabib and Drucilla Cornell, eds., *Feminism as Critique* (Minneapolis: University of Minnesota Press, 1987); Carol Pateman and Elizabeth Gross, eds., *Feminist Challenges: Social and Political Theory* (Boston: Northeastern University Press, 1986); and Eva Feder Kittay and Diana T. Meyers, eds., *Women and Moral Theory* (Totowa, N.J.: Rowman & Littlefield, 1987). On psychoanalysis and reason see Sigmund Freud, "Fixation to Traumas: The Unconscious," in Sigmund Freud, *Introductory Lectures on Psychoanalysis*, trans. James Strachey (New York: W. W. Norton, 1965). On the concept and functions of metanarrative,

see Jean-Francǫis Lyotard, *The Postmodern Condition: A Report on Knowledge* (Minneapolis: University of Minnesota Press, 1984), especially pp. 27–37.

4. I realize this is a drastic reduction of complex ideas. For more nuanced views of the Enlightenment, see Steven Seidman, *Liberalism and the Origins of European Social Theory* (Berkeley and Los Angeles: University of California Press, 1983); Robert Anchor, *The Enlightenment Tradition* (Berkeley and Los Angeles: University of California Press, 1967); Ernst Cassirer, *The Philosophy of the Enlightenment* (Boston: Beacon Press, 1955); and Peter Gay, *The Enlightenment: An Interpretation* (New York: Knopf, 1966).

5. Baynes, Bohman, and McCarthy develop this idea in their "General Introduction" to *After Philosophy*; the problems of the self are a central focus of the essays that follow. Cassirer provides an especially clear discussion of science and philosophy as knowledge in chaps. 2 and 3 of *Philosophy of the Enlightenment*.

6. Jacques Derrida, *Marges de la philosophie* (Paris: Editions de Minuit, 1972). Perhaps the most succinct and influential statement of Enlightenment beliefs is Immanuel Kant, "What Is Enlightenment?" reprinted with his *Foundations of the Metaphysics of Morals* (Indianapolis: Bobbs-Merrill, 1959). See also Jean Le Rond D'Alembert, *Preliminary Discourse to the Encyclopedia of Diderot* (Indianapolis: Bobbs-Merrill, 1963). For an attack on many Enlightenment beliefs, see especially Jean-Jacques Rousseau, *Discourse on the Sciences and Arts (First Discourse)* in *The First and Second Discourses*, ed. Roger Masters (New York: St. Martins, 1964).

7. Horkheimer and Adorno, *Dialectic*, especially pp. 3–42.

8. See Max Weber, "Politics as a Vocation," in *From Max Weber*, ed. and trans. H. H. Gerth and C. Wright Mills (New York: Oxford University Press, 1958).

9. Theodor Adorno, *Negative Dialectics* (New York: Seabury Press, 1973), p. 364.

10. Walter Benjamin, "Theses on the Philosophy of History," in *Illuminations*, ed. Hannah Arendt (New York: Schocken, 1969), p. 257.

11. On the idea of "foundational illusions," see Richard Rorty, *Philosophy and the Mirror of Nature* (Princeton N.J.: Princeton University Press, 1979), p. 6.

12. Ibid., p. 7.

13. See Norman Jacobson's interesting discussion of political theory and its functions in *Pride and Solace* (Berkeley and Los Angeles: University of California Press, 1978), chap. 1.

14. A successor project would be isomorphic to (and on the same scale as) the failed "grand theory."

15. Sigmund Freud, "Constructions in Analysis," in *Collected Papers*, vol. 5 (New York: Basic Books, 1959).

Chapter Two

1. Cf. the diametrically opposed views of the "true" Freud in Frank Sulloway, *Freud: Biologist of the Mind* (New York: Basic Books, 1979); and Bruno Bettelheim, *Freud and Man's Soul* (New York: Knopf, 1983). For examples of confrontations, see Clay Whitehead, "Additional Aspects of the Freudian-Kleinian Controversy: Towards a 'Psychoanalysis' of Psychoanalysis," *International Journal of Psychoanalysis* 56 (1975): 383–396; and Marie Balmary, *Psychoanalyzing Psychoanalysis: Freud and the Hidden Fault of the Father* (Baltimore: Johns Hopkins University Press, 1982).

2. Such considerations are lacking, for example, in the otherwise excellent review of psychoanalytic theory by Jay R. Greenberg and Stephen A. Mitchell, *Object Relations in Psychoanalytic Theory* (Cambridge, Mass.: Harvard University Press, 1983).

3. Works by Jacques Lacan include *Speech and Language in Psychoanalysis*, trans. Anthony Wilden (Baltimore: Johns Hopkins University Press, 1968); *The Four Fundamental Concepts of Psychoanalysis* (New York: W. W. Norton, 1973); *Ecrits: A Selection* (New York: W. W. Norton, 1977); and *Feminine Sexuality*, ed. Juliet Mitchell and Jacqueline Rose (New York: W. W. Norton, 1985). Object relations theorists include D. W. Winnicott, *The Maturational Processes and the Facilitating Environment* (New York: International Universities Press, 1965); and Michael Balint, *The Basic Fault* (New York: Brunner/Mazel, 1979).

4. A representative sample of recent feminist theories would include Barbara Smith, ed., *Home Girls: A Black Feminist Anthology* (New York: Women of Color Press, 1983); Cherrie Moraga and Gloria Anzaldua, eds., *This Bridge Called My Back* (Watertown, Mass.: Persephone Press, 1981); Elizabeth Abel, Marianne Hirsch, and Elizabeth Langland, *The Voyage In: Fictions of Female Development* (Hanover, N.H., and London: University Press of New England, 1983); Zillah R. Eisenstein, ed., *Capitalist Patriarchy and the Case for Socialist Feminism* (New York: Monthly Review Press, 1979); Hunter College Women's Studies Collective, *Women's Realities, Women's Choices* (New York: Oxford University Press, 1983); Sherry B. Ortner and Harriet Whitehead, eds., *Sexual Meanings: The Cultural Construction of Gender and Sexuality* (New York: Cambridge University Press, 1981); Nancy C. M. Hartsock, *Money, Sex and Power* (New York: Longman, 1983); Ann Snitow, Christine Stansell, and Sharon Thompson, eds., *The Powers of Desire: The Politics of Sexuality* (New York: Monthly Review Press, 1983); Sandra Harding and Merill B. Hintikka, eds., *Discovering Reality: Feminist Perspectives on Epistemology, Metaphysics, Methodology and Philosophy of Science* (Boston: D. Reidel, 1983); Alison M. Jagger, *Feminist Politics and Human Nature* (Totowa, N.J.: Rowman & Allanheld, 1983); Elaine Marks and Isabelle de Courtivron, *New French Feminisms* (New York: Schocken Books, 1981); Joyce Trebilcot, ed., *Mothering: Essays in Feminist*

Theory (Totowa, N.J.: Rowman & Allanheld, 1984); Alice Jardine, *Gynesis: Configurations of Woman and Modernity* (Ithaca, N.Y.: Cornell University Press, 1985); Carol Gilligan, *In a Different Voice* (Cambridge, Mass.: Harvard University Press, 1982).

5. Max Weber, "Science as a Vocation," in *From Max Weber*, ed. H. H. Gerth and C. Wright Mills (New York: Oxford University Press, 1958).

6. See the work of Evelyn Fox Keller on the gendered character of our views of the "natural world," especially her essays "Gender and Science," reprinted in Harding and Hintikka, *Discovering Reality*; and "Cognitive Repression in Physics," *American Journal of Physics* 47 (1979): 718–721.

7. On the problem of the Archimedes point, see Myra Jehlen, "Archimedes and the Paradox of Feminist Criticism," *Signs* 6, no. 4 (Summer 1981): 575–601.

8. Especially influential works include Friedrich Nietzsche, *Beyond Good and Evil* (New York: Vintage, 1966), and his *The Will to Power* (New York: Vintage, 1968); Michel Foucault, *Power/Knowledge: Selected Interviews and Other Writings 1972–77*, ed. Colin Gordon (New York: Pantheon, 1980), and his *Language, Counter-Memory, Practice*, ed. Donald F. Bouchard (Ithaca, N.Y.: Cornell University Press, 1980); Jacques Derrida, *Marges de la philosophie* (Paris: Editions de Minuit, 1972), and his *Writing and Difference*, trans. Alan Bass (Chicago: University of Chicago Press, 1978); Giles Deleuze and Felix Guattari, *On the Line* (New York: Semiotext[e], 1983), and their *Anti-Oedipus: Capitalism and Schizophrenia* (Minneapolis: University of Minnesota Press, 1983); Stanley Cavell, *The Claim of Reason* (New York: Oxford University Press, 1979); Roland Barthes, *S/Z*, trans. Richard Miller (New York: Hill & Wang, 1974), and his *The Fashion System*, trans. Matthew Ward and Richard Howard (New York: Hill & Wang, 1983). Already there is a large and ever-growing literature on and in postmodernism. Among the works I have found most helpful are Terence Hawkes, *Structuralism and Semiotics* (Berkeley and Los Angeles: University of California Press, 1977); Herbert L. Dreyfus and Paul Rabinow, *Michel Foucault: Beyond Structualism and Hermeneutics* (Chicago: University of Chicago Press, 1982); Harvey West, ed., *The Idea of the Post-Modern* (Seattle: Henry Art Gallery, University of Washington, 1981); Quentin Skinner, ed., *The Return of Grand Theory in the Human Sciences* (New York: Cambridge University Press, 1985); Michael Ryan, *Marxism and Deconstruction: A Critical Articulation* (Baltimore: Johns Hopkins University Press, 1982); Vincent Descombes, *Modern French Philosophy* (New York: Cambridge University Press, 1982); Fredric Jameson, "The Cultural Logic of Capital," *New Left Review* 146 (July–August 1984): 53–92; Henry Louis Gates, Jr., ed., *'Race,' Writing and Difference* (Chicago: University of Chicago Press, 1986); John Rajchman and Cornel West, eds., *Post-Analytic Philosophy* (New York: Columbia University Press, 1985);

Christopher Norris, *Derrida* (Cambridge, Mass.: Harvard University Press, 1987); and *Feminist Studies* 14, no. 1 (Spring 1988).

9. What follows is a summary of some of the ideas of Derrida, Foucault, Lyotard, and Rorty. For more detail and differentiation see Chapter 6.

10. Cf. Jacques Derrida, "Positions," in Jacques Derrida, *Positions*, trans. Alan Bass (Chicago: University of Chicago Press, 1981); and Foucault, "Two Lectures," in Foucault, *Power/Knowledge.*

11. Jean-François Lyotard, *The Postmodern Condition: A Report on Knowledge* (Minneapolis: University of Minnesota Press, 1984), pp. 27–41.

12. Derrida, "Violence and Metaphysics," in Derrida, *Writing and Difference.*

13. David Hoy draws many interesting parallels between hermeneutics and deconstruction in his essay, "Derrida," in Skinner, *The Return of Grand Theory.*

14. Derrida, "Positions," in Derrida, *Positions.*

15. These "normalizing discourses" are the subject of the essays and interviews in Foucault, *Power/Knowledge.*

Chapter Three

1. For Horney's views, see Karen Horney, *New Ways in Psychoanalysis* (New York: W. W. Norton, 1939); and Susan Quinn, *A Mind of Her Own: The Life of Karen Horney* (New York: Summit Books, 1987), especially chap. 15. Kohut moves somewhat from this position in Heinz Kohut, *How Does Analysis Cure?* (Chicago: University of Chicago Press, 1984).

2. A previous return was made by the critical theorists of the "Frankfurt School" after their (at least partial) disillusionment with Marxist theory and practice. Cf. Max Horkheimer, "Authority and the Family," in Max Horkheimer, *Critical Theory* (New York: Herder & Herder, 1972). An interesting history of contemporary Western thought could be written by tracking intellectuals' alternating loyalties between Marx and Freud.

3. Frederick M. Watkins, "Political Theory as a Datum of Political Science," in *Approaches to the Study of Politics*, ed. Roland Young (Evanston, Ill.: Northwestern University Press, 1958), p. 154.

4. Freud uses this evocative phrase in his essay "Analysis Terminable and Interminable," in *Collected Papers*, ed. James Strachey (New York: Basic Books, 1959), 5:357. The collection will be abbreviated in this chapter as *CP.*

5. As in "Analysis Terminable," in which Freud discusses the new difficulties the discovery of the "modification of the ego" creates for analytic technique. See also Sigmund Freud, *The Ego and the Id*, ed. James Strachey (New York: W. W. Norton, 1960), pp. 7–17.

6. Freud, "Female Sexuality," in *CP* 5:253–254.

7. Sigmund Freud, *The Interpretation of Dreams*, trans. James Strachey (New York: Avon, 1965), pp. 642–643. Freud never abandons this idea. Cf. one of his very last works, *An Outline of Psychoanalysis*, trans. James Strachey (New York: W. W. Norton, 1949), p. 2.

8. The exact relation between the constancy principle, the pleasure principle, and the nirvana principle remains unclear in Freud's work. Cf. his essay "The Economic Problem in Masochism" in *CP* 2:255–257.

9. Freud, "Instincts and Their Vicissitudes," in *CP* 4:63, 65.

10. Sigmund Freud, *Civilization and Its Discontents*, trans. James Strachey (New York: W. W. Norton, 1961), p. 23.

11. Freud, "On Narcissism: An Introduction," in *CP* 4:47; see also his "Instincts," in *CP* 4:81.

12. Freud, "Mourning and Melancholia," in *CP* 4:162.

13. Freud, "Instincts," in *CP* 4:82.

14. Freud, *The Ego*, p. 19.

15. One later object relations theorist is Harry Guntrip, *Personality Structure and Human Interaction* (New York: International Universities Press, 1964), chap. 6.

16. Freud, "The Passing of Oedipus Complex," in *CP* 2:272, 72.

17. Freud, "Mourning," in *CP* 4:159.

18. Sigmund Freud, *An Autobiographical Study*, trans. James Strachey (New York: W. W. Norton, 1952), p. 74.

19. Sigmund Freud, *Three Essays on the Theory of Sexuality*, trans. James Strachey (New York: Basic Books, 1962), pp. 78, 63–66; Freud, "The Passing of Oedipus," in *CP* 2:270.

20. Freud, *Three Essays*, p. 63.

21. Ibid, p. 29

22. Ibid., pp. 77, 74, 29, 27, 11.

23. Ibid., p. 34.

24. Freud, "The Unconscious," in *CP* 4:120.

25. Freud, *The Ego*, p. 8.

26. Ibid., p. 25.

27. Ibid., p. 46.

28. Ibid., p. 38.

29. Ibid., pp. 15, 14, 16, 38, 42.

30. Ibid., pp. 38, 39.

31. For example, Husserl's transcendental phenomenology, especially the *epoche*. Cf. Edmund Husserl, *The Crisis of European Sciences and Transcendental Phenomenology* (Evanston, Ill.: Northwestern University Press, 1970), especially part 3B, #69. René Descartes, *Discourse on Method and Other Writings*

(Baltimore: Penguin, 1968), especially Second and Third Meditations; Jean-Paul Sartre, *Being and Nothingness*, trans. Hazel Barnes (New York: Washington Square Press, 1966), especially part 2, chap. 1. Thomas Hobbes, *Leviathan* (Baltimore: Penguin, 1987), part 1.

32. Freud, *An Autobiographical Study*, p. 111.

33. Sigmund Freud, "Explanations, Applications and Orientations," in Sigmund Freud, *New Introductory Lectures on Psychoanalysis*, trans. James Strachey (New York: W. W. Norton, 1965), pp. 156–157.

34. Freud, *An Autobiographical Study*, p. 109.

35. Sigmund Freud, "The Question of a Weltanschauung," in Freud, *New Introductory Lectures*, pp. 179, 158.

36. Ibid., p. 159.

37. Freud, *An Outline*, pp. 16, 53.

38. Ibid., pp. 53–54.

39. Ibid., p. 54.

40. Ibid., p. 16.

41. Ibid., p. 15.

42. Freud, "The Question of a Weltanschauung," in Freud, *New Introductory Lectures*, p. 159.

43. Freud, *An Outline*, p. 15.

44. Freud, "The Question of a Weltanschauung," in Freud, *New Introductory Lectures*, p. 159.

45. Ibid., p. 170.

46. Ibid., pp. 166, 175, 174–175, 171.

47. Cf. Jürgen Habermas, *Knowledge and Human Interests* (Boston: Beacon Press, 1971), especially chap. 10; and his *Communication and the Evolution of Society* (Boston: Beacon Press, 1979), chaps. 1–3; and Donald Spence, *Narrative Truth and Historical Truth: Meaning and Interpretation in Psychoanalysis* (New York: W. W. Norton, 1982).

48. Sigmund Freud, "Observations on 'Wild' Psychoanalysis," in *CP* 2:301–302.

49. Adolf Grünbaum, "Epistemological Liabilities of the Clinical Appraisal of Psychoanalytic Theory," *Psychoanalysis and Contemporary Thought* 2 (1979): 451–526.

50. Cf. Merton M. Gill, *Analysis of Transference*, vol. 1 (New York: International Universities Press, 1982).

51. Freud uses martial imagery frequently. Cf. Sigmund Freud, *The Question of Lay Analysis* (New York: W. W. Norton, 1965), pp. 61–62; and his "Analysis Terminable," in *CP* 5:343. Freud uses the metaphor of a surgeon in his "Recommendations for Physicians on the Psychoanalytic Method of Treatment," in *CP* 2; and in his "Turnings in the Ways of Psycho-analytic Therapy,"

in *CP* 2. On the influences of medical practices on Freud's understanding of himself and psychoanalysis, see Leo Stone, *The Psychoanalytic Situation* (New York: International Universities Press, 1961), pp. 9–66.

52. Freud, "Analysis Terminable," in *CP* 5:351–352.

53. Sigmund Freud, "Constructions in Analysis," in *CP* 5, presents both these claims.

54. Freud, "Analytic Therapy," in Freud, *Introductory Lectures*, p. 282.

55. Sigmund Freud, "Further Recommendations in the Technique of Psycho-Analysis. Recollection, Repetition and Working Through," in *CP* 2:374–376.

56. Ibid., p. 331.

57. Freud, *An Outline*, p. 43.

58. Freud, "Constructions in Analysis, " in *CP* 5:368.

59. Sigmund Freud, "Dynamics of Transference," in *CP* 2:319.

60. Ibid., pp. 314–319.

61. Cf. the accounts of patients' experiences with Freud in Hendrix M. Ruitenbeek, ed., *Freud as We Knew Him* (Detroit: Wayne University Press, 1973): and HD, *Tribute to Freud* (New York: McGraw-Hill, 1956).

62. I discuss this debate and its limitations in Jane Flax, "Philosophy and the Philosophy of Science: Critique or Resistance?" *Journal of Philosophy* 78, no. 10 (October 1981): 561:569. See also Louis Breger, *Freud's Unfinished Journey* (Boston: Routledge & Kegan Paul, 1981).

63. Cf. Peter Gay, *Freud, Jews and Other Germans* (Berkeley and Los Angeles: University of California Press, 1981), chap. 1.

64. On the ideas of container and containing, see W. R. Bion, *Attention and Interpretation* (London: Tavistock, 1970). On patients' and analysts' feeling states see Harold Searles, *Counter-transference and Related Subjects: Selected Papers* (New York: International Universities Press, 1979); and Michael Balint, *The Basic Fault* (New York: Brunner/Mazel, 1979).

65. I am thinking here of Ludwig Wittgenstein, *Philosophical Investigations* (New York: Macmillan, 1970), especially part 2, sec. 9; G. W. F. Hegel, *The Phenomenology of Mind* (New York: Harper & Row, 1967), parts A and B; Hans-Georg Gadamer, *Philosophical Hermeneutics* (Berkley and Los Angeles: University of California Press, 1976); Habermas, appendix to *Knowledge*; Thomas Kuhn, *The Structure of Scientific Revolutions* (Chicago: University of Chicago Press, 1962); Freidrich Nietzsche's playfulness in *Thus Spoke Zarathustra* (New York: Viking Press, 1954) and his attempt to recapture and revalue the "dionysian" also provide important clues.

66. Freud, *Question of Lay Analysis*, pp. 93–94.

67. Kate Millet, *Sexual Politics* (New York: Doubleday, 1969), represents an early and influential example of the first approach. Juliet Mitchell, *Psychoanalysis and Feminism* (New York: Pantheon, 1974), especially pp. xv–15, rep-

resents an example of the third. Recently Mitchell seems to have become less comfortable with this position. See her essays, "Psychoanalysis: Child Development and Femininity" and "The Question of Femininity and the Theory of Psychoanalysis," in Juliet Mitchell, *Women: The Longest Revolution* (London: Virago Press, 1984). My own work represents the second approach. I am referring to the following essays by Freud: "Female Sexuality," in *CP* 5; "Femininity," in Freud, *New Introductory Lectures*; and "Some Psychological Consequences of the Anatomical Distinction Between the Sexes," in *CP* 5.

68. The recent works by Spence, *Narrative Truth*, Gill, *Analysis of Transference*, and Breger, *Freud's Unfinished Journey*, although excellent in many ways, make no mention of the distorting effects of gender on Freud's work or psychoanalytic theory as a whole. Such absences also pervade another highly praised recent work, Jay R. Greenberg and Stephen A. Mitchell, *Object Relations in Psychoanalytic Theory* (Cambridge, Mass.: Harvard University Press, 1983).

69. Sigmund Freud, *Civilization and Its Discontents* (New York: W. W. Norton, 1961), pp. 50–51.

70. Contrary to the (non–gender conscious) claims of such writers as Peter Gay or Norman Jacobson, *Pride and Solace: The Functions and Limits of Political Theory* (Berkeley and Los Angeles: University of California Press, 1978). These writers portray Freud as a "ruthlessly honest" revealer of the "secrets" of modern culture. In Peter Gay's recent book, *Freud: A Life for Our Time* (New York: W. W. Norton, 1988), he mentions the powerful ties between Freud and his mother and that this relationship remained largely untouched by Freud's self-analysis. Although Gay suggests that this material may have affected Freud's writing on women, he does not explore such a possibility in any depth. Gay does not seem to find gender a very significant factor in the content of Freud's work as a whole, cf. especially pp. 501–522 of his *Freud*.

71. Freud, "Femininity," in Freud, *New Introductory Lectures*, p. 134.

72. Freud, *Civilization*, p. 19.

73. Ibid., pp. 12, 15.

74. Melanie Klein puts special emphasis on these aspects of early infantile experience. See "Love, Guilt and Reparation," in her *Love, Guilt and Reparation* (New York: Dell, 1975). For a powerful feminist application of these insights, see Dorothy Dinnerstein, *The Mermaid and the Minotaur: Sexual Arrangements and the Human Malaise* (New York: Harper & Row, 1976).

75. Freud, "Analysis Terminable," in *CP* 5:357.

76. Freud, *Civilization*, pp. 51, 50.

77. Ibid., p. 118.

78. Freud, "Analysis Terminable," in *CP* 5:357.

79. Freud, *Civilization*, p. 50.

80. Freud, "Femininity," in Freud, *New Introductory Lectures*, p. 133.

81. Freud, "Analysis Terminable," in *CP* 5:356–357.

82. Freud, *An Outline*, p. 50.

83. Freud, "Analysis Terminable," in *CP* 5:355.

84. Ibid., pp. 354–355.

85. Sigmund Freud, "Fragment of an Analysis of a Case of Hysteria," in *CP* 3 (the case of Dora), reveals clearly the contributions of unanalyzed countertransference to the failure of the analysis.

Chapter Four

1. This happens, for example, when commentators treat these premises as evidence of the radical (if unpalatable) "truth" of Lacan's work. Some commentators on Lacan ignore the fact that a narcissistic ontology is by definition self-enclosed and other excluding, hence not open to disproof within its own premises. Among the writers who are too uncritical of or are captured within Lacan's premises (and style), I would include Jane Gallop, *The Daughter's Seduction: Feminism and Psychoanalysis* (Ithaca, N.Y.: Cornell University Press, 1982); Stuart Schneiderman, *Jacques Lacan: The Death of an Intellectual Hero* (Cambridge, Mass.: Harvard University Press, 1983); Juliet Mitchell, "Introduction-I," and Jacqueline Rose, "Introduction-II," to Jacques Lacan, *Feminine Sexuality*, trans. Jacqueline Rose (New York: W. W. Norton, 1985). Catherine Clément, *The Lives and Legends of Jacques Lacan*, trans. Arthur Goldhammer (New York: Columbia University Press, 1983), presents a more distanced and complex view of Lacan's work. Sherry Turkle, *Psychoanalytic Politics: Freud's French Revolution* (Cambridge, Mass.: MIT Press, 1981), is still very helpful in placing Lacan and his ideas in their historical and social context.

2. Jacques Lacan, *Ecrits: A Selection*, trans. Alan Sheridan (New York: W. W. Norton, 1977), p. 24.

3. Clément, *The Lives*, stresses the centrality of this concept within Lacan's work. See especially her discussion of the mirror stage on pp. 84–92. For Winnicott's view, see D. W. Winnicott, "Mirror Role of Mother and Family in Child Development," in D. W. Winnicott, *Playing and Reality* (New York: Basic Books, 1971). In this essay Winnicott mentions Lacan's discussion of the same subject and some of his differences with Lacan. Heinz Kohut discusses the meanings and importance of mirroring extensively in his *The Analysis of the Self* (New York: International Universities Press, 1983), part 2.

4. Lacan, *Ecrits*, p. 2.

5. Ibid., p. 4.

6. Ibid., p. 2.

7. Ibid., p. 4.

8. Ibid., pp. 5–6. Obviously, Lacan is drawing heavily on Hegel's ideas

here, especially Hegel's notions of dialectics and the "unhappy conscious-ness." Cf. G. W. F. Hegel, *The Phenomenology of Mind*, trans. J. B. Baillie (New York: Harper & Row, 1967), part 3B. However, unlike Hegel, Lacan does not believe that any *Aufhebung* of this phase is possible. In Lacan's work self-consciousness can never go any further than a recognition of its permanently split (and stuck) state. See also Jacques Lacan, "The Subject and the Other: Aphanisis," in his *The Four Fundamental Concepts of Psychoanalysis*, trans. Alan Sheridan (New York: W. W. Norton, 1981), pp. 219–220.

9. Lacan, "The Meaning of the Phallus," in Lacan, *Feminine Sexuality*, pp. 80–81. My understanding of narcissism depends not only on Freud's account but also on the work of Kohut, Kernberg, and Masterson. In the work of the last three writers, narcissism is treated not as an ontological given but rather as a potentially pathological and changeable condition. On narcissism see Sigmund Freud, "On Narcissism: An Introduction," In his *Collected Papers*, vol. 4, trans. Joan Riviere, ed. James Strachey (New York: Basic Books, 1959). This collection will be abbreviated in this chapter as *CP*. Kohut, *Analysis of the Self*; Otto Kernberg, *Borderline Conditions and Pathological Narcissism* (New York: Jason Aronson, 1975), part 2; James F. Masterson, *The Narcissistic and Borderline Disorders* (New York: Brunner/Mazel, 1981). Kohut also distin-guishes between healthy and self-affirming forms of narcissism and patholog-ical and self-isolating ones.

10. Jacques Lacan, "The Subject and the Other: Alienation," in Lacan, *Four Fundamental Concepts*, p. 207.

11. Lacan, "The Meaning," in Lacan, *Feminine Sexuality*, p. 80. See also Jacques Lacan, "From Love to the Libido," in Lacan, *Four Fundamental Con-cepts*, p. 188.

12. Lacan, "From Love," in Lacan, *Four Fundamental Concepts*, p. 191.

13. Lacan, "The Meaning," in Lacan, *Four Fundamental Concepts*, p. 79. My critique of Lacan's theory of language is derived partially from Hanna Pitkin's treatment of the parallel moves in social science toward nominalism, formal-istic concepts, and a pseudo-emptying out or neutralizing of the social history and meanings of language and language use. See Hanna Pitkin, *Wittgenstein and Justice* (Berkeley and Los Angeles: University of California Press, 1972), especially chaps. 5–6, 10–11. Ludwig Wittgenstein, *Philosophical Investiga-tions*, trans. G. E. M. Anscombe (New York: Macmillan, 1970), presents a very different theory of language than that of Lacan. He too moves from a purely representational theory of language but locates subsequent discus-sions of language in relation to "forms of life," not an abstract, ahistoric "bi-nary logic."

14. Lacan, "The Meaning," in Lacan, *Four Fundamental Concepts*, p. 79.

15. Ibid., p. 78.

16. Ibid., p. 79. See also Lacan, "The Subject," in Lacan, *Four Fundamental*

Concepts, p. 203: "The Other is the locus in which is situated the chain of the signifier that governs whatever may be made present of the subject—it is the field of that living being in which the subject has to appear," and p. 207.

17. Lacan, "Seminar of 21 January 1975," in Lacan, *Feminine Sexuality,* p. 165.

18. Lacan, "The Subject," in Lacan, *Four Fundamental Concepts,* p. 203.

19. Lacan, "The Meaning," in Lacan, *Four Fundamental Concepts,* p. 78.

20. Jacques Lacan, "Guiding Remarks for a Congress on Feminine Sexuality," in Lacan, *Feminine Sexuality,* p. 91.

21. Lacan, "The Meaning," in Lacan, *Four Fundamental Concepts,* p. 83.

22. Ibid.

23. Ibid.

24. Jacques Lacan, "From Interpretation to the Transference," in Lacan, *Four Fundamental Concepts,* p. 246.

25. Lacan is basing his argument here on a parallel one by Claude Levi-Strauss, *The Elementary Structures of Kinship* (Boston: Beacon Press, 1969), especially pp. 3–68, 478–497.

26. Jacques Lacan, "God and the Jouissance of the Woman. A Love Letter," in Lacan, *Feminine Sexuality,* p. 144.

27. Ibid., p. 145.

28. Ibid., pp. 144–145.

29. Lacan, "The Meaning," in Lacan, *Four Fundamental Concepts,* p. 89.

30. Ibid., p. 75.

31. Cf. Gallop, *Daughter's Seduction;* Mitchell and Rose, "Introduction."

32. Lacan, "The Subject," in Lacan, *Four Fundamental Concepts,* p. 203.

33. Jacques Lacan, "Intervention on Transference," in *In Dora's Case: Freud-Hysteria-Feminism,* ed. Charles Bernheimer and Claire Kahane (New York: Columbia University Press, 1985), p. 99.

34. See especially D. W. Winnicott, "Mind and Its Relation to the Psyche-Soma," in his *Through Paediatrics to Psycho-analysis* (New York: Basic Books, 1975).

35. For an example of his clinical work, see D. W. Winnicott, *The Piggle: An Account of the Psychoanalytic Treatment of a Little Girl* (New York: International Universities Press, 1977).

36. For Lacan's view of the psychoanalytic situation, see his "Intervention on Transference," in Bernheimer and Kahane, *In Dora's Case.* Schneiderman gives an account of his own analysis with Lacan in *Jacques Lacan.*

37. Sigmund Freud, "Mourning and Melancholia," in *CP* 4:154.

38. Sigmund Freud, *Inhibitions, Symptoms and Anxiety,* trans. Alix Strachey (New York: W. W. Norton, 1959), p. 96.

39. For a discussion of some of the differences among object relations theorists, see Jay R. Greenberg and Stephen A. Mitchell, *Object Relations in*

Psychoanalytic Theory (Cambridge, Mass.: Harvard University Press, 1983), part 2. In addition to Winnicott's writings, I have also drawn upon Harry Guntrip, *Personality Structure and Human Interaction* (New York: International Universities Press, 1961), and his *Psychoanalytic Theory, Therapy and the Self* (New York: Basic Books, 1971); Melanie Klein, *Love, Guilt and Reparation* (New York: Dell, 1977), *Envy and Gratitude* (New York: Dell, 1975), *Narrative of a Child Analysis* (New York: Dell, 1975); and W. R. D. Fairbairn, *Psychoanalytic Studies of the Personality* (Boston: Routledge & Kegan Paul, 1952).

40. Lacan's denial of the possible existence of a true self and of the possibility and power of early social relatedness helps account for his hostility to the object relations theorists. Lacan is transparently eager to replace the object relations analysts' emphasis on the concrete relations between mother and child with his focus on the "phallic function." See, for example, Lacan's opening comments in "Guiding Remarks," in Lacan, *Feminine Sexuality,* p. 87.

41. D. W. Winnicott, "Anxiety Associated with Insecurity," in Winnicott, *Through Paediatrics,* p. 99.

42. This phrase is Margaret Mahler's. See Margaret Mahler, Fred Pine, and Anni Bergman, *The Psychological Birth of the Human Infant* (New York: Basic Books, 1975). Mahler's work has a complex status. She wants to retain and rescue Freud's drive theory, but her observations and the developmental scheme she derives from them do not really confirm or accord with drive theory. Her work has been utilized most successfully by object relations–oriented clinicians and theorists (e.g., Masterson).

43. Winnicott, "Mind and Its Relation," in Winnicott, *Through Paediatrics,* pp. 246–247.

44. For a sensitive account of how adult eating disorders may occur, see Hilda Bruch, *The Golden Cage: The Enigma of Anorexia Nervosa* (New York: Vintage, 1979).

45. Winnicott, "Mind and Its Relation," in Winnicott, *Through Paediatrics,* pp. 246–247.

46. Recent infant research indicates that even the neonate is a much more complex and competent being than scientists and many analysts (including Lacan) used to (or still do) believe. For excellent summaries of recent research on infant development, see Kenneth Kaye, *The Mental and Social Life of Babies* (Chicago: University of Chicago Press, 1982); and Daniel Stern, *The Interpersonal World of the Infant* (New York: Basic Books, 1985).

47. The concepts of symbiosis and separation-individuation are Mahler's. Winnicott objects to the term *symbiosis* because it is too well rooted in biology to be acceptable to him. Cf. Winnicott, "Interrelating Apart from Instinctual Drive and in Terms of Cross Identifications," in Winnicott, *Playing and Reality,* p. 130.

48. D. W. Winnicott, "Ego Distortion in Terms of True and False Self," in

D. W. Winnicott, *The Maturational Processes and the Facilitating Environment* (New York: International Universities Press, 1965).

49. Winnicott, "Anxiety Associated," in Winnicott, *Through Paediatrics*, p. 99.

50. Mahler, Pine, and Bergman, *Psychological Birth*, p. 48.

51. D. W. Winnicott, "Primary Maternal Preoccupation," in Winnicott, *Through Paediatrics*.

52. Ibid., p. 305.

53. D. W. Winnicott, "Aggression in Relation to Emotional Development," in Winnicott, *Through Paediatrics*, p. 216.

54. Winnicott, "Mind and Its Relation," in Winnicott, *Through Paediatrics*, p. 245.

55. Winnicott, "Primary Maternal," in Winnicott, *Through Paediatrics*, p. 304.

56. Winnicott, "Aggression in Relation," in Winnicott, *Through Paediatrics*, p. 215. See also his "The Use of an Object," in Winnicott, *Playing and Reality*, pp. 93–94.

57. D. W. Winnicott, "Primitive Emotional Development," in Winnicott, *Through Paediatrics*, p. 153.

58. Cf. D. W. Winnicott, "The Capacity to Be Alone," in Winnicott, *Maturational Processes*.

59. D. W. Winnicott, "The Depressive Position in Normal Emotional Development," in Winnicott, *Through Paediatrics*, pp. 270–271.

60. Winnicott, "Creativity and Its Origins," in Winnicott, *Playing and Reality*, p. 71.

61. D. W. Winnicott, "Transitional Objects and Transitional Phenomena," in Winnicott, *Playing and Reality*, p. 11.

62. Ibid.

63. Ibid., p. 12.

64. Ibid.

65. D. W. Winnicott, "The Use of an Object and Relating Through Identifications," in Winnicott, *Playing and Reality*, p. 89.

66. Winnicott, "Transitional Objects," in Winnicott, *Playing and Reality*, p. 13.

67. Winnicott, "The Use of an Object," in Winnicott, *Playing and Reality*, p. 94.

68. D. W. Winnicott, "The Location of Cultural Experience," in Winnicott, *Playing and Reality*, p. 97.

69. Ibid., p. 102.

70. Winnicott, "Transitional Objects," in Winnicott, *Playing and Reality*, p. 13.

71. This point has been made by feminist theorists such as Nancy Chodorow, *The Reproduction of Mothering: Psychoanalysis and the Sociology of Gender*

(Berkeley and Los Angeles: University of California Press, 1978); Dorothy Dinnerstein, *The Mermaid and the Minotaur: Sexual Arrangements and the Human Malaise* (New York: Harper & Row, 1976); and Juliet Mitchell, *Psychoanalysis and Feminism* (New York: Pantheon, 1974), and her *Women: The Longest Revolution* (London: Virago, 1984), part 3. Winnicott does have some interesting things to say about gender in "Creativity and Its Origins," in Winnicott, *Playing and Reality,* pp. 76–85; and *The Family and Individual Development* (New York: Tavistock, 1968), pp. 163–165.

72. On gender and core identity see Robert Stoller, "Facts and Fancies: An Examination of Freud's Concept of Bisexuality," in *Women & Analysis,* ed. Jean Strouse (New York: Dell, 1974); and John Money and Anke A. Ehrhardt, *Man and Woman, Boy and Girl* (Baltimore: Johns Hopkins University Press, 1972), especially pp. 176–194.

73. Mahler, Pine, and Bergman, *Psychological Birth,* p. 102.

74. Examples of this blaming include Frankfurt Institute for Social Research, "The Family," in Frankfurt Institute for Social Research, *Aspects of Sociology* (Boston: Beacon Press, 1972); and Christopher Lasch, *Haven in a Heartless World* (New York: Harper & Row, 1977), especially chap. 8. On the tendency to blame the mother, see also Nancy Chodorow and Susan Contratto, "The Fantasy of the Perfect Mother," in *Rethinking the Family: Some Feminist Questions,* ed. Barrie Thorne with Marilyn Yalom (New York: Longman, 1982); and Bonnie Dill, "The Dialectics of Black Womanhood," *Signs* 4, no. 3 (Spring 1979): 543–555.

75. Chodorow, *The Reproduction of Mothering,* and Dinnerstein, *The Mermaid and the Minotaur,* discuss some of the reasons for this in more detail. See also Jane Flax, "Contemporary American Families: Decline or Transformation?" in *Families, Politics and Public Policy,* ed. Irene Diamond (New York: Longman, 1983).

76. Sigmund Freud discusses this in "Some Psychological Consequences of the Anatomical Distinction Between the Sexes," in *CP* 5. See also Chodorow, *The Reproduction of Mothering,* chap. 11.

77. Winnicott has an interesting discussion of the good enough mother's inevitable and necessary "hate" of her infant in his "Hate in the Countertransference," in Winnicott, *Through Paediatrics,* pp. 201–202.

78. Sigmund Freud, "The Question of a Weltanschauung," in Sigmund Freud, *New Introductory Lectures on Psychoanalysis,* trans. James Strachey (New York: W. W. Norton, 1965), p. 176.

Chapter Five

1. Simone de Beauvoir, *The Second Sex* (New York: Bantam, 1961), p. 667.

2. A representative sample of contemporary feminist theorists would include Barbara Smith, ed., *Home Girls: A Black Feminist Anthology* (New York:

Kitchen Table: Women of Color Press, 1983); Cherrie Moraga and Gloria An-
zaldua, eds., *This Bridge Called My Back* (Watertown, Mass.: Persephone Press,
1981); Elizabeth Abel, Marianne Hirsch, and Elizabeth Langland, *The Voyage
In: Fictions of Female Development* (Hanover, N.H., and London: University
Press of New England, 1983); Zillah R. Eisenstein, ed., *Capitalist Patriarchy and
the Case for Socialist Feminism* (New York: Monthly Review Press, 1979); Vivian
Gornick and Barbara K. Morgan, eds., *Woman in Sexist Society* (New York:
Mentor, 1971); Annette Kuhn and Ann Marie Wolpe, eds., *Feminism and Ma-
terialism* (Boston: Routledge & Kegan Paul, 1978); Hunter College Women's
Studies Collective, *Women's Realities, Women's Choices* (New York: Oxford Uni-
versity Press, 1983); Elaine Marks and Isabelle de Courtivron, eds., *New
French Feminisms* (New York: Schocken Books, 1981); Joyce Trebilcot, ed.,
Mothering: Essays in Feminist Theory (Totowa, N.J.: Rowman & Allanheld,
1984); Sherry B. Ortner and Harriet Whitehead, eds., *Sexual Meanings: The
Cultural Construction of Gender and Sexuality* (New York: Cambridge University
Press, 1981); Nancy C. M. Hartsock, *Money, Sex and Power* (New York: Longman, 1983); Ann Snitow, Christine Stansell, and Sharon Thompson, eds., *The
Powers of Desire: The Politics of Sexuality* (New York: Monthly Review Press,
1983); Sandra Harding and Merill B. Hintikka, eds., *Discovering Reality: Feminist Perspectives on Epistemology, Metaphysics, Methodology and Philosophy of Sci-
ence* (Boston: D. Reidel, 1983); Carol C. Gould, *Beyond Domination: New Per-
spectives on Women and Philosophy* (Totowa, N.J.: Rowman & Allanheld, 1984);
Allison M. Jagger, *Feminist Politics and Human Nature* (Totowa, N.J.: Rowman
& Allanheld, 1983); Martha Blaxall and Barbara Reagan, eds., *Women and the
Workplace* (Chicago: University of Chicago Press, 1976); Isaac D. Balbus, *Marxism and Domination* (Princeton, N.J.: Princeton University Press, 1982); Bell
Hooks, *Feminist Theory: From Margin to Center* (Boston: South End Press, 1984);
Audre Lorde, *Sister Outsider* (Trumansberg, N.Y.: Crossing Press, 1984); Glo-
ria T. Hull, Patricia Bell Scott, and Barbara Smith, *All the Women Are White, All
the Blacks Are Men, But Some of Us Are Brave: Black Women's Studies* (Old Westbury, N.Y.: Feminist Press, 1982); Sandra Harding, *The Science Question in Feminism* (Ithaca, N.Y.: Cornell University Press, 1986); and Virginia Sapiro, *The
Political Integration of Women* (Urbana: University of Illinois Press, 1984). On
the history of the "second wave" of feminism, see Vicky Randall, *Women and
Politics: An International Perspective*, 2nd ed. (Chicago: University of Chicago
Press, 1987); Ethel Klein, *Gender Politics* (Cambridge, Mass.: Harvard University Press, 1984); and Sara Evans, *Personal Politics* (New York: Vintage, 1980).

3. Helene Cixous, "The Laugh of the Medusa," in Marks and de Courtivron, *New French Feminisms*.

4. De Beauvoir, *Second Sex*, p. 673. See also Betty Friedan, *The Feminine
Mystique* (New York: Dell, 1963), pp. 332–364.

5. On the reconsideration of the quotidien, see Nancy Hartsock, "The

Feminist Standpoint: Developing the Ground for a Specifically Feminist Historical Materialism," in Harding and Hintikka, *Discovering Reality;* Caroline Whitbeck, "Afterword to the 'Maternal Instinct,'" in Trebilcot, *Mothering;* Dorothy Smith, "A Sociology for Women," in *The Prism of Sex: Essays in the Sociology of Knowledge,* ed. J. Sherman and E. T. Beck (Madison: University of Wisconsin Press, 1979); and Sara Ruddick, "Maternal Thinking," in Trebilcot, *Mothering.*

6. Friedan, *Feminine Mystique,* chap. 1.

7. This is Richard Rorty's phrase in his *Philosophy and the Mirror of Nature* (Princeton, N.J.: Princeton University Press, 1979), pp. 389–394.

8. For discussion of the feminist standpoint, see Hartsock, "The Feminist Standpoint," in Harding and Hintikka, *Discovering Reality,* and her *Money, Sex and Power;* and Harding, *The Science Question,* chaps. 6 and 7.

9. In Sandra Harding, "The Instability of the Analytical Categories of Feminist Theory," *Signs* 11, no. 4 (Summer 1986): 645–664. I think her argument rests in part on a too uncritical appropriation of a key Enlightenment equation of knowing, naming, and emancipation. Feminists who are more critical of the Enlightenment legacy include Alice A. Jardine, *Gynesis: Configurations of Woman and Modernity* (Ithaca, N.Y.: Cornell University Press, 1985); Julia Kristeva, "Women's Time," *Signs* 7, no. 1 (Autumn 1981): 13–35; Kathy E. Ferguson, *The Feminist Case Against Bureaucracy* (Philadelphia: Temple University Press, 1984); and Luce Irigaray, *Speculum of the Other Woman,* trans. Gillian C. Gill (Ithaca, N.Y.: Cornell University Press, 1985).

10. See Max Weber, "Politics as a Vocation," in *From Max Weber,* ed. H. H. Gerth and C. Wright Mills (New York: Oxford University Press, 1958); and Max Horkheimer and Theodor W. Adorno, *Dialectic of Enlightenment* (New York: Herder & Herder, 1972).

11. Jean-François Lyotard, *The Postmodern Condition: A Report on Knowledge* (Minneapolis: University of Minnesota Press, 1984), pp. 81–82.

12. On the concept of "grand theory," see Quentin Skinner, ed., *The Return of Grand Theory in the Human Sciences* (New York: Cambridge University Press, 1985). In Skinner's introduction to this book, he mentions the "women's movement" as a source of insights for the resurgence of grand theorizing (p. 6) but, as is often the case, fails even to cite any work in feminist theory, *much less* include a review of such theorizing in this collection. These "gaps and omissions" are replicated in all the essays printed in this volume.

13. Gayle Rubin, "The Traffic in Women: Notes on the 'Political Economy' of Sex," in *Toward an Anthropology of Women,* ed. Rayna Rapp Reiter (New York: Monthly Review Press, 1975), pp. 159, 166, 168, 169.

14. Ibid., p. 177.

15. Ibid., p. 178.

16. Ibid., pp. 183, 197.

17. Radical feminist works that have a determinist tenor include Mary Daly, *Gyn/Ecology: The Metaethics of Radical Feminism* (Boston: Beacon Press, 1978); and Andrea Dworkin, *Woman Hating* (New York: Dutton, 1974).

18. For a more complete critique of Rubin's structuralism, see the appendix to Hartsock, *Money, Sex and Power.*

19. Rubin, "The Traffic in Women," p. 205.

20. Ibid., pp. 209–210.

21. Ibid., p. 203.

22. Juliet Mitchell, *Women's Estate* (New York: Pantheon, 1971), pp. 101, 171–172.

23. Jean Bethke Elshtain, *Public Man, Private Woman* (Princeton, N.J.: Princeton University Press, 1981), pp. 314, 328–329, 331–333, 310.

24. Ibid., p. 311.

25. In Charlotte Perkins Gilman, *Women and Economics* (New York: Harper & Row, 1966), written in 1898, there is a brilliant discussion of the social transformations and uses of women's physical characteristics. Female athletes' recent achievements make one wonder about the "natural" limits of female bodies.

26. See the collections of essays in Eisenstein, *Capitalist Patriarchy,* and Kuhn and Wolpe, *Feminism and Materialism,* for some of the best work by socialist feminists; see also Lydia Sargent, ed., *Women and Revolution* (Boston: South End Press, 1981).

27. On Marx's method see Karl Marx and Frederick Engels, *The German Ideology* (New York: International Publishers, 1970), especially part 1. For an application and extension of his method, see Karl Marx, *Capital* (New York: International Publishers, 1967), vol. 1, especially part 1.

28. On productive and nonproductive labor see Marx, *Capital,* pp. 84–94, 177–211.

29. On the sexual division of labor, see the essays in Blaxall and Reagan, *Women in the Workplace.*

30. On the "double day" see the essays by Hartmann and Boulding in ibid.

31. Ann Ferguson, "On Conceiving Motherhood and Sexuality: A Feminist Materialist Approach," in Trebilcot, *Mothering.*

32. See Phyllis Marynick Palmer, "White Women/Black Women: The Dualism of Female Identity and Experience in the United States," *Feminist Studies* 9, no. 1 (Spring 1983): 151–170, on the economic differences between black and white women.

33. Cf. Gloria Joseph's critique in "The Incompatible Menage a Trois: Marxism, Feminism, and Racism," in Sargent, *Women and Revolution.*

34. Cf. Balbus, *Marxism,* especially chap. 1; Jane Flax, "Do Feminists Need Marxism?" in *Building Feminist Theory,* ed. Quest Staff (New York: Longman,

1981); and Jane Flax, "The Family in Contemporary Feminist Thought: A Critical Review," in *The Family in Political Thought*, ed. Jean Bethke Elshtain (Amherst: University of Massachusetts Press, 1982), pp. 232–239.

35. Cf. Albert O. Hirschman, *The Passions and the Interests* (Princeton, N.J.: Princeton University Press, 1977), for an interesting discussion of the historical emergence and construction of a specifically *capitalist* mentality.

36. Annette Kuhn, "Structures of Patriarchy and Capital in the Family," in Kuhn and Wolpe, *Feminism and Materialism*, p. 53.

37. Cf. Balbus, *Marxism*, on the ecological problems of Marxism; and Hilde Scott, *Does Socialism Liberate Women?* (Boston: Beacon Press, 1974); Judith Stacey, *Patriarchy and Socialist Revolution in China* (Berkeley and Los Angeles: University of California Press, 1983); and Gail Warshofsky Lapidus, *Women in Soviet Society* (Berkeley and Los Angeles: University of California Press, 1978), on women in socialist societies.

38. Ferguson, *The Feminist Case*, pp. 160–161.

39. Karl Marx, *Economic and Philosophical Manuscripts of 1844*, in *The Marx-Engels Reader*, 2nd ed., ed. Robert C. Tucker (New York: W. W. Norton, 1978), p. 116. Balbus, *Marxism*, chaps. 1–3, stresses Marx's relation to and repetition of Enlightenment assumptions, especially those concerning nature and history. He also persuasively reveals the blindnesses to gender relations without which basic categories in Marxist analysis (such as labor) would collapse.

40. Adrienne Rich, *Of Woman Born: Motherhood as Experience and Institution* (New York: W. W. Norton, 1976).

41. Dorothy Dinnerstein, *The Mermaid and the Minotaur: Sexual Arrangements and the Human Malaise* (New York: Harper & Row, 1976), especially pp. 76–82, 207–228.

42. Juliet Mitchell, *Psychoanalysis and Feminism* (New York: Pantheon, 1974), pp. xv–xxiii, 113–119.

43. The primary alternative theories Mitchell discusses in *Psychoanalysis* are those of Wilhelm Reich and R. D. Laing. Even in her more recent work, for example, the essays on psychoanalysis in her *Women and Revolution* (London: Virago, 1984), there is no sustained grappling with any type of psychoanalysis other than the work of Freud and Lacan.

44. Mitchell, *Psychoanalysis*, p. 413.

45. Dinnerstein, *The Mermaid and the Minotaur*, p. 20.

46. Nancy Chodorow, *The Reproduction of Mothering: Psychoanalysis and the Sociology of Gender* (Berkeley and Los Angeles: University of California Press, 1978), p. 10.

47. Ibid., pp. 169–170.

48. Ibid., p. 218.

49. Lilian B. Rubin, *Worlds of Pain: Life in the Working-Class Family* (New York: Basic Books, 1976), is a good example of this approach.

50. For an example of such arguments, cf. Balbus, *Marxism,* pp. 303–352. Balbus still seems under Marx's (metatheoretical) spell in his search for *a* cause or ordering principle structuring all of human history.

51. The theorists of difference themselves differ, of course. In this rather broad category I would include the work of Luce Irigaray; Hélène Cixous; Sara Ruddick; Carol Gilligan, *In a Different Voice* (Cambridge, Mass.: Harvard University Press, 1982); Julia Kristeva, *Desire in Language* (New York: Columbia University Press, 1980), and her essays in *The Future of Difference,* ed. Hester Eisenstein and Alice Jardine (New Brunswick, N.J.: Rutgers University Press, 1985). Furthermore some American feminists work with a Lacanian framework. Cf., for example, most of the essays in Charles Bernheimer and Claire Kahane, eds., *In Dora's Case: Freud-Hysteria-Feminism* (New York: Columbia University Press, 1985).

52. The work of Cixous; Irigaray; and Toril Moi, *Sexual Textual Politics* (London: Methuen, 1985), exemplifies the first emphasis; that of Carol Gilligan, Sara Ruddick, and Caroline Whitbeck, "The Maternal Instinct," in Trebilcot, *Mothering,* exemplifies the second.

53. Judith Stacey, "The New Conservative Feminism," *Feminist Studies* 9, no. 3 (Fall 1983): 559–583; and Domna Stanton, "Difference on Trial: A Critique of the Maternal Metaphor in Cixous, Irigaray and Kristeva," in *The Poetics of Gender,* ed. Nancy Miller (New York: Columbia University Press, 1986).

54. Hélène Cixous, "Sorties," in Hélène Cixous and Catherine Clément, *The Newly Born Woman* (Minneapolis: University of Minnesota Press, 1986), p. 93.

55. Luce Irigaray, "Questions," in Luce Irigaray, *This Sex Which Is Not One* (Ithaca, N.Y.: Cornell University Press, 1985), p. 28.

56. Ibid., p. 199. On woman as mirror for man, see also Virginia Woolf, *A Room of One's Own* (Harmondsworth, England: Penguin, 1963), pp. 37–38.

57. Irigaray, *This Sex,* pp. 25, 196.

58. Cixous and Clément, *Newly Born Woman,* p. 68.

59. Catherine Clément, "The Guilty One," in Cixous and Clément, *Newly Born Woman,* p. 29.

60. Irigaray, *This Sex,* pp. 108–109.

61. Cixoux and Clément, *Newly Born Woman,* p. 67; Irigaray, *This Sex,* pp. 128–130.

62. Cixous and Clément, *Newly Born Woman,* pp. 64, 65; also Irigaray, *Speculum of the Other Woman,* esp. pp. 13–66, 203–240.

63. Irigaray, *This Sex,* p. 74; see also Cixous and Clément, *Newly Born Woman,* pp. 70–71, 78–83.

64. Irigaray, *This Sex,* p. 171.

65. Ibid., p. 166.

66. Cixous and Clément, *Newly Born Woman*, p. 93.

67. Irigaray, *This Sex*, p. 196.

68. Cixous and Clément, *Newly Born Woman*, p. 97.

69. Hélène Cixous and Catherine Clément, "Exchange," in Cixous and Clément, *Newly Born Woman*, p. 157. This emphasis on libido and the revolutionary qualities of imagination recalls Herbert Marcuse's romantic-aesthetic period. Cf. Herbert Marcuse, *An Essay on Liberation* (Boston: Beacon Press, 1969); and his *The Aesthetic Dimension* (Boston: Beacon Press, 1978).

70. I develop this critique further in "Re-membering the Selves," *Michigan Quarterly Review* 26, no. 1 (Winter 1987): 92–110.

71. Irigaray, *This Sex*, p. 164.

72. Jessie Redmond Fauset, *Plum Bun: A Novel Without a Moral* (London: Pandora Press, 1985), p. 54. This novel, originally published in 1928, is the story of a woman light enough to "pass" for white, what she discovers of the benefits and cost of doing so, and of the painful perversities of the social relations of race and selfhood in the United States. On the centrality and diversity of race relations in the lives of women of color, see also the essays in Smith, *Home Girls*; Moraga and Anzaldua, *This Bridge*; and Hooks, *Feminist Theory*.

73. Barbara Smith, "Introduction," in Smith, *Home Girls*, p. xlv. For a historical overview of the "sexual history" of the United States and black women's place within it, see Barbara Omolade, "Hearts of Darkness," in Snitow, Stansell, and Thompson, *Powers of Desire*.

74. Alice Walker, "In Search of Our Mothers' Gardens," in her *In Search of Our Mothers' Gardens: Womanist Prose* (New York: Harcourt, Brace, Jovanovich, 1983), p. 237. On the misconstruing of black women's qualities and experiences, see Bonnie Thornton Dill, "The Dialectics of Black Womanhood," *Signs* 4, no. 3 (Spring 1979): 543–555; Michele Wallace, *Black Macho and the Myth of the Super Woman* (New York: Dial, 1978); and Angela T. Davis, *Women, Race and Class* (New York: Random House, 1981), especially pp. 3–29.

75. Audre Lorde, "Eye to Eye," in Lorde, *Sister Outsider*, p. 158; see also Bernice Johnson Reagon, "My Black Mothers and Sisters or on Beginning a Cultural Autobiography," *Feminist Studies* 8, no. 1 (Spring 1982): 81–96.

76. Paule Marshall, *Brown Girl, Brownstones* (Old Westbury, Conn.: Feminist Press, 1981), p. 46. See also Lorde, "Eye to Eye," in Lorde, *Sister Outsider*; and Gloria I. Joseph and Jill Lewis, *Common Differences* (Garden City, N.Y.: Doubleday, 1981), pp. 75–126.

77. On the barriers to and costs of not "speaking differences," see Maxine Baca Zinn, Lynn Weber Cannon, Elizabeth Higginbotham, and Bonnie Thornton Dill, "The Costs of Exclusionary Practices in Women's Studies," *Signs* 11, no. 2 (Winter 1986): 290–303; Marie C. Lugones and Elizabeth V.

Spelman, "Have We Got a Theory for You! Feminist Theory, Cultural Imperialism and the Demand for the Woman's Voice," in *Women and Values,* ed. Marilyn Pearsall (Belmont, Calif.: Wadsworth, 1986); Palmer, "White Women/ Black Women"; Audre Lorde, "Age, Race, Sex and Class," in Lorde, *Sister Outsider;* and Margaret A. Simons, "Racism and Feminism: A Schism in the Sisterhood," *Feminist Studies* 5, no. 2 (Summer 1979): 384–401. However I do not think the solution to these exclusionary practices is, as Donna Haraway does in "A Manifesto for Cyborgs," *Socialist Review* 80 (1983): 65–107, to create a mythic "most oppressed" woman (Third World, working in a multinational corporate factory in a repressive, poor state) and to have her represent woman as such. This tactic results in the reification of the incredibly diverse experiences of women of color and hence recreates their absence from feminist theory as concrete beings.

78. Moi, *Sexual Textual Politics,* p. 23.

79. Elaine Marks and Isabelle de Courtivron, "Introductions," in Marks and de Courtivron, *New French Feminisms,* p. 4.

80. The work of Cixous and Irigaray seems to exemplify this tendency and its problems.

81. Elshtain makes these arguments in *Public Man,* chap. 6, and in her "Introduction," in Elshtain, *The Family in Political Thought.*

82. Stacey, "The New Conservative Feminism," provides a sensitive discussion of the often muddled feminist views of families.

83. As Smith points out in her "Introduction," in Smith, *Home Girls.*

84. Catherine MacKinnon, "Feminism, Marxism, Method and the State: An Agenda for Theory," *Signs* 7, no. 3 (Spring 1982): 531.

85. Cf. Cixous's work; also Adrienne Rich, "Compulsory Heterosexuality and Lesbian Existence," *Signs* 5, no. 4 (Summer 1980): 515–544. Stanton provides a sharp critique of the ontological and essentialist assumptions of these writers.

86. Iris Young, "Is Male Gender Identity the Cause of Male Domination?" in Trebilcot, *Mothering,* p. 140. In this essay Young replicates the split Mitchell posits in *Psychoanalysis and Feminism* between kinship/gender/superstructure and class/production/base.

87. As in Shulamith Firestone, *The Dialectic of Sex* (New York: Bantam, 1970); MacKinnon, "Feminism"; and Dworkin, *Woman Hating.*

88. On this point see the essay by Nancy Chodorow and Susan Contratto, "The Fantasy of the Perfect Mother," in *Rethinking the Family,* ed. Barrie Thorne with Marilyn Yalom (New York: Longman, 1983).

89. Trebilcot, *Mothering;* and Thorne and Yalom, *Rethinking the Family.*

90. I consider MacKinnon's essay, "Feminism," an example of this viewpoint. See also Jeffner Allen, "Motherhood: The Annihilation of Women," in Trebilcot, *Mothering.*

91. Important recent sources for such work include Haleh Afshar, ed., *Women, State and Ideology: Studies from Africa and Asia* (Albany: State University of New York Press, 1987); Paula S. Rothenberg, ed., *Racism and Sexism: An Integrated Study* (New York: St. Martin's Press, 1988); Janet Henshall Momsen and Janet Townsend, *Geography of Gender in the Third World* (Albany: State University of New York Press, 1987); and Johnnetta B. Cole, ed., *All American Women: Lines that Divide, Ties that Bind* (New York: Free Press, 1986).

92. Exceptions to the lack of self-reflection by white women about the impotance of race include Palmer, "White Women/Black Women"; see also the dialogues between Joseph and Lewis, *Common Differences;* and Lugones and Spelman, "Have We Got a Theory for You!"

93. Michel Foucault, *Power/Knowledge,* ed. Colin Gordon (New York: Random House, 1981), pp. 109–133.

94. Sigmund Freud, *Civilization and Its Discontents* (New York: W. W. Norton, 1961), pp. 50–51.

Chapter Six

1. I am indebted to the following essays, which clarify the relationships between postmodernism, modernism, and the "crisis" of philosophy: Richard J. Bernstein, "Introduction," in *Habermas and Modernity,* ed. Richard J. Bernstein (Cambridge, Mass.: MIT Press, 1985); Kenneth Bayes, James Bohman, and Thomas McCarthy, "General Introduction," in *After Philosophy: End or Transformation,* ed. Kenneth Baynes, James Bohman, and Thomas McCarthy (Cambridge, Mass.: MIT Press, 1978); Alice A. Jardine, *Gynesis: Configurations of Women and Modernity* (Ithaca, N.Y.: Cornell University Press, 1985); Jonathan Culler, *On Deconstruction: Theory and Criticism After Structuralism* (Ithaca, N.Y.: Cornell University Press, 1982); Andreas Huyssen, "Mapping the Postmodern," in *The Crisis of Modernity: Recent Critical Theories of Culture and Society in the United States and West Germany,* ed. Gunter H. Lenz and Kurt L. Shell (Boulder, Colo.: Westview Press, 1986); Samuel Weber, "Demarcations: Deconstruction, Institutionalization and Ambivalence," in Lenz and Shell, *Crisis of Modernity;* John Rajchman, *Michel Foucault: The Freedom of Philosophy* (New York: Columbia University Press, 1985); Jonathan Arac, "Introduction," in *Postmodernism and Politics,* ed. Jonathan Arac (Minneapolis: University of Minnesota Press, 1986); David Hoy, "Jacques Derrida," in *The Return of Grand Theory in the Human Sciences,* ed. Quentin Skinner (New York: Oxford University Press, 1985); Mark Philp, "Michel Foucault," in Skinner, *The Return;* Hubert L. Dreyfus and Paul Rabinow, *Michel Foucault: Beyond Structuralism and Hermeneutics,* 2nd ed. (Chicago: University of Chicago Press, 1982); and Vincent Descombes, *Modern French Philosophy* (New York: Cambridge University Press, 1980).

2. For arguments about the need to protect, redeem, or fulfill the promises of Enlightenment and modernity, see Jürgen Habermas, "Neo-Conservative Culture Criticism in the United States and West Germany: An Intellectual Movement in Two Political Cultures," and "Questions and Counterquestions," both in Bernstein, *Habermas and Modernity;* Herbert Marcuse, "On Hedonism," in his *Negations* (Boston: Beacon Press, 1968); and also Martin Jay, "Habermas and Modernism," in Bernstein, *Habermas and Modernity.*

3. Most notably in Max Horkheimer and Theodor Adorno, *The Dialectic of Enlightenment,* trans. John Cumming (New York: Herder & Herder, 1972); but see also Max Horkheimer, *Critique of Instrumental Reason* (New York: Seabury, 1974).

4. The work of Adolf Grünbaum; for example, his "Epistemological Liabilities of the Clinical Appraisal of Psychoanalytic Theory," *Psychoanalysis and Contemporary Thought* 2 (1979): 451–526, is an instance of the reassertion of the philosopher's role as adjudicator of knowledge claims.

5. Karl Marx, "Theses on Feuerbach," reprinted in *The Marx-Engels Reader,* ed. Robert C. Tucker (New York: W. W. Norton, 1978), p. 145.

6. "Defiance and infatuation are one and the same thing, and whoever defies them is thereby lost to the myth against which he set himself," Horkheimer and Adorno, *The Dialectic,* pp. 58–59. This is a note from "Excursus I," in Horkheimer and Adorno, *The Dialectic,* in which the authors utilize the story of Odysseus and the Sirens as a metaphor for the complex relations between myth, enlightenment, and the seduction or cunning of reason. On the relation(s) between postmodernism and earlier themes in critical theory, see Rainer Nagele, "The Scene of the Other: Theodor W. Adorno's Negative Dialectic in the Context of Post-structuralism," in Arac, *Postmodernism and Politics;* and Albrecht Wellmer, "Reason, Utopia, and the *Dialectic of Enlightenment,*" in Bernstein, *Habermas and Modernity.*

7. Richard Rorty, "Pragmatism and Philosophy," in Baynes, Bohman, and McCarthy, *After Philosophy,* p. 47.

8. See, for example, Melanie Klein, "The Importance of Symbol-Formation in the Development of the Ego," in Melanie Klein, *Love, Guilt and Reparation* (New York: Delta, 1975). I am not claiming Klein's approach is the correct one; however I mention her work to suggest there may be many far more radical ways to "displace philosophy" than internal critiques or theories of writing.

9. I owe a great debt to Naomi Schor, "Dreaming Dissymmetry: Barthes, Foucault and Sexual Difference," in *Men in Feminism,* ed. Alice Jardine and Paul Smith (New York: Methuen, 1987), for alerting me to some of these gaps.

10. Jacques Derrida, "Positions," in Jacques Derrida, *Positions,* trans. Alan Bass (Chicago: University of Chicago Press, 1981), p. 51. I will quote Derrida

extensively in this section because he emphasizes the importance of style as content; my own style of writing is quite different from his.

11. Jacques Derrida, "Violence and Metaphysics," in Jacques Derrida, *Writing and Difference*, trans. Alan Bass (Chicago: University of Chicago Press, 1978), pp. 91–92, 96.

12. Ibid., pp. 103–104. In its being as "face," and "absence," Derrida's "other" has strong similarities to Lacan's "mother."

13. Ibid., pp. 147, 103.

14. Jacques Derrida, "Freud and the Scene of Writing," in Derrida, *Writing and Difference*, pp. 196, 200. On being, writing, and other, see also Jacques Derrida, "Difference," in Jacques Derrida, *Margins of Philosophy*, trans. Alan Bass (Chicago: University of Chicago Press, 1982), especially pp. 25–27.

15. Derrida, "Freud," in Derrida, *Writing and Difference*, pp. 211–212.

16. Ibid., pp. 230, 227. On this point see also Jacques Derrida, "Signature Event Context," in Derrida, *Margins*.

17. Jacques Derrida, "From Restricted to General Economy: A Hegelianism Without Reserve," in Derrida, *Writing and Difference*, pp. 259–260, 263, 268.

18. Ibid., pp. 269–272.

19. Derrida, "Violence," in Derrida, *Writing and Difference*, p. 147.

20. Derrida, "From Restricted to General Economy," in Derrida, *Writing and Difference*, p. 274.

21. Jacques Derrida, "Implications," in Derrida, *Positions*, p. 14.

22. Derrida, "Positions," in Derrida, *Positions*, p. 45.

23. Richard Rorty, "Pragmatism and Philosophy," in Baynes, Bohman, and McCarthy, *After Philosophy*, p. 28.

24. Derrida, "Positions," in Derrida, *Positions*, n. 32, p. 105.

25. Rorty, "Pragmatism," in Baynes, Bohman, and McCarthy, *After Philosophy*, p. 60.

26. Ibid., pp. 32–33, 57.

27. Ibid., p. 28.

28. Ibid.

29. Ibid., pp. 30–31.

30. Ibid., pp. 32, 54.

31. Richard Rorty, *Philosophy and the Mirror of Nature* (Princeton, N.J.: Princeton University Press, 1979), p. 379.

32. Rorty, "Pragmatism," in Baynes, Bohman, and McCarthy, *After Philosophy*, p. 62.

33. Jean-François Lyotard, *The Postmodern Condition: A Report on Knowledge*, trans. Geoff Bennington and Brian Massumi (Minneapolis: University of Minnesota Press, 1984), p. 30.

34. Ibid., p. xxiii.

35. Ibid., p. 31.

36. Ibid., pp. 32, 35.

37. Ibid., pp. 33–35.

38. Michel Foucault, "Truth and Power," in Michel Foucault, *Power/Knowledge*, ed. Colin Gordon (New York: Pantheon, 1980), p. 131.

39. Lyotard, *The Postmodern Condition*, pp. xxiv, 81.

40. Ibid., p. 127.

41. Michel Foucault, "What Is an Author?" in Michel Foucault, *Language, Counter-memory, Practice*, ed. Donald F. Bouchard (Ithaca, N.Y.: Cornell University Press, 1977), p. 120. Rorty is also critical of Derrida's concept of writing. He does not believe there is any "beyond," and his concept of "language" is very different than Derrida's. Cf. Richard Rorty, *Consequences of Pragmatism* (Minneapolis: University of Minnesota Press, 1982), chaps. 6, 8.

42. Cf. Richard Rorty, "Postmodernist Bourgeois Liberalism," in *Hermeneutics and Praxis*, ed. Robert Hollinger (Notre Dame, Ind.: University of Notre Dame Press, 1985).

43. Foucault, "Truth and Power," in Foucault, *Power/Knowledge*, p. 114.

44. Michel Foucault, "Nietzsche, Genealogy, History," in Foucault, *Language*, p. 142.

45. Michel Foucault, "The Discourse on Language," in the appendix to Michel Foucault, *The Archaeology of Knowledge*, trans. A. M. Sheridan Smith (New York: Harper Colophon, 1976), p. 229.

46. Ibid.

47. Foucault, "Nietzsche," in Foucault, *Language*, p. 151.

48. Ibid., p. 163.

49. Michel Foucault, "Revolutionary Action: 'Until Now,'" in Foucault, *Language*, pp. 221–222.

50. Foucault, "Truth and Power," in Foucault, *Power/Knowledge*, p. 119.

51. Ibid., p. 125.

52. Michel Foucault, "On the Genealogy of Ethics: An Overview of Work in Progress," in Dreyfus and Rabinow, *Michel Foucault*, pp. 235–237.

53. Richard J. Bernstein, "Philosophy in the Conversation of Mankind," in Hollinger, *Hermeneutics and Praxis*; Paul A. Bove, "The Ineluctibility of Difference: Scientific Pluralism and the Critical Intelligence," in Arac, *Postmodernism and Politics*; and Cornel West, "The Politics of American Neo-Pragmatism," in *Post-Analytic Philosophy*, ed. John Rajchman and Cornel West (New York: Columbia University Press, 1985), discuss this problem from nonfeminist viewpoints.

54. Kathy Ferguson's work suggests some of the alterations that would result. See especially her *The Feminist Case Against Bureaucracy* (Philadelphia: Temple University Press, 1984), chap. 2.

55. It would be interesting, for example, to compare Linda Gordon, *Woman's Body, Woman's Right: A Social History of Birth Control in America* (New York: Viking Press, 1976), with Foucault's methods and histories in relation to gender; see also Ferguson, *The Feminist Case*, especially the preface and chap. 5; and Susan Rubin Suleiman, ed., *The Female Body in Western Culture* (Cambridge, Mass.: Harvard University Press, 1985).

56. Jacques Derrida, *Spurs: Nietzsche's Styles*, trans. Barbara Harlow (Chicago: University of Chicago Press, 1979), p. 51. My reading of this text has benefited from Jardine's analysis of it in *Gynesis*, chap. 9. However I find her reading insufficiently critical of the gendered nature of Derrida's categories.

57. Derrida, *Spurs*, pp. 101, 103.

58. Jardine, *Gynesis*, p. 194.

59. Derrida, *Spurs*, pp. 61, 65, 67, 107.

60. Schor, "Dreaming Dissymmetry," p. 110.

61. For a discussion of Plato, cf. Luce Irigaray, *Speculum of the Other Woman*, trans. Gillian C. Gill (Ithaca, N.Y.: Cornell University Press, 1985), especially "Plato's Hysteria." On Rousseau cf. Susan Moller Okin, *Women in Western Political Thought* (Princeton, N.J.: Princeton University Press, 1979), especially part 2. I have also discussed the (unconscious) effects of gender relations on Plato and Rousseau's philosophies in Jane Flax, "Political Philosophy and the Patriarchal Unconscious: A Psychoanalytic Perspective on Epistemology and Metaphysics," in *Discovering Reality: Feminist Perspectives on Epistemology, Metaphysics, Methodology and Philosophy of Science*, ed. Sandra Harding and Merill Hintikka (Boston: D. Reidel, 1983).

62. Cf. Okin, *Women in Western*, for an extended discussion of this point.

63. Luce Irigaray, "Commodities Among Themselves," in Luce Irigaray, *This Sex Which Is Not One*, trans. Catherine Porter (Ithaca, N.Y.: Cornell University Press, 1985).

64. This is Schor's suggestion. See her "Dreaming Dissymmetry," p. 109.

65. Lyotard, *The Postmodern Condition*, p. 82.

66. Cf. Richard Rorty's apt critique of Lyotard in his "Habermas and Lyotard on Postmodernity," in Bernstein, *Habermas and Modernity*.

67. One could not integrate the traits of the good enough mother as presented by D. W. Winnicott (cf. Chapter 4) with Foucault's aesthetic subjectivity.

68. Cf. Jean-Paul Sartre, *Being and Nothingness* (New York: Washington Square Press, 1966), especially pp. 747–748. Foucault tries to distinguish his views from Sartre's in his "On the Genealogy of Ethics," in Dreyfus and Rabinow, *Michel Foucault*, p. 237.

69. On the problems of reconciling Foucault's politics and ideas, see Rajchman, *Michel Foucault*, chap. 2; and Dreyfus and Rabinow, *Michel Foucault*, pp. 253–264. Problems of gender or child rearing are not addressed in

either of these works. Foucault was evidently rethinking some of his ideas about subjectivity shortly before his death. See Luther H. Martin, Huck Gutman, and Patrick H. Hutton, *Technologies of the Self* (Amherst: University of Massachusetts Press, 1988).

70. Richard Rorty, "Freud and Moral Reflection," in *Pragmatism's Freud: The Moral Disposition of Psychoanalysis,* ed. Joseph H. Smith and William Kerrigan (Baltimore: Johns Hopkins University Press, 1986). Derrida naturally reconstructs the unconscious as the scene of "writing," the other, and chance. See his "My Chances/*Mes chance:* A Rendezvous with Some Epicurean Stereophonies," in *Taking Chances: Derrida, Psychoanalysis and Literature,* ed. Joseph H. Smith and William Kerrigan (Baltimore: Johns Hopkins University Press, 1984).

71. Rorty, "Freud," in Smith and Kerrigan, *Pragmatism's Freud,* pp. 5, 7.

72. I discuss part of the treatment of a borderline patient in Jane Flax, "Remembering the Selves: Is the Repressed Gendered?" *Michigan Quarterly Review* 26, no. 1 (Winter 1987): 92–110.

73. Rorty, "Pragmatism and Philosophy," in Baynes, Bohman, and McCarthy, *After Philosophy,* p. 52, suggests, "some intuitions should be deliberately repressed."

74. Hanna Pitkin, "Justice: On Relating Private and Public," *Political Theory* 9, no. 3 (August 1981): 327–352.

Chapter Seven

1. Sandra Harding has suggested to me in private correspondence that the dualism true/false is in need of deconstruction. She argues that perhaps there could be concepts of falsehood that are not dependent on a notion of truth. I find her suggestion interesting but not immediately useful for my purposes.

2. On Jürgen Habermas's notion of communicative competence and some of the problems with it from a feminist point of view, see Nancy Fraser, "What's Critical About Critical Theory: The Case of Habermas and Gender," in *Feminism as Critique,* ed. Seyla Benhabib and Drucilla Cornell (Minneapolis: University of Minnesota Press, 1987). For Habermas's own views see Jürgen Habermas, *The Theory of Communicative Action* (Boston: Beacon Press, 1984).

3. Cf. Julia Kristeva, *Desire in Language* (New York: Columbia University Press, 1980). Kristeva is ambivalent about the meanings of *feminism* and its relation to her work. See also Luce Irigaray, *Speculum of the Other Woman,* trans. Gillian C. Gill (Ithaca, N.Y.: Cornell University Press, 1985).

4. Luce Irigaray, *This Sex Which Is Not One,* trans. Catherine Porter (Ithaca, N.Y.: Cornell University Press, 1985), pp. 95–96.

5. Ibid., p. 94.

6. Donald McIntosh, "The Empirical-Bearing of Psychoanalytic Theory,"

International Journal of Psychoanalysis 60 (1979): 405–431, provides an excellent commentary on this literature.

7. Cf. Naomi Scheman, "Individualism and the Objects of Psychology," and Jane Flax, "Political Philosophy and the Patriarchal Unconscious," both in *Discovering Reality*, ed. Sandra Harding and Merill Hintikka (Dordrecht, Netherlands: D. Reidel, 1983); and Sandra Harding, *The Science Question in Feminism* (Ithaca, N.Y.: Cornell University Press, 1986), especially chaps. 7–9.

8. Susan Moller Okin, *Women in Western Political Thought* (Princeton, N.J.: Princeton University Press, 1979), especially chaps. 7, 10, 11.

9. A recent example is Carol Pateman, *Participation and Political Theory* (New York: Cambridge University Press, 1970).

10. Cf. Richard Rorty, "Postmodernist Bourgeois Liberalism," in *Hermeneutics and Praxis*, ed. Robert Hollinger (Notre Dame, Ind.: University of Notre Dame Press, 1985); and Jean-François Lyotard and Jean-Loup Thebaud, *Just Gaming* (Minneapolis: University of Minnesota Press, 1985).

11. See, for example, Judith Stacey, *Patriarchy and Socialist Revolution in Socialist China* (Berkeley and Los Angeles: University of California Press, 1983); Hilda Scott, *Does Socialism Liberate Women?* (Boston: Beacon Press, 1974); and Sheila Rowbotham, *Women, Resistance and Revolution* (New York: Vintage, 1974).

12. Herbert Marcuse, *Eros and Civilization* (Boston: Beacon Press, 1955); Heinz Hartmann, *Ego Psychology and the Problem of Adaptation* (New York: International Universities Press, 1958); Jacques Lacan, *Ecrits: A Selection* (New York: W. W. Norton, 1977); and D. W. Winnicott, *The Maturational Process and the Facilitating Environment* (New York: International Universities Press, 1965).

13. Irigaray, *This Sex*, chaps. 9, 11.

14. This question of doing right initiates the dialogue on justice in Plato, *The Republic*, trans. Allan Bloom (New York: Basic Books, 1968).

15. Richard Rorty, "Habermas and Lyotard on Postmodernity," in *Habermas and Modernity*, ed. Richard J. Bernstein (Cambridge, Mass.: MIT Press, 1985), p. 174.

Index

Compositor:	Graphic Composition
Text:	$11/13$ Palatino
Display:	Palatino
Printer:	Maple-Vail Book Mfg. Group
Binder:	Maple-Vail Book Mfg. Group